The New Zealanders at Gallipoli

BY

MAJOR FRED WAITE, D.S.O., N.Z.E.

Adjutant Divisional Engineers, N.Z. & A. Division, 1914-15
Chief Engineer Instructor, N.Z.E.F. Training Camps, 1916-18

1919

To the Memory
of
Our Glorious Dead.

They went with songs to the battle, they were young,
Straight of limb, true of eye, steady and aglow.
They were staunch to the end against odds uncounted,
They fell with their faces to the foe.

They shall grow not old, as we that are left grow old;
Age shall not weary them, nor the years condemn,
At the going down of the sun and in the morning
We will remember them.

—*Laurence Binyon*

Contents.

		PAGE
The New Zealand Popular History Series, by Sir James Allen, K.C.B.		v.
The New Zealanders of Anzac, by General Sir Ian Hamilton		vii.
To My Old Comrades, by General Sir Wm. Birdwood		xv.

CHAPTER

I.	The Concentration of the Expeditionary Force	1
II.	The Voyage to Egypt	14
III.	Training in Egypt	32
IV.	The Defence of the Suez Canal	47
V.	The Rendezvous at Mudros	64
VI.	The Anzac Landing	74
VII.	The First Week	86
VIII.	At the Head of Monash Gully	102
IX.	The Battle of Krithia	119
X.	The Coming of the Mounteds	132
XI.	Supplying the Needs of the Army	152
XII.	Midsummer at Anzac	166
XIII.	The Preparations in July	182
XIV.	The Battle of Sari Bair	192
XV.	The Battle of Kaiajik Aghala	245
XVI.	Preparing for the End	259
XVII.	The Evacuation	278
XVIII.	The Return to Anzac	294

APPENDIX

I.	The Main Body Transports	302
II.	N.Z. and A. Division Transports	303
III.	Main Body Establishments	304
IV.	The Men of Anzac. Decorations and Mentioned in Despatches	307
V.	The Place-Names of Anzac	317
VI.	A Gallipoli Diary	325

Trench Map of Anzac at end of Volume.

The New Zealand Popular History Series.

These popular histories of New Zealand's share in the Great War are designed to present to the people of New Zealand the inspiring record of the work of our sons and daughters overseas.

It was recognized that the Official History would necessitate considerable research, would take a long time to write, and then must be largely a study of strategy and tactics; but something—that would be concise and interesting, not expensive, and available at once—seemed desirable. It was decided to avoid the style of an Official History and select as writers soldiers who had themselves fought with the N.Z.E.F. through the several campaigns; soldiers recognized by their comrades as authorities on the campaigns with which they deal; soldiers who themselves have experienced the hopes and fears, the trials and the ultimate triumph of the men in the ranks.

The volumes—of which this story of Anzac is the first published—are four in number:

Vol. I. "The New Zealanders at Gallipoli," by Major Fred Waite, D.S.O., N.Z.E., who served with the Main Body and the N.Z. & A. Division as a Staff Officer of Engineers.

Vol. II. "The New Zealanders in France," by Colonel Hugh Stewart, C.M.G., D.S.O., M.C., who served through the campaigns in Gallipoli and France with the N.Z. Infantry.

Vol. III. "The New Zealanders in Palestine," by Lieut.-Colonel C. Guy Powles, C.M.G., D.S.O., who as a Staff Officer of the N.Z. Mounted Rifles served through the campaigns in Gallipoli and Palestine. The material for this volume was collected by Major A. Wilkie, W.M.R.

Vol. IV. "The War Effort of New Zealand," will deal with:
  (a) The minor compaigns in which New Zealanders took part;
  (b) Services which are not fully dealt with in the campaign volumes;
  (c) The story of the work at the Bases—the efforts of our Women abroad and in New Zealand, our Hospitals, the raising and the training of the men.

Without rhetoric, without needless superlatives—for the stories do not need them—these volumes are placed before the people of New Zealand in the hope that a fuller realization of the difficulties encountered and eventually triumphed over will act as an inspiration to those of us who were not privileged to fight for the cause of Freedom on the battlefields of the World.

J. Allen,

Minister of Defence.

Parliamentary Buildings,
  Wellington,
    1-12-19.

The New Zealanders of Anzac.

As I was on the point of starting to pay a long-promised visit to the Commander-in-Chief of our Army of the Rhine, a cabled message from the Government of New Zealand was put into my hands—a message asking me to write a Preface to the Gallipoli volume of the "HISTORY OF NEW ZEALAND'S SHARE IN THE GREAT WAR." This preface was to be written and posted to Wellington without loss of time, as the work had already gone to press.

When I set out for the Dardanelles on Friday, March 13, 1915, to command an unknown army against an unknown enemy, in an unknown country, that was an original undertaking. To write a preface to an unknown book being printed in another hemisphere—to write it from memory—in the train and in a hurry, that also is an original undertaking, and it is necessary to begin by setting forth these facts in order that my many omissions and shortcomings may have a better chance of forgiveness.

Crossing the German frontier, with the edict of the New Zealand Government still in my pocket, I got out to stretch my legs at the first stop. The name of that railway station was Düren. Hardly had I alighted when my eyes fell upon the letters, "N.Z.M.R.," quite unmistakably affixed to the shoulder-strap of an officer also standing on that platform. Since the year 1915, this particular combination of capital letters has exercised upon me a certain fascination—I have to go right there. So I went, and asked the wearer of the shoulder-strap if he had been at the Dardanelles.

"I have, indeed," he said. "I am Lieut.-Colonel John Studholme. I served in the Dardanelles under you, and now I am the last New Zealander in Germany."

"You speak figuratively," said I. "You mean you are one of the last."

"Not so," he replied. "I am not one of the last; I am the last one."

Now here, thought I to myself, is a queer thing! I am told to write a preface to a history of an Army, and I meet the last item of that Army which did so much to win the

Rhineland, in Rhineland; the last man of that superb band who were raised from a population of one million and lost fifteen thousand killed; whereas, to take other standards, the Belgians, justly famous as having fought so long and so valiantly for the freedom of Europe, lost thirteen thousand killed out of a population of seven millions. Once again, too, there came to me the thought of their losses at the Dardanelles:—

Total strength landed .. .. 8,556 all ranks
Casualties in killed and wounded
 (excluding sickness) 7,447

These thoughts and the coincidence of meeting Colonel Studholme, gave me courage. I had been thinking I could not do justice to my theme, and that I must regretfully decline. Now I resolved to take my courage in both hands and go ahead; so here, with the help of my personal diary, I revive memories of my meeting with the first New Zealander.

On March 29, 1915, I motored across from Mena Camp (where I had been reviewing the Australians) to Heliopolis. There was a big dust storm blowing. Godley commanded. I wrote down on the spot, "These fellows made a real good show; superb physique. Numbers of old friends, especially amongst the New Zealanders."

Next day, March 30, I wrote to Lord Kitchener, "The physique of the rank and file could not be improved upon." Also: "They are all as keen as possible, and will, I am certain, render a very good account of themselves if the conditions encountered give them a fair chance."

Now, the force that I had seen and admired on March 29, 1915, had sailed from far-away New Zealand early in October, 1914, so each private soldier had already travelled over land and sea further than Ulysses during his ten years' Odyssey, and further than Christopher Columbus during his discovery of America; and they had voyaged thus, not for gold or glory, but to help the Old Country and to succour the weak and the oppressed.

When to-day we look round upon our wrecked and devastated world, we can see that neither the War, nor the Peace,

PREFACE. ix.

[Photo by Guy
LIEUT.-COLONEL A. BAUCHOP, C.M.G.
Otago Mounted Rifles.
(Died from wounds).

has added to the moral structure of Governments. The one great, enduring asset is this: that the rank and file of mankind, and especially the rank and file of New Zealand, let no private interest stand between them and their eagerness to strike a blow for the Right.

So the New Zealanders sailed away from their own safe islands, towards danger and death, and first cast anchor at Albany, Western Australia, a pleasant, old-fashioned spot. The little force consisted of one brigade of Mounted Rifles, a Brigade of Infantry, and one Brigade of Artillery; and there, at the south-western point of the neighbouring continent, they joined the 1st Australian Division and headed, under convoy, for Egypt, arriving at Alexandria early in December.

On the formation of Birdwood's Corps, a brigade of Australian Light Horse and a brigade of Australian Infantry were incorporated with them to form what was known as the New Zealand and

Australian Division. This formation was trained under General Godley at Zeitoun till April, 1915, during which time a small portion of the New Zealand Brigade took part in the repulse of the Turkish attack on the Suez Canal in February. Both Sir John Maxwell and General Godley assured me, at the time of my inspection in March, that the behaviour of the New Zealanders during this trying period of straining at the leash was in every way excellent.

Soon after my inspection, the last stage of the journey was begun, and leaving the mounted troops behind them, the infantry and artillery took ship and set sail for Mudros. There, for the short time remaining to them, they worked very hard at rowing, embarking, disembarking, &c., until they were almost as handy as bluejackets in the boats. Much of the success of the landing was due to this period of special preparation.

On April 25, 1915, a date regarded in the Near East as the most memorable of the Great War, the New Zealand Brigade landed early in the day and fought valiantly on the northern or Suvla side of the Bay. Everything was strange and astonishing to these boys from the green, well-watered islands of the South—the enemy, the precipices, the thirst, the wounds and death around them; but no veterans have ever done better than they did during those first few hours. Then it was that they carried, occupied and held, under steadily-increasing shell and machine-gun fire, what was afterwards known as Plugge's Plateau (from Lieut.-Colonel Plugge, commanding the Auckland Battalion), and Walker's Ridge (from Brigadier-General Walker, General Birdwood's Chief-of-Staff, who commanded the New Zealand Infantry Brigade at the Landing in the absence of Brigadier-General Earl Johnston, sick). These are the prosaic facts of a feat of arms which will endure as long as heroic poetry and history are written or read.

An extract from my diary, dated April 25, H.M.S. "Queen Elizabeth": "They are not charging up into this Sari Bair Ridge for money, or by compulsion. There they are—all the way from the Southern Cross—earning Victoria Crosses, every one of them."

An extract from my diary dated April 26, H.M.S. "Queen Elizabeth": "Passed on the news to Birdwood: I doubt the Turks coming on again—but, in case, the 29th Division's feat of arms will be a tonic."

"I was wrong. At 3 p.m., the enemy made another effort, this time on the left of our line. We shook them badly, and were rewarded by seeing a New Zealand charge. Two battalions racing due north along the coast and foothills with levelled bayonets. Then the tumult died away."

On May 5 I brought the New Zealand Infantry down to Helles. They had been fighting hard at Anzac, making sorties against the Turks, but I could not do without them in the attack I was about to make—a three days' and nights' battle it turned out to be—on Achi Baba. In my diary is this entry :—

"May 7, 1915—At 4.30 I ordered a general assault: the 88th Brigade to be thrown in on the top of the 87th; the New Zealand Brigade in support; the French to conform. Our gunners were to pave the way for the infantry with what they thought they could afford."

In the deadly struggle which ensued, in the night-long conflict, in the supreme effort of the next day, the New Zealanders gained great glory, as was gratefully acknowledged by me to General Godley at the time.

That same month, the New Zealand Mounted Rifles Brigade was called in to the Dardanelles. We wanted every New Zealander we could get. The brigade, destined to become so famous, was commanded by Brigadier-General Russell, now Major-General Sir Andrew Russell, K.C.B., K.C.M.G. They came dismounted, torn in two betwixt grief at parting with their horses and a longing to play their part on the Peninsula. They turned up, as is their way, in the nick of time, and were put into the trenches at once.

On one of the first days of July, the Maoris appeared upon the Peninsula. General Godley had informed me that all ranks were anxious to have them, so I cabled to Lord Kitchener, and I have always been thankful that he permitted them to come along. They were received with open arms by their compatriots, and I may say here at once that they proved themselves worthy descendants of the chivalrous warriors of the olden days, and remembered, in the fiercest battles, the last words of Hongi Hika: "Be brave that you may live."

No doubt the history to which these words are a preface will tell the tale of the trench warfare of June and July; here I will only remark that the New Zealanders helped themselves to a liberal allowance of all that was going in the way of bombs, onslaughts, and generally, hard knocks.

On August 6, took place the great attack on Sari Bair. To the New Zealand Mounted Rifles (Brigadier-General Russell) fell the honour of covering the assault, and the New Zealand Infantry Brigade (Brigadier-General Earl Johnston) formed the right assaulting column. During the four days' desperate fighting, which included night marches through the worst country imaginable, steep, scrub-covered spurs, sheer cliffs and narrow winding ravines,

LIEUT.-COLONEL W. G. MALONE
Wellington Infantry Battalion
(*Killed in action.*)

these two brigades and the Maoris wrested from a brave and numerous enemy the footing on the Ridge which they held till the bitter end.

Brilliant leadership was shown by Lieut.-Colonel A. Bauchop, commanding the Otago Mounted Rifles, and Lieut.-Colonel W. G. Malone, Wellington Battalion, during this battle, wherein Corporal Bassett, of the Divisional Signal Company, won a well-earned V.C. I lay a very special stress on the deeds of Bauchop and Malone. These two heroes were killed whilst leading their men with absolute contempt of danger—Bauchop after having captured what was afterwards known as Bauchop's Hill, and Malone on the very summit of Chunuk Bair. Both Bauchop and Malone were soldiers of great mark and, above all, fearless leaders of men. Where so many, living longer, have achieved distinction, it is quite necessary that New Zealand should hear the names of these two gallant soldiers in tender remembrance.

Of the New Zealanders who survived, Russell was beyond doubt the outstanding personality on the Peninsula. Steady as a rock, with a clear head and a firm character, he belongs to the type of soldier who will shoulder responsibility and never leave either his men or his commander in the lurch.

Chaytor, who was Assistant-Adjutant-General, did excellently well also, though, through being wounded, he did not have full time to develop merits which afterwards became so conspicuous in Palestine.

The losses incurred by the brigades from this terrible and prolonged fighting for the key to the Narrows of the Dardanelles, were cruel. On September 21 and 22, Russell had further victorious fighting when he and General Cox took Kaiajik Aghala; soon afterwards the brigades were sent down to Mudros to rest and to recruit. Reinforcements arrived in due course, and, in a shorter time than would have seemed possible, the formations were ready again and keen as ever to go on. But meanwhile, in October, events had occurred which put an end to the forward fighting and extinguished the Dardanelles enterprise. The first was the sending of two of our Peninsula Divisions to Salonika. The second was an order from Home that nothing serious in the way of fighting should be undertaken. The third was the advent of a new Commander-in-Chief who was opposed to the whole of the Dardanelles idea. From that date, therefore, until the evacuation, there was no further attack. When the tragic end came, the New Zealanders, steadfast as ever, held the post of honour, and General Russell and his rearguard were the very last to leave the Northern theatre of our operations.

Owing to the conditions under which my preface is being written, it will be understood that any attempt to make a list of distinguished names would be hopeless. I have just put down the half-dozen best remembered in full confidence that the historian will make good my failure in the body of the book. But there is one more officer I must mention, for although he is not a New Zealander born, he had the advantage of living there and getting to know both islands long before the War. I refer, I need hardly say, to Sir Alexander Godley, who commanded the New Zealand and Australian Division during the Dardanelles campaign. He has devoted some of the best years of his life to New Zealand, and with all his courtesy and charm of manner, has never had any traffic with indiscipline or inefficiency. If he wants his monument, let him look round at the glories won by the division in the laying of whose foundations he played a leading part.

One last word: the New Zealanders have been feared by the enemy; in quarters they have made themselves beloved. Wherever they have been billeted, all the civilians say: "We want to have them again."

Ian Hamilton

General.
Lieutenant of the Tower of London

G.H.Q., Army of the Rhine,
17/8/'19.

To My Old Comrades.

I have been asked to write a foreword to "THE NEW ZEALANDERS AT GALLIPOLI," and it gives me the greatest pleasure to do so, providing, as it does, an opportunity of recording the affection and admiration I have, and shall always have, for those who were my comrades on the Gallipoli Peninsula.

It was as a comparatively small force that we started our soldiering in Egypt towards the end of 1914. And I am sure that no soldier was ever prouder of his command than I was when, on the orders of Lord Kitchener, I took over the command of the Australian and New Zealand troops who were then arriving from their homes.

Not a moment of the time spent in Egypt was wasted, for all ranks instinctively realized what was before us, and put their best work into the necessary training. I doubt if any but those who were present can conceive all that this training meant to us, and in what wonderfully good stead it stood us when the time of trial came at Gallipoli. When that time arrived, we felt that we were a really formed military body, and not merely a collection of units hastily thrown together and without any military cohesion. During that period, a strong feeling of esprit de corps was engendered throughout the force, and perhaps most important of all, a spirit of discipline, the necessity of which was realized, was inculcated in all ranks.

I so well remember on that early morning of April 25, 1915, the intense keenness and anxiety on the part of all to get ashore and capture the Turkish positions without a moment's delay; and it was, I know, a source of great regret to the New Zealanders that it was to the 1st Australian Division that the honour of the first landing fell. Transports, however, followed each other rapidly, and the day had not worn long when the New Zealand infantry were ashore and attacking what afterwards became known as Russell's Top, on the left of the Australians. There and thereabouts it was destined to continue this fighting through thick scrub for many a long day, and to prove to the Turks how impossible it was to throw such men back into the sea, as they had confidently anticipated doing.

A short foreword like this is no place for a history of the doings of the force, to which I know full credit will be done in this and other volumes depicting New Zealand's share in the Great War. I will only say here what complete confidence I always had—without one moment of hesitation—throughout the campaign in the bravery, the steadfastness and the efficiency of the New Zealand troops. Their

[Photo by Bartlett & Andrew
MAJOR-GENERAL SIR A. J. GODLEY, K.C.B., K.C.M.G.

discipline was admirable, while never have I seen troops more willing or determined.

I would that I could here mention by name even half of those who were such real comrades to me, such as General Godley, Colonels Russell, Napier Johnston, F. E. Johnston, Chaytor; Colonel McBean Stewart, of the Canterbury

To My Old Comrades. xvii

Battalion, who, to my great regret, was killed on the day of the landing; and Colonels Findlay, Mackesy, and Meldrum, of the Canterbury, Auckland, and Wellington Mounted Rifles respectively.

There are two others who gave their lives on the Peninsula, and whom I would especially record.

One of the most difficult points which we had to hold was known as Quinn's Post. The Turkish trenches there were certainly not more than ten yards from our own, and it can easily be imagined how the battle raged furiously

[*Photo by Bartlett & Andrew*]
BRIGADIER-GENERAL SIR A. H. RUSSELL., K.C.B.

between the two systems. The gallant Quinn, after whom the post was named, had been killed, and, later on, the Australians were replaced in their turn by the Wellington Battalion under Colonel Malone. This officer at once set himself the task of making his post as perfect and impregnable as he could, and in this task he fully succeeded. I shall never forget the real pleasure it gave me when visiting the post from time to time to realize the keenness and energy which Colonel Malone put into his work, and on every visit I found myself leaving it with greater confidence that, come what may, Quinn's Post could never be taken by an enemy, however strong. Shortly after this, Colonel Malone was, to my deep regret, and to that, I know, of his many comrades, killed while leading his battalion most gallantly in the main attack on Sari Bair on August 8. A thorough and keen soldier, his loss was great to the whole force, and I personally felt I had lost not only an excellent officer, but a really true friend.

The other officer to whom I cannot refrain from making especial reference, was Colonel Bauchop, of the Otago Mounted Rifles: a more gallant and cheerier gentleman never lived. Always full of high spirits and courage—ready to undertake any enterprise, and refusing to acknowledge difficulties, he was just the type of man wanted to ensure the maintenance of high morale in such a campaign as we were carrying out at Gallipoli. For a very long time Colonel Bauchop held command of our extreme semi-detached outposts, and I know how proud he was of the great game of war in which he played so prominent a part. Perfectly fearless, he came through the fighting unscratched until August 8, when he was killed at the head of his regiment, leading it in a gallant charge on the extreme left of our old position. Surely it would be impossible for any commander not to be devoted to such men as these!

What seemed to me as one of the best features of our fighting at Gallipoli was the mutual confidence and esteem which it engendered between the New Zealand and the Australian soldiers. Before this, they had had little opportunities of knowing each other. Going round, as I did, the trenches of all, it was to me a constant source of satisfaction and delight to find New Zealanders and Australians confiding in me the highly favourable opinion which, apparently to their surprise, they had formed of each other! May such a feeling continue for all time, to the great advantage of the British race in the Southern Seas.

To My Old Comrades.

I am sure that the New Zealand troops would not wish me to conclude this foreword without mentioning the British Navy, to whom we all owe so much, and memories of whom will remain for ever with all those who served alongside of them.

On our return from Gallipoli to Egypt, in 1916, the arrival of the New Zealand Rifles Brigade and the large reinforcements which had been sent from New Zealand enabled us to expand the original New Zealand Expeditionary Force into a complete division—than which, I can say with confidence, no finer or better organized division served in France. I had the honour to take this division with me to the Western Front in April, 1916. But, alas! I was not to have the honour of retaining it long under my command, for on the reconstitution of the Australian and New Zealand divisions, it was decided that the latter should leave my army corps: I need scarcely say it was a matter of the deepest personal regret to me.

I sincerely wish all my old comrades happiness and success. None of us are ever likely to forget the times we spent together on Gallipoli. We sincerely mourn for those who so willingly gave their lives for the great cause in which we were fighting; but we know they have not died in vain, for they have ensured freedom and right for our children and our children's children. New Zealand may well be—as I am sure she is—justly proud of her magnificent sons, who so bravely upheld her flag and fought for her honour on the shores of the Gallipoli Peninsula.

W. R. Birdwood.

UNDER THE SHADOW OF THE "SPHINX": GRAVES OF MEN KILLED AT THE ANZAC LANDING.
The valiant dead that gazed upon the skies,

The New Zealanders at Gallipoli

CHAPTER I.

The Concentration of the Expeditionary Force.

THE pioneer settlers of New Zealand left the Mother Country for many reasons, but primarily because they wished for a freer existence. They certainly did not choose an easy path for themselves. They could have settled in English-speaking countries comparatively near, but they deliberately left England, Scotland, Wales and Ireland for a land thirteen thousand miles away—a land covered with virgin forest and inhabited by a proud and warlike native race.

In communities that governed themselves according to their own advanced ideas, away from the baneful influence of large cities and the trammelling tendencies of hoary tradition, they wrestled with the giants of the bush, literally hewing out their homes in the wilderness. Not sparing themselves, they created a desirable and a healthy environment for their sons and daughters. Many had given up comfortable homes in the old lands so that their children and their children's children might have that freedom of life and thought and speech for which they themselves had been willing to make so many sacrifices.

Would it be natural, then, when Autocracy and Greed again threatened the free peoples of Europe, that a young nation born of the early settlers of New Zealand should stand aloof? A few weeks after the dreadful tragedy of Serajevo, realizing that the freedom of the world was again challenged, and recognizing to the full the gravity of the step, New Zealand placed all her resources at the disposal of the Mother Land.

The martial instincts of Maori and Pakeha were at once aroused. In the town enthusiasm was infectious; newspaper offices were besieged, and eager volunteers thronged the headquarters of each territorial unit; every shop, office and factory sent its representatives, and before the services of the Expeditionary Force were accepted by the Imperial Government the lists were full to overflowing.

From the country men crowded in. The musterer and station owner alike forsook their flocks; the bushman put away his crosscut and axe; the flaxmill hand left swamp and mill and hurried to the nearest railway station. Quiet men up on the hillside watched the train coming across country with the eagerly awaited newspapers. The strain of waiting was unendurable. With the call of Old England throbbing in their ears, they left their stock unattended in the paddocks and swelled the procession to the railway station. Here eager crowds discussed the situation. It was instinctively recognised that Britain must stand by France and Belgium, and when the news of that momentous decision did come the great wave of enthusiasm swept anew over the country side.

The Mobilization.

In those early days of August, the naval position in the Pacific was shrouded in mystery. Rumour was alarmingly busy. It was possible that the German Pacific fleet of heavily armed cruisers might appear at any moment off the New Zealand coast. Their only superior in these waters at the outbreak of war was the battle cruiser "Australia," the "New Zealand," of course, being in the North Sea. On August 6, a message from the Secretary of State for War was received by His Excellency the Governor: "If your Ministers desire and feel themselves able to seize the German wireless station at Samoa, we should feel that this was a great and urgent Imperial service. . . ." A force of 1,413 men immediately volunteered from territorial units in Auckland and Wellington, and sailed for their unknown destination on August 15, convoyed by three obsolescent "P" class cruisers —"Philomel," "Psyche," and "Pyramus"; joined by H.M.A.S. "Australia," H.M.A.S. "Melbourne," and the

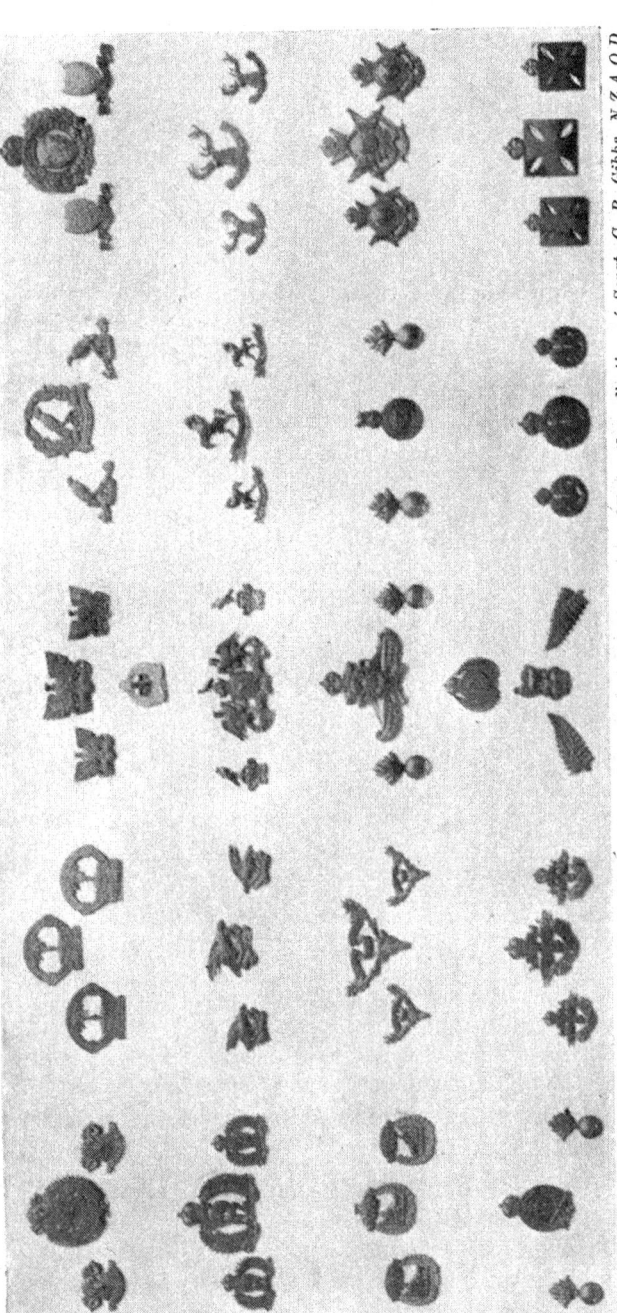

BADGES OF NEW ZEALAND MOUNTED RIFLES AND DIVISIONAL UNITS THAT SERVED AT SAMOA AND GALLIPOLI.

[*From the collection of Sergt. C. B. Gibbs, N.Z.A.O.D.*]

1st Canterbury Yeomanry Cavalry M.R.
6th Manawatu M.R.
11th North Auckland M.R.
Railway Battalions, N-Z.E.

2nd Wellington West Coast M.R.
7th Southland M.R.
12th Otago M.R.
Post and Telegraph Corps, N.Z.E.

3rd Auckland M.R.
N.Z. Army Nursing Service.
8th South Canterbury M.R.
N.Z. Field Artillery
N.Z. Staff Corps.
N.Z. Permanent Staff

4th Waikato M.R.
9th Wellington East Coast M.R.
Field Engineers, N.Z.E.
N.Z. Veterinary Corps.

5th Otago Hussars M.R.
10th Nelson M.R.
Signal Service, N.Z.E.
N.Z. Chaplains Dept.

French cruiser "Montcalm" at New Caledonia, the expedition proceeded on its way, occupying German Samoa on August 29 without firing a shot. Thus early in the Great War were New Zealand soldiers, supported by the allied navies, the first to take possession of German territory in the name of King George V.

On August 7, 1914, the New Zealand Government cabled to the Imperial authorities offering the services of an Expeditionary Force. On August 12 the offer was accepted, and preparations were made to have the force ready to embark for Europe on August 28. More and more men offered their services. Those declared unfit by the doctor in Auckland caught the train to Wellington, and if not successful there, went on and on until they found a loophole. Family men of fifty-five shaved their faces clean and enlisted with an "apparent age" of thirty-five. One man, with an artificial eye and minus two fingers, struggled into the N.Z.M.C.; while two gallant souls—veterans of previous wars—enlisted and were accepted as quartermasters, even though they had but one arm apiece.

A partial mobilization had already taken place at each regimental headquarters. The drafts, consisting mostly of men who had served in the Territorial Force and in previous wars, were sent to district concentration camps. The Auckland Mounted Rifles, Auckland Infantry Battalion, and the No. 1 Field Ambulance of the New Zealand Medical Corps were quartered in Alexandra Park, Auckland. The Wellington Mounted Rifles and the Wellington Infantry Battalion camped at the Awapuni Racecourse, near Palmerston North; here, also, were organized the N.Z. Field Artillery, the Field and Signal Troops of New Zealand Engineers, the company of Divisional Signallers, and the Mounted Field Ambulance, the men for these units being drawn in proportion from the territorial troops of the four Military Districts. Addington Park, Christchurch, was the rendezvous for the troops of the Canterbury Military District—the Canterbury Mounted Rifles Regiment and the Canterbury Infantry Battalion. The Otago Mounted Rifles Regiment and the Otago Infantry Battalion concentrated in Tahuna Park, near the Ocean Beach, Dunedin.

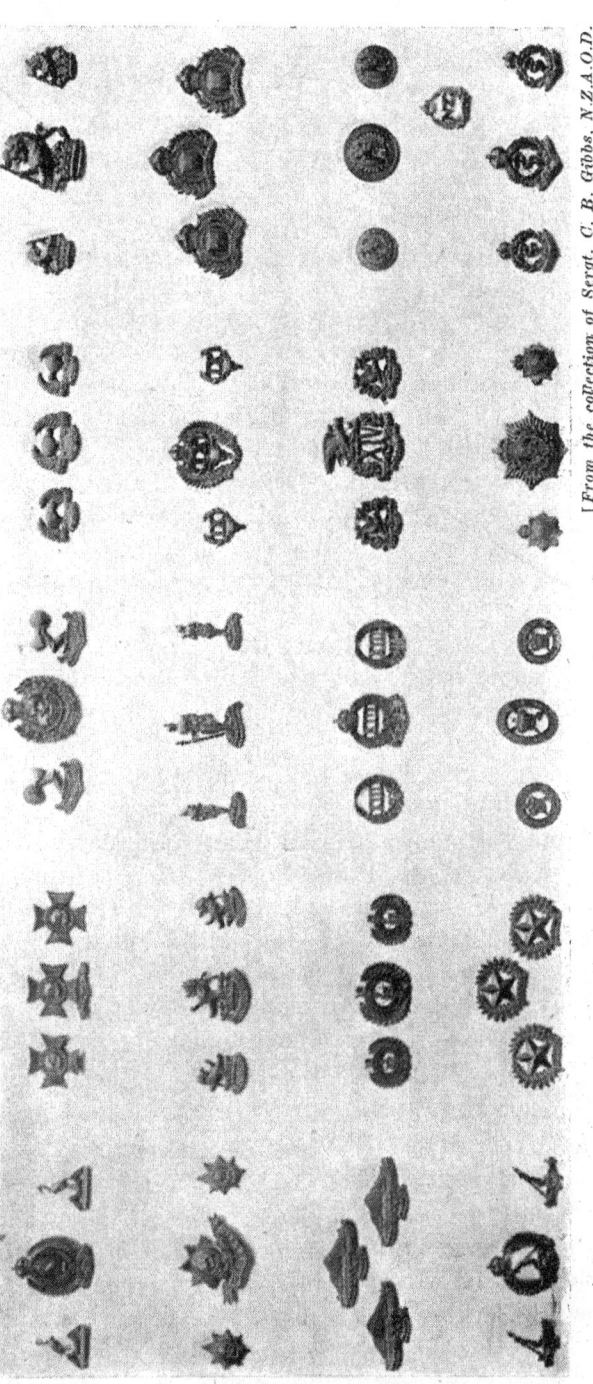

BADGES OF INFANTRY REGIMENTS THAT SERVED AT SAMOA AND GALLIPOLI.

[*From the collection of Sergt. C. B. Gibbs, N.Z.A.O.D.*

1st Canterbury Regiment.
6th Hauraki Regiment.
11th Taranaki Rifles Regiment.
16th Waikato Regiment.

2nd South Canterbury Regiment.
7th Wellington West Coast Regiment.
12th Nelson Regiment.
17th Ruahine Regiment.

3rd Auckland Regiment.
8th Southland Regiment.
13th North Canterbury and Westland Regiment.
N.Z. Maori Contingent.

4th Otago Regiment.
9th Hawkes Bay Regiment.
14th South Otago Regiment.
N.Z. Army Service Corps.

5th Wellington Regiment.
10th North Otago Regiment.
16th North Auckland Regiment.
N.Z. British Section.
N.Z. Medical Corps.

The territorial system of compulory training was still in its infancy, but it was considered advisable to retain the territorial distinctions. Each of the four Military Districts was asked to supply one regiment of mounted rifles and one battalion of infantry. Each territorial regiment and battalion supplied to the Expeditionary Force a squadron and a company respectively, and these units retained their badges and the customs of their parent organisations.

The organisation of the Expeditionary Force was that of the headquarters of a division, divisional troops, a mounted rifles brigade, and an infantry brigade. The Auckland, Wellington, and Canterbury Mounted Rifles Regiment made, with the Field and Signal Troops and Mounted Field Ambulance, a complete mounted brigade. The Otago Mounted Rifles Regiment became divisional cavalry, and did not form part of the brigade. The four infantry battalions—Auckland, Wellington, Canterbury, and Otago—made a complete infantry brigade.

The characteristic slouch hat, with the brim down all round, was adopted by the whole force; but the Otago Mounted Rifles, the New Zealand Field Artillery, and the Wellington Infantry Battalion wore their hats peaked and with four dents. After the evacuation of the Gallipoli Peninsula the entire New Zealand Division wore peaked hats, but the New Zealand Mounted Rifles remained faithful to the old style. A further distinguishing mark was the different coloured puggaree for each branch of the service. The troopers of the Mounted Rifles wore khaki and green; the gunners, red and blue; the sappers, khaki and blue; the infantry, khaki and red; the Army Service Corps, khaki and white; and the men of the Field Ambulance, khaki and maroon.

Equipping the Force.

The equipment of the force was no easy matter, though valuable material was obtained from the Territorial Force, which was being fitted out at the time. Most of the mounted riflemen brought their own horses to the place of concentration. If the animals were suitable, they were paid for, and became the property of the Government, but each man was

Otago Infantry entraining at Tahuna Park, Dunedin.

[Photo by Guy

allowed to ride the horse that he had brought. The saddles and equipment were mostly made in the Dominion. Day by day more material came to hand, and the men became more accustomed to manoeuvring in troops and squadrons; gradually but surely the mounted regiments evolved from very keen individual horsemen and shots to efficient military units. With the traditions of the South African campaign and the enthusiasm of the New Zealander for a good horse, the excellence of the mounted rifles was not at all surprising.

The field artillery were fortunate in that they had the nucleus of batteries in the officers and men of the Royal New Zealand Artillery—professional soldiers, who, in time of peace, trained the territorial batteries and garrisoned the artillery provided for coast defence. Thanks to the energy and foresight of the dominion artillerists, the old 15-pounders had been replaced by modern 18-pounders, and more fortunate still, New Zealand had, in 1914, some of the newest 4.5 howitzers, which guns above all others were to prove their worth in the closing days of April, 1915. The horses for the gun teams were procured mostly in the Wellington District—some were well broken, others were broken to chains in the plough, a number had hardly been handled at all; but the drivers set to with a will, and soon the roads of Palmerston North were enlivened with spirited six-horse teams jingling along with their businesslike guns and limbers.

The sappers of the field troop were drawn in equal proportions from the territorial field companies. There were no divisional field engineers, only a mounted brigade troop. In order to keep up with the cavalry, light collapsible boats were substituted for the heavy pontoons of the ordinary field company. No boats were available in New Zealand, the intention being to pick them up in England when the Expeditionary Force landed there. The signal troop and divisional signallers were all territorials, most of the operators being highly skilled men from the Post and Telegraph Department.

Owing to the large numbers available for selection, the infantry were a magnificent body of men. Born of freedom-loving parents in a free country, nurtured in a land of plenty with a climate unsurpassed on earth, it is not surprising that the trained New Zealander is modelled like a Greek statue. To see a battalion of infantry bathing in the Manawatu River was a wonderful sight. The clean blue sky, the waving toi toi on the fringe of native bush, the river rippling and sprawling over its gravelly bed, the thousand beautiful athletes splashing in the sun-kissed water, made an ineffaceable impression. The New Zealand infantry soldier trained at Alexandra Park, Awapuni, Addington, and Tahuna Park has long since proved his courage and steadfastness to be equal to his undeniable physique and fitness.

[*Lent by Capt. Boxer, N.Z.M.C.*]
LOADING HORSES ON THE "STAR OF INDIA" AT AUCKLAND.

The matter of transport was a difficult one. As yet the New Zealand Army Service Corps of the Territorial Force was not organized. Men and horses were forthcoming, but suitable waggons were hard to procure. Eventually a number of waggons—some suitable and some otherwise—were purchased. Many were only a quarter-lock, and the angry drivers were sometimes heard to murmur that no place but the wide deserts of Egypt would have been sufficient to turn—much less manoeuvre—in!

The personnel of the New Zealand Medical Corps was from the outset most efficient. The senior officers had mostly seen service in former campaigns; the men were enthusiastic territorials and keen young medical students who had forsaken their classes when the call came.

In all branches of the service discipline was very strict. Men realized that if they transgressed they would cease to be members of the Main Body. There was no crime. All ranks understood they were chosen to represent New Zealand in the eyes of the world.

Passed by the doctor, the recruit was fitted out with that wonderful receptacle, the soldier's kit bag. This was soon filled to overflowing by the combined efforts of a paternal Government and committees of enthusiastic ladies. All the uniforms and purely military kit came from the ordnance stores, but the woollen stuff — socks, underclothing and woollen caps—were the handiwork and gift of the women of New Zealand. Surely never before in history had an army so many socks and shirts! It must be admitted that in the first flush of enthusiasm some good folks showed more energy than skill in the matter of shirt making. The soldier is nothing if not adaptable, so he cut off the superfluous portion of sleeve. One was not surprised that the sergeant-major, wanting the men for physical drill, daily shouted "Fall in the kimonos."

Waiting for the Escort.

Through August and the first weeks of September the training and equipping went on. Four transports were lying alongside the Wellington wharves, and two ships at each of the other three ports of embarkation—Auckland, Lyttelton and Port Chalmers. Day and night carpenters laboured fitting up the troop and horse decks.

On September 24, the people of Wellington assembled at Newtown Park to witness the farewell parade of the divisional troops, the Wellington Mounted Rifles Regiment, and the Wellington Infantry Battalion. After an inspection by His Excellency the Governor, the Prime Minister and the Minister of Defence, the troops marched through cheering crowds to the transports, and at half-past five that evening all but the "Maunganui" pulled out into the stream, ready

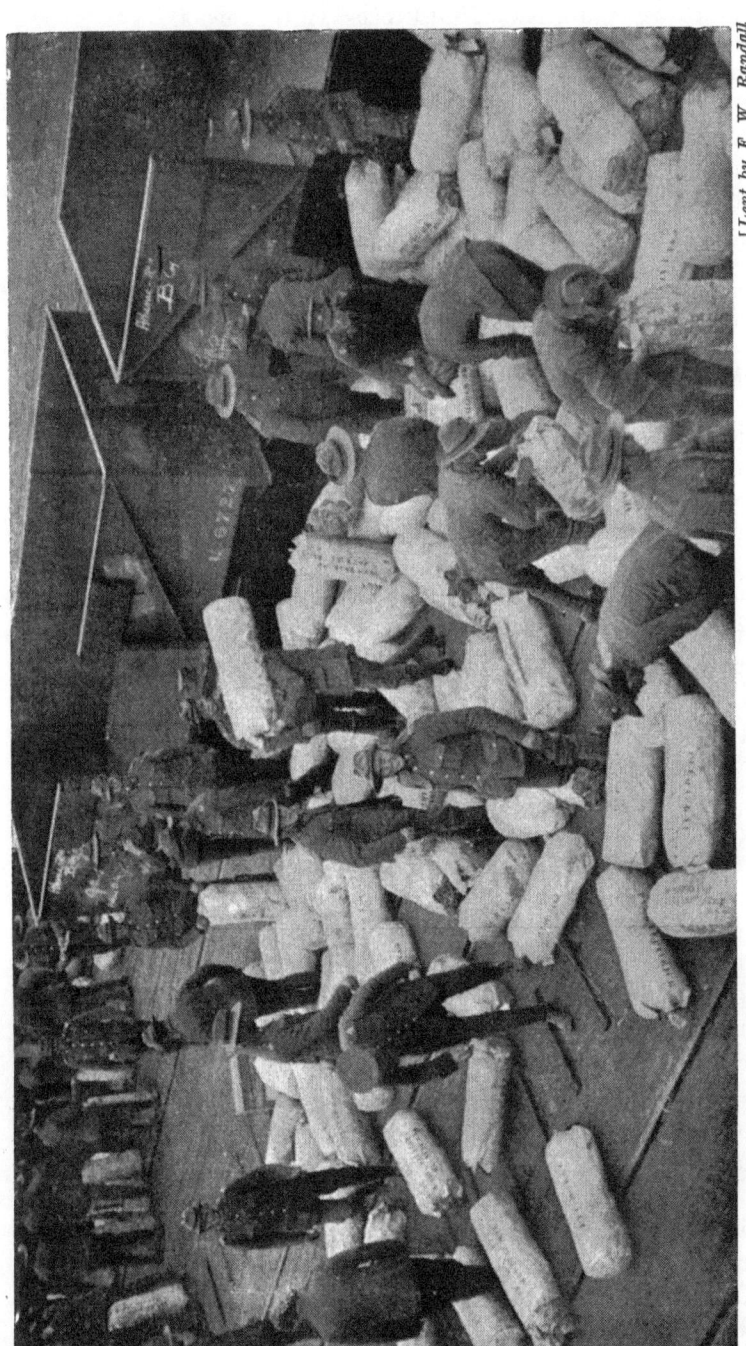

SORTING KIT-BAGS ALONGSIDE THE "ATHENIC," LYTTELTON.

[*Lent by F. W. Randall*

to sail early next morning to join the Auckland ships at sea. During the evening of the 24th the four ships from Lyttelton and Port Chalmers joined the Wellington quota in the harbour. All night anxious relatives made endeavours to get aboard the vessels in the stream to say a last farewell or deliver a parting gift, while the people of Wellington went betimes to bed to awaken early and see the fleet steam out.

But early next morning a wireless message recalled H.M.S. "Philomel," the "Waimana," and the "Star of India," which had left Auckland the night before. In Wellington the seven transports in the harbour rejoined the "Maunganui" alongside the wharves. The mounted units and horses were disembarked and scattered to camps round Wellington, there to remain until a more powerful naval escort was available.

For three weeks the troops, chafing at the delay, were exercised in musketry and route marching. At nights they crowded into Wellington for a little amusement. The women of Wellington rose splendidly to the occasion. Concert parties entertained the men every night in "U" shed on the wharf. At this time the well-known Sydney Street Soldiers' Club was started. The soldier realizes that he may never come back, and that sacrifice he is prepared to make willingly. He sings and is happy because he feels—though often in an indefinite way—that he did the right thing in enlisting. But the times of waiting—whether at the base or in the front-line trench—are most irritating. Being a healthy animal, he must be doing something. It is here that soldiers' clubs, managed by understanding, sympathetic women, prove of inestimable value. For their untiring efforts the women of Wellington are entitled to the thanks of all the mothers of men concentrated in Wellington throughout the four long years of war.

On October 14, the troops exercising their horses in the surf at Lyall Bay were delighted to see a big grey four-funnelled cruiser, flying the white ensign, closely followed by a huge black three-funnelled monster with the rising sun displayed. Past Somes Island and Evans Bay they steamed and dropped anchor, proving to be H.M.S. "Minotaur" and H.I.J.M.S. "Ibuki," the escort which the army was anxiously expecting.

Waiting for the Escort.

Next day the "Star of India" and "Waimana," escorted by the "Philomel," arrived in Wellington from Auckland, and proceeded to water and coal. The ten transports were now assembled, and the four cruisers made ready to convoy the precious freight on the first stage of its long journey. Many are the valuable cargoes that have left these shores, but for the first time in the history of New Zealand were nine thousand gallant souls—the flower of the young nation's manhood—going down to the sea in ships.

[Lent by F. W. Randall

The "Ibuki" and "Minotaur" in Wellington Harbour.

By half-past three on the afternoon of Thursday, October 15, the mounted units were again embarked. The last good-byes were exchanged with relatives ashore, and night fell on Wellington Harbour with its fleet of fourteen historic ships. The morning broke beautifully fine. The fleet weighed anchor at 6 o'clock. Crowds of early risers saw the ships go out, preceded by the "Minotaur" and the "Ibuki." The first division of ships was led by the cruiser "Psyche" and the second division by the "Philomel." So the watchers on Mount Victoria saw the long grey line slip silently down the Straits.

CHAPTER II.

The Voyage to Egypt.

While confined to the narrow waters of Cook Strait, the fleet preserved its line ahead formation, but after passing Cape Farewell the two divisions of five ships each steamed in parallel lines eight cable lengths apart. Miles ahead raced the "Minotaur," a speck on the horizon; the "Philomel" was four miles astern; while on either beam, six miles away, were the other two cruisers—the "Ibuki" to starboard and the "Psyche" to port.

The weather was typical of the Tasman Sea, and both men and horses suffered a good deal from seasickness. Where there were many horses, particularly on ships like the "Orari," those who were well enough had plenty to do cleaning the horse decks and setting unsteady animals on their feet. That only four horses died out of the 3815 on board speaks volumes for the care taken in selection and the solicitude of the seasick troopers and drivers.

[Lent by Major Brunt, W.I.R.

Resting on the Boat Deck.

A Great Welcome at Hobart.

After six weary days at sea no one was sorry to see Wednesday morning break with the rugged coast of Tasmania ahead; little wonder that the prospect of a three hours' route march on the morrow was received with jubilation. Next morning it seemed that all Hobart was astir. With packs up the infantry cut a fine figure. All along the route women and children showered flowers on the troops. Wherever a halt was made the people brought out bunches of beautiful roses, which the soldiers carried back to grace their none too ornamental quarters. Thousands of the famous Tasmanian apples were pressed upon the men. Some enthusiasts presented the artillery with a garland on a pole, which the proud gunners carried before them as a colour. Back again at the wharf, the sellers of apples and crayfish did brisk business, and many were the commissions handed over by the sportsmen aboard to be dealt with by the celebrated Hobart house of Tattersall. When the gangways were up the people thronged the wharves, handing up parcels of cakes, sweets and apples. The regimental bands struck up "It's a long way to Tipperary," and the ships pulled out to the accompaniment of tumultuous cheering.

It was three o'clock that afternoon when the ships again put to sea. The "Psyche" returned to New Zealand, and her place was taken by the "Pyramus." The long rolling swell common to the Great Australian Bight again made things very uncomfortable for the horses; to make matters worse, a thick fog descended, speed was reduced, and every few minutes the ear was assailed by the blasts of the "Minotaur" syren and the answering shrieks from the vessels of the fleet.

Gradually the weather moderated and the men became steadier on their legs. Musketry practice at floating targets was initiated; where there was room on the crowded decks physical training was carried on, while the mounted men had their horses with the never-ending stables—it being recognized that the habit of absolute cleanliness in regard to both the men's and the horses' quarters should become second nature before the really hot weather was encountered.

THE WELL SET UP INFANTRY OF THE MAIN BODY PARADING AT HOBART FOR A ROUTE MARCH.

[*Lent by F. W. Randall*

A private of the New Zealand Medical Corps died on Sunday, October 26, and next day a most impressive burial service was conducted on the "Ruapehu." At three o'clock she steamed out of her line and took station in the centre of the parallel divisions. At half-past three, when colours were hoisted and lowered to half-mast, the troops in each transport paraded with their bands. The flagship having made the signal to "Stop engines," the troops on all ships stood to attention, whereupon the "Dead March" was played, followed by a short funeral service; the body of the first soldier of the New Zealand Expeditionary Force to die overseas was reverently committed to the deep. The firing party having fired its three volleys, the solemn notes of the "Last Post" floated over the sunlit waters, the flagship signalled "11 knots," and the convoy proceeded on its way.

Young Australia greets Young New Zealand.

Thirteen days after leaving Wellington the New Zealand ships crept into the spacious harbour of Albany, Western Australia. Here were gathered innumerable vessels of every line trading in the Southern oceans. Not painted uniformly grey like our ships, but taken in all their glory of greens, blues and yellows, they rode on the calm water of King George's Sound packed with the adventurous spirits of the First Australian Division. The cheering and counter-cheering, the Maori war cries and answering coo-ees would have moved a stoic. Young Australia was welcoming Young New Zealand in no uncertain manner in the first meeting of those brothers-in-arms soon to be known by a glorious name as yet undreamed of.

After a few days spent in replenishing supplies, the wonderful armada put out to sea. The twenty-six Australian transports steamed in three parallel divisions, being joined a day out by two Westralian transports from Fremantle. The New Zealand ships retained their old formation, the two divisions covering off the blank spaces of the Australian convoy. We parted company from the old "P" class cruisers, but got in return the two new Australian ships, the "Sydney" and the "Melbourne," long, snakey-looking craft with four

AN IMPRESSIVE SUNDAY SERVICE ON THE "ATHENIC."
[Lent by F. W. Randall

rakish funnels. The "Minotaur" was still steaming away ahead, while to starboard was our old friend the "Ibuki," evidently burning bad coal, her three black funnels belching forth tremendous volumes of the blackest smoke.

Great attention was now paid to the masking of all lights by night. It was known that German cruisers were at large—notably the "Scharnhorst," "Gneisenau" and "Emden." In order to evade these ocean highwaymen the usual course was not set through the Indian Ocean. For the same reason, a strict censorship in regard to movements of ships prevailed in Australia and New Zealand. At Hobart and Albany the greatest precautions were taken. Ample proof was ultimately forthcoming that this trouble was not in vain.

But the convoy was a very cumbersome thing. The cruiser leading and the cruiser acting as a rearguard were both hull down on the horizon. There was an Australian transport that most days could do nine knots with an effort; one or two erratic performers like this sorely trying the practised station-keepers of the Imperial Navy. Characteristic sailor messages were being constantly transmitted. The following is a sample:—"From H.M.S. 'Minotaur' to all transports: The attention of masters of Australian transports is again drawn to the extreme importance of keeping accurate station, especially at night. During last night the Second Division straggled to seven miles, whereas their line should be three miles in length. The Third Division straggled to six miles, whereas their line should be three miles and a half. By this careless station-keeping the masters expose their ships to an increased risk of being torpedoed by an enemy, and also involve the New Zealand convoy in the same danger. The New Zealand convoy are keeping stations at three cables apart in excellent order, and their great attention to convoy orders as regards reduction of power of lights merits my warm approval. The 'Medic' and 'Geelong' were signalling last night with lights visible at least ten miles. I again point out the necessity of reducing the power of lights by blue bunting or other means."

A strange ship on the horizon always aroused great speculation; never did a cloud of smoke materialize into a ship but the stranger was already attended by one of our escorting cruisers. Thus was the R.M.S. "Osterley" of the Orient line examined, and later passed the convoy on Guy Fawkes Day, homeward bound, carrying the soldiers' Christmas mails.

An air of expectancy hung over the convoy on Sunday, November 8, for on that day news arrived of the naval battle off Valparaiso, in which H.M.S. "Good Hope" and H.M.S. "Monmouth" were destroyed by a superior German force.

Early that same morning the "Minotaur" signalled to the "Maunganui": "I am ordered on another service; wish you the very best of success when you land in France. Give the Germans a good shake-up. It has been a great pleasure to escort such a well-disciplined force and convoy. Good-bye."

The Triumph of Australia.

The flagship's place ahead was now held by the "Melbourne," with the "Ibuki" to starboard and the "Sydney" to port.

With the news of the Valparaiso battle and the departure of the "Minotaur" came word that the Cocos Islands would be passed during the night, and special precautions were ordered to be taken in regard to lights. The usual sharp look-out was kept, but the hours of darkness slipped by without incident. But at 6.30 a.m. the "Melbourne" turned to port and spoke for a few minutes to her sister ship. By this time all the transports were aware of the wireless messages from the Cocos Islands signalling "S.O.S.," "Strange warship approaching." The Australian transport "Karoo" and the New Zealand transport "Arawa" picked up the following: "PNX DE WSP DE PNX NE DE NGI PFB DEO," also, "S.O.S.—Strange warship at entrance. Ignores our remarks—S.O.S., S.O.S.," then a long message, apparently in Dutch. These mixed-up messages, obviously mutilated and jammed by the hostile Telefunken, provided knotty problems for those whose duty it was to fathom the mysteries of code and cypher.

The captain of the "Melbourne," being in charge of the convoy, could not go to the Cocos Islands, sixty miles away,

THE LAST OF THE "EMDEN."

While the "Sydney" dealt with the "Emden," the "Ibuki" and "Melbourne" lay on the threatened quarter of the convoy. The action took place out of the sight and sound of the troops on the transports, which were over seventy miles away from the Cocos Group.

so ordered the "Sydney" on this service. By 7 p.m. the cruiser had worked up to her speed and was rapidly lost to sight. The "Melbourne" came down to the "Sydney's" place on the threatened flank, and then the attention of the whole convoy was rivetted on the Japanese cruiser coming across from starboard around the head of the convoy. As she forged ahead through the heavy swell a great white wave streamed over her bows, being made more conspicuous by her pitch black hull and the three black funnels belching enormous columns of dense black smoke. Tearing through the indigo Indian Ocean, with her great battle flags streaming blood-red in the breeze, she became the very personification of energy and power.

With the two cruisers lying handy on the threatened flank, the troops waited anxiously for news. All realized that just across the horizon a life and death struggle was taking place. No sound of battle could be heard but the spluttering of the wireless, from which it was learned at 9.30 that the enemy had been brought to action.

The men could hardly contain themselves for excitement This was intensified when, about 11 o'clock, the Japanese cruiser appeared to steam away in the direction of the fight. But at twenty minutes past eleven the wireless announced. "Enemy beached herself to prevent sinking." Restraint was thrown aside. The men cheered again and again. Messages then chased one another in quick succession: "Emden beached and done for. Am chasing merchant collier." The cheering burst out afresh, for this was the first mention of the "Emden." How the New Zealanders envied the Australians this momentous achievement of their young navy.

About half an hour later came the story of the price paid for admiralty—two killed and thirteen wounded. The troops shouted themselves hoarse when they learned that the "Emden" was ashore on North Cocos Isle, and had surrendered with her foremast and three funnels down. The following message was sent from the "Maunganui": "Many congratulations from the N.Z.E.F. on result of first action of the Australian Navy." Back came a typical naval answer: "Reply to your signal of yesterday. Many thanks to New

Zealand Squadron for their congratulations. It is very satisfactory that in its baptism of fire the superiority of town class cruiser over German town class light cruiser was so completely established."

Four days after this most memorable day a signal announced that H.M.S. "Hampshire" was steaming fifty miles ahead of us, and to facilitate coaling and watering at Colombo, the New Zealand squadron was ordered to steam ahead of the Australians, who were left in charge of the "Ibuki."

The line was crossed on the same day (November 13), and His Deep Sea Majesty King Neptune, attended by his consort and a numerous suite of barbers, bears, and orderlies, came aboard each of the transports. All deference and homage was paid, and the hoary old salt never had a busier day— eight thousand four hundred New Zealanders paying their tribute according to their respective popularity with His Majesty's attendants.

A Run Ashore at Colombo.

Two days steaming brought the "Hampshire" and her convoy within sight of Ceylon. This to most New Zealanders was the first far-off view of a tropical isle. As the ships steamed over an unruffled sea, the troops drank in the wonderful sight, so refreshing after the tiresome monotony of the voyage. The little brown fishing boats were thickly sprinkled over a fleckless seascape — ashore the beautiful buildings resplendent in a setting of graceful palms. Up the coast and round the breakwater the squadron picked its way through a flotilla of every conceivable variety of small craft.

Inside the crowded harbour lay our old friend the "Melbourne" and a quaint five-funnelled warship—the Russian cruiser "Askold," which we were later to know so well. The work of the "Emden" had been fairly thorough—during her career she had sunk sixteen merchant ships, the Russian cruiser "Jemtchug," and the French destroyer "Mousquet"— and here in Colombo Harbour were dozens of ships which had been held up, but were again free to sail the ocean highways.

About half an hour after our arrival, it was rumoured that the "Sydney" was coming, and sure enough, there were the familiar four funnels with their little white bands, and closely following her the big "Empress of Russia" with her cruiser stern. Slowly the gallant ship come round the breakwater to her moorings. As she passed the New Zealand transports it was evident that she was, as her captain described her, "nothing but a hospital of a most painful

[Lent by F. W. Randal
THE VICTOR.
The "Sydney" steaming round Colombo breakwater after destroying the "Emden."

description." Wounded Germans were lying on stretchers all over the deck, and on that account the soldiers, though greatly thrilled and moved by the obvious marks of battle on the ship, stood respectfully silent at attention.

The prisoners, 138 in number, were distributed over the Australian and New Zealand transports, an officer and half a dozen men being placed on each ship. Many of them could speak English, having served on British merchant ships. It then became apparent that the precautions of darkening lights and a strict censorship had indeed borne fruit, for on the night of November 8, the "Emden" actually crossed the bows of our convoy, accompanied by a captured British collier, the "Buresk," heavily laden with the best Welsh coal. The raider, knowing nothing of our presence, arrived off the Cocos group early in the morning, and sent a party ashore on Direction Island to destroy the cable and the wireless station, which barely had time to send out the S.O.S. received by the fleet. The

A Run Ashore at Colombo.

appearance of the Australian cruiser on the horizon (the Germans took her to be H.M.S. "Yarmouth") was the first intimation to the "Emden" that all was not well. The German ship put out to sea and fought her last sea fight, while the armed party ashore busied themselves with preparing the "Ayesha," a local schooner, for flight. The "Sydney" had to turn her attention to the collier, which was endeavouring to escape. On overtaking her, it was found that her sea-cocks were open, and as she could not be saved, the "Sydney" fired a couple of shots into her at the water line. Night coming on, the schooner with her adventurous crew successfully cleared the Cocos, apparently for the African coast. Such were the facts as gleaned from the German prisoners.

[Photo by Capt. Paddon, O.M.R.

PRISONERS FROM THE "EMDEN."
The 138 prisoners were distributed among the Australian and New Zealand transports.

From the transports in Colombo Harbour 200 men at a time went ashore from each ship; each party being broken up into smaller ones of twenty men with an officer. Going ashore in the boats we pulled through clouds of lemon, chrome, and golden butterflies fluttering over the water in all directions, reminding one of yellow poplar leaves drifting to the ground in an autumn wind. Once ashore the brilliant colours and fragrant flower scents seemed like fairyland after the heat and smell of the horse decks. Along the brick-red sandy roads the rickshaw coolies pattered with their slouch-hatted loads. Under the shade of the Eastern trees the soldier snatched one hour of the real joy of living. Interested parties explored the Buddhist temples, the air heavy with incense and the scent of many flowers. Down on the Galle Face, where the cocoanut palms weep over the sea, the revelation of poverty and mendicity came as a shock to the young New Zealanders—thousands of beggars, the halt, the lame and the blind—small boys begging pennies, old men with one foot in the grave complaining in broken English, "No mother, no father, sixpence please!"

[Photo by Guy
ON THE HORSE DECKS.

The New Zealand soldier away from home is prodigal with his money, and the Cingalese and Indian shopkeepers parcelled up many thousands of pounds worth of gifts, ranging from precious stones and expensive silks down to the cocoanut-wood elephants and the little green-backed beetles. The censors never left their desks, so energetic were the correspondents, but gradually the pile grew less and the mail bags more swollen; the shouting gangs of dirty coolies passed—basketful by basketful—the contents of their loaded barges into the hungry stokeholds; all water tanks were refilled, and on the morning of November 17, the New Zealand transports, escorted by the "Hampshire," headed once again for the deep water.

[*Lent by Major Brunt, W.I.B.*

The "Hampshire."
Transferring the "Emden" prisoners to the "Hampshire" at Port Said.

The Monotony of the Voyage.

In a sense this was the most wearisome stage of the journey, although there was a little to interest. By day, shoals of flying fish leaped ahead of the ships, shimmered in the sunlight, and splashed again into the depths; and in the hours of darkness the stable picket gazing out of the porthole marvelled at the mass of gleaming phosphorescence. But the monotony of the warm weather and a placid sea, together with the reaction after the glorious taste of freedom at Colombo, did not make for tranquility of spirit. Even the civilian passenger in the first saloon tires of marvellous seascapes, and ship's food, however daintily served, becomes repugnant. Pity, then, the poor soldier cramped up in a transport; necessarily living on monotonous food which he must help to prepare; tending horses and cleaning up the ship; stiff from the inoculations designed to protect him in the future, and steaming steadily on (at a rate of nine knots per hour!) to a destination only vaguely guessed at. So it was a relief to reach that rocky outpost, Aden, and to learn that just on the horizon hostile Arabs and Turks were bent on making trouble. Dicomforts were quickly forgotten in the thrill of nearing battle grounds. Away on those red sands we could picture Turk and Teuton scheming and planning to get possession of those priceless water cisterns.

No one was allowed ashore, but the harbour was full of interest. Nine big vessels packed with South Wales Borderers and Middlesex Territorials were coaling, on their way to India. The "Ibuki" here wished us good-bye and steamed away to join the Southern Japanese squadron.

[Photo by Capt. Paddon, O.M.R.
"Monday."

The voyage from Aden to Suez was commenced on Thursday, November 26, with the "Hampshire" escorting the entire Australian and New Zealand fleet in five divisions, the five leading ships all being in line. We passed Perim at 2.30 in the afternoon, the New Zealand ships having been ordered to steam five miles ahead of the Australians.

It was anticipated that the horses would be severely tried in the Red Sea. When a following wind got up the troopers were more apprehensive, but the horses seemed determined to do honour to their native land, and there was little sickness.

Ordered to Disembark in Egypt.

In the Red Sea a wireless was received instructing the Force to prepare for a disembarkation in Egypt. Turkey being at war with the Allies and already threatening the Suez Canal, this turn of affairs was not surprising, but some were disappointed that anything should occur to defer our landing in France to help the sorely tried British and French Armies.

At 5 o'clock on December 30, the first New Zealand ship, the "Maunganui," entered the Canal. Each ship had a little engine installed forward to provide for the powerful electric headlight fastened on the bows. The armed guard stationed on the starboard side strained their ears and eyes for any movement, but there was nothing evident except the beautiful

[Lent by F. W. Randall
STEAMING INTO ALEXANDRIA.

stars, the Indian sentries pacing noiselessly up and down their sandy beats, and the incessant chatter of the little engine forward.

"Who are you?" shouted a voice from the desert, and continued, "126th Baluchis here." "We're New Zealanders," was the quiet answer. "Hooray!" cried the Baluchi, "Advance Australia!" It must be said that since that December day of 1914, both Baluchi and New Zealander have

DISEMBARKING AT ALEXANDRIA.

In the foreground is a white "ramp" used for disembarking horses. On the outskirts of the group

[Lent by F. W. Randall

gained a good deal of geographical knowledge—at the same time removing an amount of ignorance, the price of previous insularity.

From Suez to the Bitter Lakes, past all the posts we were destined to know so well; past Ismailia and the fortifications of Kantara, the transports slowly steamed. It was the New Zealander's first real glimpse of Empire. Here lining the banks were the picturesque bearded Sikhs, the native cavalry and infantry from every frontier State, and the alert Ghurka with his familiar slouch hat and short trousers.

At Port Said the German prisoners of war were transferred to the "Hampshire." This was the last we saw of the famous cruiser, fated to become, on the disastrous day, July 5, 1916, off the Orkneys coast, the ocean mausoleum of that great soldier, Field-Marshal Lord Kitchener of Khartoum.

Exactly seven weeks after leaving Wellington Harbour, the look-outs saw with the dawn of December 3, the great white city of Alexandria standing in a sea of mist. Slowly we forged ahead until clustering spars resolved themselves into a multitude of transports and captured sailing ships, for here were interned most of the enemy mercantile marine captured in the Eastern Mediterranean. By 8 o'clock that morning six of the New Zealand transports were alongside, and clamouring round, the long-skirted rabble of the Egyptian seaport beheld in the stalwart colonials the same material as that which wrested victory at Tel-el-Kebir and Omdurman.

The poor horses were delighted to get ashore; groggy on their feet, they cut the most amusing capers. Soon men and stores, guns and horses, were en route to the railway station, where troop trains were waiting, and in a few hours were speeding across some of the most magnificent agricultural country in the world—the delta of the Nile.

CHAPTER III.

Training in Egypt.

The first troop train, with Divisional Headquarters on board, got away late in the afternoon, and pursued its way past old Lake Mareotis, with the little brown fishing boats dotted over its waters, into the heart of the Nile Delta. In the failing light the network of irrigation canals, the graceful date palms, and the unpretentious mud houses were dimly discernible.

All night long more trains were loaded and disappeared into the gloom. The Cairo-Alexandria express would be a credit to any English railway company, doing the journey of 133 miles in a little over three hours, but the troop trains, like their kindred all over the world, took a little more leisure, being about eight hours on the way, the first train reaching Zeitoun, four miles further on through Cairo, at 1 o'clock the next morning. The baggage and supplies were tumbled out into the darkness; guards were mounted; and horses and men trudged their weary way about a mile and a half along a dusty white road and across a sandy desert, eventually coming to a halt near a racecourse, to the picket fence of which the horses were made secure, while those who could lay down on the sand to snatch an hour or two of sleep.

It was the Egyptian winter and the nights were exceedingly cold, but the weary men slept on. More and more trains rolled in to Helmieh and Palais de Koubbeh; more and more men and horses stumbled into the bivouac, until about 5 o'clock even the heaviest sleeper was awake and endeavouring to restore circulation until the rising sun should dissipate the morning mist. A great hunger became infectious—most men had a ration of bully beef and biscuits, but the wherewithal to make the welcome billy of tea was not forthcoming. Then the New Zealanders found real friends—friends in need—the men of the East Lancashire Territorial Division, for the generous North Countrymen arrived with

Training in Egypt.

steaming dixies of tea and "summat t' eat." These were the first English troops we had "lain" alongside, and the good-fellowship so welcomely begun in the desert was strengthened later on the Gallipoli Peninsula.

Presently the sun burst triumphantly through the mist and disclosed a bivouac of thousands of men and horses lying on the edge of a limitless desert. As far as the eye could see was a yellow sandy plain. This was skirted on the Cairo side by the main Heliopolis-Suez road, which ran east and west through the camp, and was bounded on the far horizon by a range of low brown sandhills. Soon all hands were at work pitching headquarters and the supply depots south of this

"Donks."   [*Photo by the Author*

These big mules of the N.Z. Divisional Train were bred in North America.

main road and the other units north of it. A new road at right angles to the main road was constructed in a northerly direction—on the right of which the mounted rifles, artillery and ambulance placed their tents and horse lines, while the infantry occupied the whole of the left hand side. Water-pipes had been laid on and watering troughs for horses were already on the ground, and by evening some order had been evolved, though many troops had again to bivouac in the open, realizing that, notwithstanding the poets, the sands of the desert do become very cold about 2 o'clock in the morning.

By the end of a week all the ships had been cleared of men, horses and stores, and the three colonial camps had shaken down into something like order—the Australian infantry at Mena, under the shadow of the great Pyramids; the Australian Light Horse at Medi; and the New Zealanders at Zeitoun. The horses were not fit for either transport work or driving, but for a week or two were exercised in progressive work until able to stand the strain of manoeuvres. Out of nearly four thousand horses only eighty-eight failed to survive the buffetting journey through the Tasman Sea and Great Australian Bight, the sweltering heat of the Indian Ocean and the Red Sea, and the hazardous acclimatization in a hot and sandy desert—there they stood in long and polished rows, chewing the succulent berseem and munching the dry and uninviting tibbin, which apparently caused the horses much less concern than it did the anxious troopers.

Training commenced in earnest. Early every morning the infantry battalions paraded in full marching order and trudged through miles of sandy desert. Like so much of the

[Photo by the Author
THE WATER CART ON THE DESERT.

soldier's life, this work was not interesting, but it was necessary; with clothing designed for a cool climate the long columns swung out along the never-ending sands, hardening the hardy ones, the cruel desert slowly but mercilessly winnowing out the few unfit. If a man had a bad knee or a weak chest, those weary sweltering marches and misty nights sought out the weak, who were sent to the Egyptian Army Hospital at Abassia, where Australian nurses of Queen Alexandra's Imperial Nursing Service nursed them tenderly back to health, or sent them broken-hearted to convalesce at Alexandria preparatory to their long sea voyage home.

The mounted rifles, artillery and engineers daily exercised their horses and teams until it was possible to have squadron and battery training. Out in the hot sun all day, by diligence and care, men and horses became efficient units in the

[Lent by Capt. Boxer, N.Z.M.C.

IN THE SHADE OF THE DATE PALMS.

great machine. The way was not always a sandy one; sometimes the route lay along the banks of the irrigation canals, past ancient sakiehs and Archimedean screws lifting the precious water into the little tributary canals that are the life of Egypt. Past fields of wheat and tomatoes; acres of beans reminding one of Thoreau's sojourn in the wilds; down scented orange groves and acacia avenues; through acres and acres of the clover known as berseem—the soldiers went their way, marvelling at the fertility of a land that produces three crops within the year.

On those fresh dewy mornings, with the crows chattering noisily in the trees overhead, one realised what made Egypt triumph over Time. These simple fellaheen and their forbears had watched Hittite, Assyrian, Persian, Greek and Roman sweep through the country and ravish its beauty, to be followed in later days by Saracen and Turk with the same intent; and here, long years after, following in the great line of fighting men, but striving for freedom and not conquest, the soldiers from the Antipodes, glorying in their youth, pass

[Photo by the Author

CATTLE ON BERSEEM.

Berseem is a variety of lucerne, and is the staple green food of camels, horses, cattle, goats and sheep. It helps to keep the Nile Delta fertile.

the old obelisk at Heliopolis and recognize that, perhaps more than pride of race, a fertile soil and a diligent husbandry make for national longevity.

It may have been because of the church parades, where men sang the hymns they knew—hymns associated with their early life and Sunday school, or perhaps during the service men let their minds wander from the dust and glare of Egypt to the green fields and the loved ones of home—but whatever the cause, Sunday was essentially the day of letter writing. On Sunday afternoons, groups of men wandered further afield—to the mighty Pyramids of Ghizeh, there to pose on the protesting camels for the conventional photograph of tourist, sphinx and pyramid; or perchance to the Zoo at Ghezireh, with its

"LIZZIE"

quaint mosaic paths, its giraffes and the bewitching "Lizzie," with her radiant smile and open countenance. Crowds were fascinated by the collection of antiquities in the Egyptian Museum, and by those polished cases in which, surrounded by great sphinxes and pylons, sleep the former kings of four and five thousand years ago. It is difficult to conceive that these were ever people of flesh and blood, until the revelation of mummified queens with their tiny babies forces one to realize that they, too, once were really human in their hates and loves, their triumphs and disappointments.

Most of the soldiers' spare time was naturally spent in Cairo. Here everything seemed to be licensed except the drinking shops—the newsboy needed a license to sell his papers; the donkey boys and donkeys, who seemed numberless, were really carefully numbered; the futile red-tarbushed police spent much of their time chasing the bootblack who dared to ply without a permit. Owing to the war, the tourist season had failed—the rich Americans had stayed at home—

[Photo by the Author

"MILK DIET."
A Camel Study on the road to Helouan.

but in the well-paid Australians and New Zealanders the astute merchants found suitable substitutes, whom they proceeded to bleed most unmercifully. Out into the streets they came with their wares. In the natural course of affairs men hawked sugar-cane, vegetables, live poultry, sweetmeats and cakes; the clang of the liquorice-water sellers' gongs clashed with those of the lemonade man; round the cafes, where the patron sits at a little table on a footpath, men tendered their little trays of shrimps and dusty plates of strawberries—all these now supplemented by an army of boys and men trading walking-sticks and swagger canes by the thousand; antiques made out of Nile mud; ancient Dervish weapons with the dust of Birmingham still upon them; foreign postage stamps on sheets; scenic postcards and questionable pictures; dainty little fly-whisks and "pieces of the true Cross."

Watching from the balconies of the fashionable hotels (every soldier is fashionable while the money lasts) the procession filling the street below was always interesting. The Rolls-Royce of the Egyptian Pasha slowing down behind a string of heavily-laden camels; a man with a performing monkey protesting against the intrusion of a flock of turkeys shepherded ahead and astern by old women—solemnly down the main street of Cairo go the old ladies with the birds; a wedding procession with a raucous band meanders past; and jostling one another on the road, shouting arbagis with their two-horse cabs, scurrying motor cyclists of the Army of Occupation, and the quaint one-horsed lorries perambulating the closely-veiled collection of ladies that go to make the modest modern harem.

Like the schoolboy, the soldier dearly loves a tuck shop. Army fare is very monotonous. The soldier on trek and in the trenches constantly talks of his likes and dislikes in the matter of eating and drinking. So it was that the hotels were always crowded—a hot bath and a meal were always welcome—and the girls of Cairo were never treated more liberally and often to the daintiness of Sault's and Groppi's.

The Egyptian, like the Babu, is fond of bursting into print. The comedian in the colonial forces discovered a rich new field. Eating houses purveying the fried steak and eggs and tomatoes, together with imitation Scotch whisky and Greek beer, came forth in all their glory of calico signs inscribed "The Balclutha Bar," this with a fine disregard for the prohibition tendencies of the Southern town; "The Waipukurau Reading Rooms," and the "Wellington Hotel—very cheap and breezy." Every township in Australia and New Zealand was similarly honoured!

[*Lent by Capt. Boxer, N.Z.M.C.*

ON THE TOP OF THE GREAT PYRAMID.

This New Zealand officer, the two Australians, the Ghurkha officer and the two Ghurkhas are typical of the men who in August 1915, reached the highest points on the Gallipoli Peninsula—the New Zealanders on Chunuk Bair; the Australians on Abdel Rahman Bair; the Ghurkhas on Hill Q.

The most ubiquitous person was easily the bootblack. A soldier could not walk along the street without being besieged by a pestering multitude crying "Bootsa clean, sir! no good, no money; Kiwi polish, sir!" Upon sitting down in a railway station or elsewhere, one's boots would be attacked by a swarm which had to be literally kicked away.

The places of amusement were very attractive. The houses that combined refreshment with entertainment were liberally patronized; the food was much appreciated, and the efforts of the artists cheerfully tolerated. In the first flush of life in a Continental city, the casinos, dancing houses and saloons were far too popular, until the nastiness of these places became apparent through the numbers on the morning sick parades, whereupon officers and men alike realized that they could not keep fit by dancing till the small hours of the morning. The soldier knows his faults, but he strongly resents armchair criticism. It is not difficult to avoid temptation if one sits quietly at home. A cabbage is not immoral, it is unmoral. It is easy to condemn the men who sometimes are not temperate in all things, but the soldier finds it easy to live a prodigal life. He reasons, perhaps quite wrongly, that he may as well eat, drink and be merry, for to-morrow he may be in the casualty list. The soldier will not try to defend his conduct. He recognizes he is a man, with most of the human frailties, yet is prepared at a word and for an ideal, to place his body as a shield between his country and his country's enemies.

It was decided to use the New Zealand Expeditionary Force as the nucleus of a Division. The New Zealand Infantry Brigade and the New Zealand Mounted Rifles Brigade were to be joined by the 1st Australian Light Horse Brigade and the 4th Australian Infantry Brigade, at that time on the high seas, en route to Egypt. As regards divisional troops, there was a great shortage. A Divisional Ammunition Column was an urgent necessity. A cable was sent to New Zealand asking for the despatch of a second Howitzer Battery (one was already on the water) and a Howitzer Brigade Ammunition Column as the necessary complement. A Field Company of Engineers was to be formed out of surplus reinforcements, and a cable was despatched to New Zealand for a second company. The Divisional Train was to be organized as soon as the men and mechanical transport could be obtained. The Ceylon Planters' Rifle Corps was also attached and posted to the Wellington Infantry Battalion as a fifth company.

[Lent by Major Brunt, W.I.B.
NEW ZEALAND FIELD ARTILLERY PASSING BAB-EL-HADID, CAIRO.

The camp rapidly acquired a well-groomed air. Patterns in stone ornamented the surroundings of each tent. Regimental crests and mottoes, representations of New Zealand birds and Maori proverbs were picked out in little coloured pebbles gathered on the desert. It was discovered that oats, rice and other grains, if soaked in water, germinated vigorously when planted in the sand. Soon among the tents of the mounted units there appeared many green patches like miniature lawns. Round the officers' messes more elaborate gardens were attempted. From Cairene florists pot plants were procured; these were plunged, pot and all, into beds made of soil carted from the Canal banks, and there, watered by the careful Arab gardener, roses and canna bloomed profusely.

The newspaper boys were a never failing fount of amusement. Knowing no English but a few carefully taught swear words, these boys would stop the first slouch hat they met, and ask to have read over in English the gist of the headlines. Many an honest soldier would read the lines as printed, but it was too good a field for the wags to miss. Accordingly it was not uncommon to hear the news cried something like this: " 'Time-ees Egyp.' Very good news! Captain —— dead again!" One small boy made a hobby of "Very good news! 'Egyptian Times' to-morrow!"

Next to the newsboys in number and popularity were the sellers of oranges. Wherever the troops went in the desert, at smoke-oh, up would come the boys with the "oringies, very beeg, very sweet," three for a half-piastre. The oranges were little ones, but with a very meaty and juicy pulp, and were most grateful and refreshing in the desert heat. So sudden was their appearance that it seemed these people, together with the boys who sold the cakes and the ones with the hard-boiled eggs, must live in the clouds and drop straight down wherever the dust cloud settled.

"Oringies!"

Egypt was nominally a province of Turkey, but the Khedive, Abbas Hilma Pasha, having gone over to the Central Powers with Turkey, it was notified on December 18, 1914, that Egypt was placed under the protection of His Majesty the King. The suzerainty of Turkey over Egypt thus terminated. The person appointed to the place of the late Khedive was His Highness Prince Hussein Kamel Pasha, the eldest living prince of the family of Mohammed Ali. His Highness was to be proclaimed Sultan of Egypt at the Abdin Palace, Cairo, on the morning of December 20. The Australians and New Zealanders furnished representatives to line the streets—the Otago and Wellington Infantry Battalions with their bands doing duty for New Zealand. The detachment of Ceylon Planters' Rifles Corps also assisted in guard duty and were posted in the Abdin Square. The streets and buildings were gaily decorated—many Italian and Greek and French flags being displayed, but principally Union Jacks and ensigns and the new Egyptian flag, red with three white crescents and stars.

THE MARCH THROUGH CAIRO.
The Field Troop of New Zealand Engineers passing Shepheard's Hotel.

The authorities entrusted with holding Egypt and the Suez Canal were sorely troubled in early December in reference to the Turks proclaiming a Holy War. The Nationalists were active, but with the arrival of the colonial troops the anxiety of those responsible was greatly relieved. The suspected civilians and Turkish officers holding high command in the Egyptian Army were deported to Malta. The Egyptian understands armed strength and despises weakness. Being aware of this, it was deemed advisable to parade the troops as strong as possible and march through the most populous parts of the city.

The New Zealanders were ordered to march through Cairo three days after the coronation. Leaving the camp early in the morning, the parade moved down the beautiful asphalt roads; past processions of camels laden with sugar-cane; past old women with their herds of predatory flocks of sheep and goats; past Pont Limoun and Bab-el-Hadid barracks to the Opera Square, where the General Officer Commanding His Majesty's Forces in Egypt took the salute. This far was plain sailing, but presently the head of the column dived down a narrow bazaar where four men could hardly ride abreast. Into this dark slum went the mounted men; the glistening guns of the artillery; the collapsible boats of the Field Troop; the cable waggons of the signallers; then the long line of desert-trained, sun-tanned infantry, with the ambulance and some more mounted men bringing up the rear. In the bazaars it was almost dark, and in the narrower streets, where the projecting balconies seemed to meet overhead, it was not much better. It was a relief to get to wider streets and less foul air. Lining the streets were thousands of people, all seemingly in a good humour. In the open workshops, old men working at primitive loom and lathe never even looked up. Down past the schools and colleges, where hot-headed young Nationalists were wont to air their grievances, the cavalcade clattered on its noisy way; here, perhaps, there was a little scowling. The common people — the men clad in their many-coloured robes and each wearing the red, flat-topped fez worn by every male from the Sultan to the donkey driver—made quite a splash of colour as they crowded on the sidewalk in the shade of the trees and cheered and clapped with apparent earnestness. Even as the fellaheen appreciates the fact that under British rule he has to pay his taxes only once, so the poor and working class of Egypt recognized that since these bloodless conquerors arrived from overseas, even the beggar and the seller of Turkish delight had accumulated a little hoard of piastres. The disturbances of 1919, however, show that the Egyptian of the cities is a very gullible person.

[*Photo by the Author*
AN EGYPTIAN PLOUGHMAN.
The wooden plough is shod with a metal point. The furrow is not turned over. The earth is merely broken and pushed aside.

Christmas Eve saw the arrival of the British section of the New Zealanders, a contingent of six officers and 234 other ranks who had enlisted in England. These were men who were away from New Zealand when war broke out—some were gold-dredging in the East; some were working in the copper mines in Spain; but wherever they were—Pernambuco, Sarawak or the Andes—when the call came they hastened to the Old Country and enlisted. Engineers, sailors, painters, actors and gentlemen of leisure, they banded together in England and were organized as a machine-gun corps for France, but were eventually sent out to Egypt. Smart and well drilled, they made an excellent impression, and were just the men wanted for the nucleus of the new engineer and transport services, between which two branches they were equally divided.

The Christmas dinner was eaten out of doors in the hot sun, as the new dining huts were not ready. New Year was ushered in by festivals in the city, while out on the desert the regimental bands played all the old familiar tunes, the men meanwhile holding impromptu dances under the silent desert stars.

CHRISTMAS DINNER, 1915.   [*Photo by the Author*

Every week the division was becoming better organized and more like the working whole. From day to day inspections were held by the subordinate commanders. Periodically, staff officers held minute inspection of units, until on two occasions the whole division was paraded for General Maxwell, the General Officer Commanding the Force in Egypt. Each day now saw an improvement. Transport was continually arriving. The division was now officially styled "The New Zealand and Australian Division," as there would be two complete Australian Brigades incorporated—the 1st Light Horse and the 4th Infantry Brigade.

January 25 was a red-letter day, occupied by the New Zealand Infantry preparing the camp for the 4th Australian Brigade, due to arrive during the week. But at 5 o'clock that afternoon came the thrilling news from Army Corps Headquarters that the Infantry Brigade was needed hurriedly on the Suez Canal to support the Indian troops against an attack by the Turks, who were reported to be advancing. During that night seven days' supplies were carted to the railway stations of Helmieh and Palais de Koubbeh; ammunition was served out; men's kits were checked and deficiencies supplied. Far into the night excited soldiers talked, and scorning sleep, waited expectantly for the morrow.

CHAPTER IV.

The Defence of the Suez Canal.

The New Zealand troops detailed to assist in the defence of the Suez Canal were the Auckland, Wellington, Canterbury and Otago Infantry Battalions and the New Zealand Field Ambulance. At 7 a.m., on January 26, the entrainment commenced; everybody working with a will, the last train cleared Helmieh Siding at 3 in the afternoon. Brigade Headquarters, the Auckland and Canterbury Battalions, and two

[*Photo by the Author*]
EN ROUTE TO THE SUEZ CANAL.
Tel-el-Kebir is the scene of the famous battle fought by Lord Wolseley in 1882

sections of the Field Ambulance detrained at Ismailia; the Wellington and Otago Battalions and one section of the Field Ambulance going on to Kubri, about twelve miles north of Suez.

A glance at the map will show that the defence of Egypt from the Turk was strengthened by two great natural obstacles—natural from a military point of view—the arid wastes of the Sinai Desert, and the chain of salt lakes connected by the Suez Canal. In those days, when trained men were not plentiful, it was natural that this long ribbon of sea water—nowhere less than sixty-five yards wide—should be

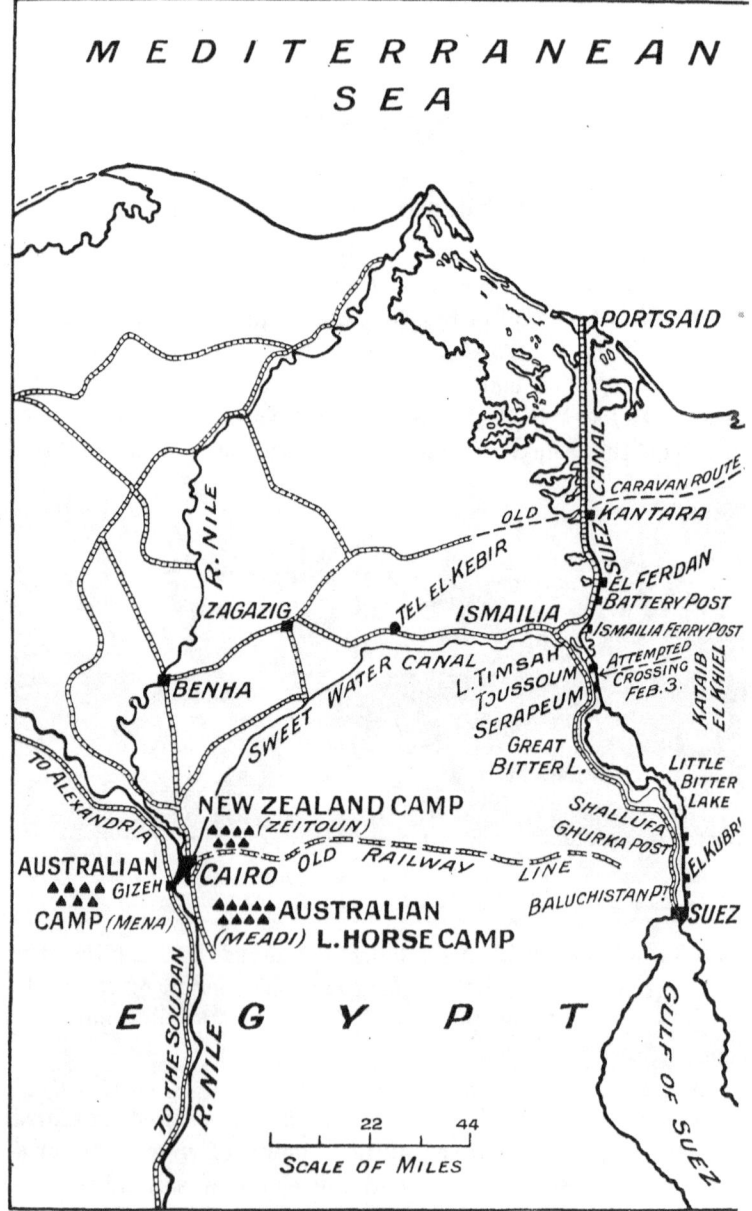

EGYPT AND THE SUEZ CANAL.
This map shows how the troops defending the Suez Canal could have been quickly reinforced from the camps near Cairo.

selected as the line of resistance, although much elaborate fortification had been made on the eastern bank, more particularly at Kantara. In the matter of heavy artillery we had the advantage, as the Turk had to bring his guns over miles of soft sand, whereas we employed ships of the Royal Navy, which, with their powerful guns, could move up and down the defence line, easily outranging the most powerful Turkish artillery.

About thirty miles south of Port Said a few low sandhills cut off Lake Menzala from the Balah Lakes. Across this narrow isthmus ran the old caravan route, through Kantara, from Syria to Egypt. This was the classical way for an army attacking Egypt. So Kantara was made extra strong and garrisoned by Indian regulars.

Based on Ismailia itself were three sets of posts. A few miles north was El Ferdan, where a company and two platoons of the Auckland and Canterbury Battalions were stationed; the second group was nearer Ismailia — two posts, one called Battery Post, with two platoons of New Zealanders as part of its garrison, the other, Ismailia Ferry, with one company; in reserve at Ismailia were Brigade Headquarters, with the remainder of the Canterbury and Auckland Battalions not absorbed by the posts.

"KUKEIS"
The Ghurka badge and weapon.

Between Lake Timsah and the Great Bitter Lake was an important stretch of the Canal, only about seven miles long, but comprising the two posts of Toussoum and Serapeum. At the latter post, two platoons of the Canterbury Battalion (the 12th Nelson Company) were instrumental in helping to stave off the most determined attack ever made by the Turks on Egypt.

South of Serapeum the Canal widens into the Great Bitter Lakes and the Little Bitter Lake, the defence of this part of the line naturally being entrusted to the Navy, assisted by two French cruisers. Between the lower lake and Suez, a distance of about fifteen miles, the Wellington and Otago Battalions were distributed—units at different times being posted at Shalouf, Baluchistan, Ghurka Posts, El Kubri and Suez.

About midnight on the night of our arrival at Kubri, a party of Turks made a great show of liveliness, evidently to draw fire and so obtain some information as to our strength and dispositions. But nothing came of these diversions, which occurred periodically.

Waiting for the Turk.

Some of our posts were on the Sinai side of the Canal, some on the Egyptian side. Up and down we were connected by telephone to all these posts and the batteries. The Turkish intelligence system was very active, whatever its efficiency, for on one night the wires from Kubri were cut no less than five times, although the line was being specially watched.

IN THE SUEZ CANAL.

The provision of desert patrols, post guards, Canal patrols, listening and examination posts, took up most of the time. The work was hard but full of interest. The Turk was not far away, and it was exhilarating making preparations for his downfall. On both sides of the Canal, trenches had to be dug and sandbagged, and strong posts of tactical importance constructed. Every day it was regretted that though the Turks were quiescent, armies of mosquitoes were extremely active. Ships of all the Allies and the neutral nations passed slowly through the Canal, carrying many civilian Australians and New Zealanders to and from the south. After the heat of Cairo, the daily dip was a great boon, particularly as the ladies on the passing vessels threw many luxuries to the soldiers in the water. Especially at Ismailia were the surroundings agreeable. The men in their spare time bathed in Lake Timsah, lolled in the shade of the high acacias, and marvelled at the masses of bougainvillea climbing in its purple glory among the dark green trees.

On January 28, the "Willochra" discharged the infantry of the Second Reinforcements at Suez, from whence they travelled by rail to Cairo. The ships carrying the 4th Australian Infantry Brigade, together with the New Zealand transports "Verdala" and "Knight of the Garter," steamed

[*Lent by Major Brunt, W.I.R.*
TRENCHES ON THE CANAL BANK.

up through the Canal to the accompaniments of tumultous cheering, which burst forth anew when their escort was discovered to be the Australian submarine AE2, steaming awash between the banks lined with enthusiastic East Lancashires, Indians, Australians and New Zealanders.

The end of January drew near and still the Turks did not attack. Occasionally the outposts on either side saw shadowy

forms and fired into the dark. Our Intelligence Department
had gleaned some knowledge of the enemy's dispositions. It
was known that about forty miles east of the Canal, opposite
Serapeum, he was concentrating in a deep valley, from whence
it was believed he intended to advance in two columns—one
on Kantara and the other on Serapeum. These were the
obvious routes, the only other feasible one being by way
of Kubri.

The troops were very fit and well dug in. Every man—
English, Indian, and Colonial—was a volunteer in the strictest
sense and eager to try conclusions with the enemy. On the
last day of the month we were greatly cheered by the news
that the "Blucher" had been sunk in the North Sea.

It was discovered that the Turkish column, marching by
way of the old caravan road towards Kantara, moved at
nights, using the telegraph line as a guide. The Indians had
prepared elaborate fortifications and wire entanglements out
from Kantara, then skilfully altered the direction of the
telegraph line, so that it might end in carefully concealed
barbed wire and pointed stakes.

[*Lent by Major Brunt, W.I.R.*
THE TARANAKI SECTION OF KUBRI FORT.
The wire running out is an alarm wire connected with the wire
entanglements in front.

Affairs of outposts gradually became matters of frequency
over the length of the line. The Turk was making a show of
reconnaissance from Kantara to Kubri, but everywhere a
warm welcome was awaiting him.

Our First Battle.

At last, on the night of February 2/3, it was obvious that
the great attack had commenced. At Kantara the enemy

made an early morning attack on the outposts, which was easily repulsed. Then their main body came down the deceiving telegraph line. To the intense delight of the Indians the enemy walked straight into the trap, and were scattered to the four winds of the desert by carefully posted machine guns. It was quite evident that Kantara would not fall. But the enemy maintained a certain measure of activity, advancing and digging in just out of range. He showed no anxiety for a closer acquaintance, but appeared content to throw a few shells at the posts and occasionally at the shipping on Lake Timsah. This continued all day, until he was evidently ordered to the attack. It was a miserably feeble effort, which rapidly converted itself into a hasty retirement.

Some of the Canterburys were at El Ferdan, upon which post four small enemy field guns opened a desultory fire, but were quickly put out of action by a few well directed rounds from H.M.S. "Clio."

Down at Kubri the troops were on the alert. H.M.S. "Himalaya" used her searchlights all night, flinging her ghostly beams of light far over the desert and preventing any surprise attack. A few shots were fired by the outposts, but well-directed fire from the "Himalaya" deterred the Turk from making any organized advance.

The only place at which a comparatively serious attack was pressed home was in the neighbourhood of Toussoum and Serapeum. On the evening of February 2, the 12th Nelson Company of the Canterbury Battalion was holding a section of 800 yards. On their left the line was taken up by the 62nd Punjabis. At about 3.25 next morning the enemy opened fire with machine guns, and at 3.30 it was evident that

[Lent by Capt. Saunders, 12th Nel. Reg.
WHERE THE ATTACK CAME.
This is the part of the Canal where the pontoons were launched. The 12th Nelson Company was holding a line near the fir trees.

he was making an attack a few hundred yards on our left. Thirty men of the Nelsons were at once doubled over to assist the Indians, but were surprised to find no troops there! The enemy, in five pontoons, was already crossing the Canal! The handful of New Zealanders opened fire and drove back the boats. The other platoons of the Nelsons kept up a steady long-range fire. Soon both banks of the Canal were ablaze with the spluttering of rifles fired by soldiers undergoing their baptism of fire. The rival artilleries now came into action, and by dawn the battle raged over the two and a half miles

LIFTING THE PONTOONS.
The fir trees on our side of the Canal are discernible. The pontoons were sunk by rifle fire. The large holes were made with axes to render the boats unserviceable.

of Canal in the neighbourhood of Toussoum and Serapeum. The Turk made attempt after attempt, but our infantry easily accounted for the men in the pontoons; the field artillery scattered the bridge-making squads; and when it was fully light, the ships' guns caused such consternation in the enemy's reserves that gradually the attack melted away.

Everywhere in front of the line between Toussoum and Serapeum lay dozens of enemy dead.

At noon the Punjabis counter-attacked with considerable effect, took many prisoners, and cleared a large area of the enemy. In the afternoon the New Zealanders were ordered to close on the 22nd Indian Brigade Headquarters, and during this movement we suffered our first New Zealand casualties—one sergeant being wounded and a private of the 12th Nelson Company died as the result of wounds received in action—the first soldier of the New Zealand Expeditionary Force to be killed on the field of battle. The troops spent an expectant night, but nothing further materialized.

THE FIRST MAN KILLED IN ACTION. The last resting place of 6/246 Private William Arthur Ham, 12th (Nelson) Company of the Canterbury Infantry Battalion.

Captured Turkish Orders.

From daylight on the morning of the 4th, parties cleared up the battlefield, burying hundreds of Turks. Captured orders showed that the attempt was to have been made on a grand scale, but something must have sadly miscarried. The following extracts dealing with the main attack reveal Turkish Orders at their best: "By the grace of Allah we shall attack the enemy on the night of February 2/3, and seize the Canal. Simultaneously with us the right column will attack Kantara; the 68th Regiment will attack El Ferdan and Ismailia; the left column will attack Suez; and one company from the 10th Division will attack Shallufa. The champions of Islam, from Tripoli in Africa, from the left wing will

[*Photo by the Author*]
CAPTURED PONTOONS AT ISMAILIA.

advance to Serapeum and the south of Serapeum. . . . As soon as it is dark the heavy artillery battery will take up its position. Its task is to destroy the enemy's warships in Lake Timsah. If it gets the opportunity, it is to sink a ship at the entrance to the Canal. . . . .

[*Lent by Capt. Boxer, N.Z.M.C.*]
A TURKISH PRISONER.

Three regiments will proceed to the Camp of the Bridgemakers; the detachments will take pontoon and engineer soldiers from the companies selected as attack column . . . The advances from the 'place of preparation' is to be made simultaneously in eight columns at a place to be fixed, and in a straight line; a pontoon is to be given to each squad; each squad is to send forward a party to reconnoitre. . . . .

The march to the Canal is about four or five kilometres, and is to be accomplished without halt. The pontoons are to be launched in the Canal and the passage across is to begin immediately. . . . The first duty of the detachments which cross is to occupy the slope of the western bank. The two companies collected on the western bank are to advance 500 or 1000 metres from the Canal and take up a favourable position facing west. After all the battalions in the first line have been mustered they are to continue the march. The 2/75th Regiment is to seize Toussoum and occupy the hill with small force. The 74th Regiment is to

[*Photo by the Author*
BOWS OF TURKISH PONTOONS.
The pontoons are of German make, as the spelling of "the home port" indicates.

take the direction towards Timsah and the west, and is to advance as far as the railway line. . . .If the regiments meet with opposition from the enemy while occupying these positions, they are at once to execute a fierce bayonet charge. . . . At first I will be at the little hill on which are two sandhills; later on I shall go towards Toussoum." All of which showing that even early in the War the best laid plans of Turk and Hun went very much astray. Instead of executing fierce bayonet charges and taking up favourable positions facing west, the broken remnants of the champions of Islam had in large measure fled a considerable distance east—going so far and so quickly that an aeroplane reconnaisance of sixty miles showed great clouds of dust still hastening towards the desert sanctuary.

The enemy's total casualties were about 3000 in killed, wounded and prisoners. The British loss was 18 killed and 83 wounded. The naval casualties were also infinitesimal—

TURKISH PRISONERS CAPTURED ON THE CANAL.
This picture, which shows the physique of the Turk, was taken by Lieut. A. E. Forsythe, (12th Nelsons) who was killed on Gallipoli.

one man killed on the "Swiftsure" and ten wounded on the "Hardinge." Thus was the enemy's much-heralded attack brought to confusion. From that day the Suez Canal, thanks to the efforts of the British and Indian troops and the Allied navies, has been open day and night to the ships of friendly nations.

Three weeks of waiting ensued. There was certainly work to be done, but the Canal is just the Canal, and men get very sick of it. Any change is welcome to the soldier. It was a relief to climb into the troop trains on February 26 and eventually arrive in the old encampment near Zeitoun.

Return to Zeitoun.

The New Zealand and Australian Division was now feeling its feet, and towards the end of March the Third Reinforcements arrived and were promptly drafted to the units requiring them, particularly the Field Engineers and Divisional Train. Among them was a Maori contingent of 14 officers and 425 other ranks, eager to prove that they were too good for garrison duty. Egypt had never seen their betters as regards drill, physique and discipline.

About this time the Mediterranean Expeditionary Force came into being. The air was full of rumours; soon it became manifest that the two Colonial Divisions—the 1st Australian Division and the New Zealand and Australian Division —were, as the Australian and New Zealand Army Corps, to be called on to engage in a most important enterprise. Bustling administrative officers from the two Divisions commenced addressing their letters to Army Headquarters as A.N.Z.A.C., little realizing they were unconsciously creating a word destined to ring with glory down the ages.

How the prospect of humbling the Turk appealed to these young crusaders from the far South! What an atmosphere of anticipation pervaded the camp when it was learned that the Division was to be paraded for the last searching inspec-

[*Photo by the Author*

A COSMOPOLITAN ARMY.
In this picture are Australian Signallers, Ceylon Rifle Planters, British, French, and Australian Officers.

tion by the illustrious soldier to whom Britain had entrusted the confounding of the Turk. There was a certain element of romance in these young, untried divisions from the New World daring to confront one of the oldest and most warlike of the Old World races.

An Inspection on the Desert.

Just a year before, Sir Ian Hamilton, reviewing the New Zealanders and Australians in their own lands, expressed the wish that some day these wonderful horsemen might be shown to the world. By a strange chance, here they were in Africa, soon to be led by him in their first great visit to Europe. Surrounded by his staff, here again he sees them in the desert. Squadron after squadron go the 1st Light Horse Brigade, the pride of all Australia; then the New Zealand Mounted Rifles—men from the Waikato, the Wairarapa, the Waitaki, and every country district in between—prance gaily past in a cloud of dust and locusts; following the mounted rifles come the divisional artillery, all New Zealanders—with their cap badges blackened for war and their guns bedaubed with multi-coloured paints in a manner to make an old battery sergeant-major go crazy. Here are the handy men of the army—the divisional engineers with their great pontoons, and their confreres the signallers—wise men with buzzers and telephones and other signalling paraphernalia bedecking their horses and waggons. Following the "fancy troops," in solid ranks of khaki and with bayonets flashing in the desert sun, come the infantry brigades of the Division. These are the men who trudge all day in the desert and at night dig themselves in, bivouacking and trudging on again next morning. The New Zealand Brigade marches brilliantly; every man is a prouder man than when he left New Zealand, for the infantry alone out of our Division participated in the defence of the Canal.

Now come the newly joined 4th Australian Infantry Brigade, and, closely following, the waggons of the divisional train; finally the field ambulance, flying their great Red Cross flags. By this time everybody is covered with grey desert dust and the plain is obscured as if with the smoke of a great bush fire. The march past over, units make for home by the shortest route. Soon the horses are rubbed down and are munching their tibbin and crushed barley, while the men are crowding the showers preparatory to the call of the cookhouse.

That night we realized that at last the long-desired standard was attained—the New Zealand and Australian Division was pronounced fit for active service.

A Riot in the Ezbekieh Quarter.

Good Friday was a bad day for Australia and New Zealand. This was the occasion of the great riot. There were reasons for this outburst. On that holiday morning all troops were given leave for the day. There was nothing to do in

[Photo by the Author

DIVISIONAL HEAD-QUARTERS.
Showing Head-quarters cars and signallers on the old Suez Road. The officer in the foreground is Lt. Col. G. R. Pridham, D.S.O., R.E., the talented C.R.E. of the Division in Gallipoli and France.

the town, so some men got more than was good for them of the wretched liquors sold in those tenth-rate cafes and dancing houses. Soldiers under the influence of drink do not behave any better than their civilian brothers. They are necessarily high-spirited people and very fit. In retaliation for some real or fancied grievance, a few irresponsibles commenced throwing things out of a top-storey window. The red caps were not popular, and both sides receiving reinforcements, a melee ensued. Some fool fired the broken furniture lying in the street, and from this it was only a stage to firing the houses. An Egyptian fire brigade arrived, but the soldiers, by this time numbering thousands, cut the hoses and pelted the unfortunate firemen with their own gear. Realizing that only disgrace could come of the affair, the sane people gradually got the rioters away, and after about four hours of Bacchanalian revelry the city was again quiet. A legend has grown up that the work was a good one, and that the soldiers had determined to rid the city of those sinks of iniquity. It is almost suggested that the good work was the result of a religious revival among the troops. It must be admitted that it was a bad business; but without apologizing in any way, it may be honestly set down that throughout the four years of War this is almost only the only instance of excess participated in by the New Zealand troops.

Leaving Cairo.

The men of the Maori contingent were disappointed to find that they were not to join up at once with the Division, and after an entertainment and haka before Sir John Maxwell, the High Commissioner of Egypt, one of their officers made an eloquent plea to be sent on active service. The promise

[*Lent by Capt. Boxer, N.Z.M.C.*
KIT INSPECTION IN THE FIELD AMBULANCE LINES.

was made that the request would be acceded to after a short term of garrison duty at Malta, for which station they left Zeitoun Camp on the evening of Easter Monday, embarking on the s.s. "Runic" at Port Said.

Easter Monday was a most trying day. The khamseen blew, the breakfast dishes were full of grit, horses were

Leaving Cairo.

fidgety in the driving sandstorm, everyone's temper was on edge. Egypt is a delightful place for the tourist, who can amuse himself indoors if the conditions be undesirable without. The soldier, on the contrary, must soldier on, khamseen or no khamseen, so over the drifting wastes of sand, artillery, engineers, infantry, divisional train and ambulance, wended their several ways to their different rendezvous in the desert. This was a new idea in the matter of parades—parading by ships—all to go on the "Lutzow" mustering in one place, those for the "Katuna" in another, and so on. Men, horses and vehicles were carefully checked by the known capacity of the transports already waiting in Alexandria Harbour.

Because the country was known to be mountainous and almost devoid of water it was recognized that in the initial stages of the campaign the mounted men must be left behind. This reduced the fighting strength of our division from four brigades to two. The mounted rifles for once were sorry they had horses, but hardly envied the infantrymen the daily long-distance route marches with the seventy pounds of pack and a rifle, dusty tracks, and an angry sun.

Everything comes to an end, even training in Egypt. In the week following Easter, all ranks were thankful to get aboard the troop trains in the dark and disappear into the black Egyptian night. The only regret was that their comrades of the New Zealand Mounted Rifles and Australian Light Horse were left fretting in the desert camps.

CHAPTER V.

The Rendezvous at Mudros.

Alexandria Harbour was alive with shipping — British, French, Greek, Italian and many captured vessels. Some of the latter—the "Lutzow," the "Annaberg," the "Haidar Pasha," and the "Goslar"—were requisitioned to make up the fleet of thirteen ships necessary to carry our Division. They ranged from liners like the "Lutzow," down to dirty, lice-infested tramps like the "Goslar," and had mostly lain in Alexandria Harbour for about eight months, tended only by a few Greeks, who, scrupulously observing the regulations, had thrown nothing overboard, but dumped the galley ashes

ON THE QUAY AT ALEXANDRIA
Vehicles, Stores, and a mountain of Hay for the Mediterranean Expeditionary Force.

and refuse on the once immaculate decks. The carpenters were still in possession of some of them, improvising horse boxes and fitting the tramps to carry more passengers than they had previously been accustomed to. As the journey took only about three days, a little congestion was not of great moment.

Going out to take over one of the transports, two New Zealand officers had an amusing illustration of patriotism not peculiar to Egypt. The usual picket boat of the Ports and Lighthouses Administration not being available, recourse was made to one of the bumboats selling Turkish Delight and other delicacies. The two boatmen—a stolid Nubian at the bow oar, and a flashy Arab at the other—were both quite sure of one thing: "German, no good—English, very good." The Arab was a fascinating person, who gripped the thwart with his big toe at every stroke. Listening to the eloquent and reiterated denunciation of the Hun, one officer noticed that part of the stock-in-trade was brown boot polish with a German label, and drew the attention of his companion to the

EMBARKING HORSES.
The Otago Mounted Rifles putting horses on board at Alexandria.

fact. The Arab overheard the conversation. "What!" he said, pointing to the offending polish, "that German?" "Yes," said the New Zealander. Without more ado, the Arab scooped the lot into the harbour. "That's true patriotism," the officers agreed, but were puzzled by the grinning of the suppositious patriot. "What are you laughing at, you fool? That must have cost you a lot of money!" "Aha!" came the answer, and pointing to the black man in the bows, who seemed a trifle angry, the Arab said, " It is not mine, it's hees!"

Lying at anchor was the United States cruiser "Tennessee," with her huge "paper-basket" masts. For some time

she had been employed around the coast of Asia Minor safe
guarding American interests. Greek and Italian ships wer
busy bringing refugees—English, French, Jews and Arme
nians—fleeing from their homes in Palestine and Syria. Jus
outside Alexandria these unfortunates were housed in concen
tration camps, at one of which many Jews, mostly Russia
subjects, enlisted in a transport corps styled "the Zion Mul
Transport Corps," the members of which certainly looke
most unhappy with their big, rough, North American pac
mules.

Through the Ægean Sea.

On April 10, our first ships got away—the "Achaia,"
"Katuna," and "Itonus." The headquarters transpor
"Lutzow" sailed on the evening of the 12th, while th
"Goslar," the lame duck of the fleet, after many vexatiou
troubles with her internal fittings, her messing, and her crew
finally cleared Alexandria at sunset on April 17, with th
New Zealand Infantry Brigade Headquarters on board.

During the three days of the voyage the troops had man
experiences. Every day fire and boat drill was practised. Thi
required a good deal of ingenuity, because on none of th
transports was there much deck room. On some of the ship
there were lifeboats to hold only about 20 per cent. of th
troops, to say nothing of the crews. One ship had not enoug
lifebelts to go round. So an order was given that any ma
drawing a seat in a boat could not have a lifebelt as well
Yet some Germans insist that we, not they, prepared ur
ceasingly for war!

The journey was through a sea full of islands of classi
interest. Some of the islands set in the clear Ægean blu
were startlingly beautiful. Passing Patmos, the old monaster
on the top of the rocky height stood out, clear cut, white an
gleaming in the morning light. The padres were quite in
terested, for it was here, tradition says, that the Apostle Joh
wrote the Book of Revelations. Past island after island ric
in mythological lore, the smoking transports laboured; no
and then British and French destroyers mysteriously appeare
from behind a barren islet; and interesting beyond measur

we saw a good example of maritime camouflage—a town-class cruiser painted grey and black and white to resemble a storm-tossed sea. Ceaseless vigilance was imperative, as Turkish torpedo boats were wont to issue from harbours in the Asiatic coast and threaten the safety of transports. The "Manitou," carrying British troops, lost a good many killed and drowned in the confusion ensuing on the sudden appearance of a Turkish destroyer.

Parading by echelon, boat and fire drill, slinging of horses and waggons—all things tending to ensure a rapid disembarkation in the face of the enemy—were assiduously practised on the voyage. Past the fertile island of Nikaria the transports picked their way and anchored one by one in the spacious outer harbour of Mudros.

Mudros Harbour.

Mudros is a land-locked harbour, the entrance easily controlled by a boom and a minefield. Here were gathered merchantmen from the ends of the earth—conveying the five

[Photo by the Author
BATTLESHIPS IN MUDROS HARBOUR.

divisions of French and British soldiers that comprised the Mediterranean Expeditionary Force. Here, too, were ancient and modern battleships, every pattern of torpedo boat, cruisers protected and unprotected, submarines and trawlers from the far North Sea.

It was the flush of the Ægean spring, and the shore parties cutting grass for the horses revelled in meadows that reminded them of home. But the gaunt grey battleships and black destroyers in the bay struck a vastly different note.

From one side of the ship could be seen cows and sheep and stacks of hay; from the other, the grim realities of war. Overhead the engines droned incessantly as the seaplanes circled the harbour preparatory to a reconnaissance of the Peninsula. The tents of the French gleamed white on the hillside below the group of ancient windmills, and floating

[Photo by Sister M. Jeffery, N.Z.A.N.S.
MILLS FOR GRINDING CORN AT MUDROS.

across the rippling water came the stirring notes of the trumpets calling the French Territorials and Senegalese to their frequent battle practice.

Daily the mosquito fleet steamed out to gather information of the Turk, and returned to find more and more transports anchored in the stream. The representative of the young Australian Navy, AE2, passed down one afternoon, amid tumultuous cheering, she being recognised as the convoy to one of the early reinforcement drafts. She went out through the minefields, and in running the gauntlet of the Dardanelles, died fighting. Whenever a French ship passed, the New Zealanders lined the rails, the bands played the "Marseillaise," cheers and counter-cheers were given.

The Attack on the Dardanelles.

The newcomers were at once informed of the present situation and the intention of the High Command. It is not advisable here to discuss the political and strategical considerations that determined an attack on the Dardanelles—whether the campaign failed because of faulty strategy, staff

MAP OF GALLIPOLI AND SURROUNDING ISLANDS.
From Bulair to Cape Helles is about 50 miles; from Anzac to Kephalos 15 miles; from Anzac to Helles 14 miles.

work, or tactics, or because the whole conception of the operation was unsound. This is simply a soldier's narrative of events, and not a detailed and critical examination of a political and military effort. This much, however, is known: that in order to help Russia, to relieve the attacks on the Suez Canal, and to influence the wavering Balkan States, some action was imperative.

It had been laid down in England that the British commander should not land his army until a naval attack had been attempted and failed. Further, he was not to commit himself to any adventurous undertakings on the Asiatic shore.

On February 19 the outer defences of Sedd-el-Bahr and Kum Kale were demolished by the fleet. For a time success seemed within our grasp, but the flat trajectory of the naval guns availed them little against the forts and land defences situated inside the Straits, and on March 18, the carefully laid minefields and mobile field guns gave the coup-de-grace to the naval plan by destroying in one day the "Irresistible," the "Inflexible," and the "Ocean," together with the French battleships "Bouvet" and "Gaulois."

Begotten of vacillation and hesitancy at Home, a period of local inactivity ensued. It was finally decided that a combined land and sea attack should be attempted. It was known that early in the year the Turk had six divisions distributed between Bulair, Gaba Tepe, Helles, and Kum Kale. Since then reinforcements had been constantly arriving and the fortifications greatly strengthened. The situation in France was serious—men and more men, guns and more guns, were being clamoured for. After some delay the last division of British Regulars—the 29th—were detailed for the service, and now in Mudros Harbour they were waiting in their transports.

The Allied troops composing the M.E.F. were five divisions, as follows:—

> A French Division (Territorials and coloured troops).
> The 29th Division (British Regulars).
> The Royal Naval Division.
> The 1st Australian Division.
> The N.Z. and A. Division (two brigades only).

Of these it may be said that as seasoned soldiers the 29th

Preparing for the Attack.

Division had no superiors on earth, being of the same calibre as the famous "First Seven Divisions" of the early days in France. The remainder of the British troops were practically untried, but keen, and volunteers to a man. For heavy artillery, reliance had to be placed on the Allied Navies. For the first time in history a British army was to be supported by 12-inch and 15-inch naval guns, the latter carried by the "Queen Elizabeth."

Preparing for the Attack.

The troops were organised into three groups, labelled Echelon A, B, and C. Echelon A was composed of the portion first to land—men who carried three days' rations and water, 200 rounds of ammunition, their packs and entrenching

A FRENCH SENEGALESE AT MUDROS.
The children, of course, are Greek.

tools—whose orders were to secure enough territory to enable the other troops to disembark with their horses, guns and heavy vehicles. The 18-pounders and 4.5 howitzers were also in Echelon A. Echelon B consisted of first-line transport, hold parties, and officers' horses. They would be brought ashore as the situation developed. In Echelon C were the pontoons of the Engineers, the waggons of the Field Ambulance, motor cars, cycles, and supply trains.

Day by day the soldiers in Echelon A assembled on the troop deck for disembarkation practice. The men with their loads seemed bulky enough, but the officers looked even worse. When trussed up with bulging haversacks, two full water bottles, a heavy Webley and ammunition, a big map case, field glasses, prismatic compass, a note book and message forms—not to mention the dozen and one small articles that they, in their innocence, considered necessary—is it any wonder that they stepped gingerly? For, once having fallen, they would have found it difficult, as did the knights of old, to rise again.

About four times a day the soldier crept into his Webb equipment, struggled over the side, swayed violently on the frail rope ladder, tumbled into the waiting boat, and pulled slowly to the shore.

[*Photo by the Author*

THE "QUEEN ELIZABETH."
The warships and transports leaving Mudros Harbour for the attack on the Peninsula.

The days passed all too quickly. Conference upon conference was held on the flagship; much interest was awakened by the issue of maps; and the thrill of intense anticipation was quickened by Sir Ian Hamilton's famous Force Order:—

"Soldiers of France and the King—

> Before us lies an adventure unprecedented in modern war. Together with our comrades of the fleet we are about to force a landing upon an open beach in face of positions vaunted by our enemy as impregnable.

Preparing for the Attack.

> The landing will be made good by the help of God and the Navy, the positions will be stormed, and the war brought one step nearer to a glorious close.
>
> 'Remember,' said Lord Kitchener, when bidding adieu to your commander, 'remember, once you set foot upon the Gallipoli Peninsula, you must fight the thing through to a finish.' The whole world will be watching your progress. Let us prove ourselves worthy of the great feat of arms entrusted to us."
>
> IAN HAMILTON, General.

Let it never be said that the Mediterranean Expeditionary Force held its opponent cheaply. The seriousness of the situation was obvious, but the troops were imbued with the fact that with proper backing they could not fail, and whatever sacrifice should be demanded, that sacrifice would be gladly made.

At 2 o'clock on the afternoon of April 24, there steamed from Mudros Harbour that great armada, led by the "Queen Elizabeth," with Sir Ian Hamilton on board. As the New Zealand transports rode at anchor near the entrance, ship after ship passed out at a few cable lengths' distance. The destroyers fussed and fumed about, while the battleships steamed steadily on to take up their position for the early morning bombardment. As each battleship, cruiser, transport and trawler slipped past, great cheers were exchanged; then night came quietly on; lights blinked and twinkled over the expanse of the great harbour; and a great hush fell on the place until about midnight, when the New Zealand ships lifted their anchors and picked their way through the minefields towards the open sea.

CHAPTER VI.

The Anzac Landing.

Early on Sunday morning the intention of Army Headquarters was made clear by the issue of orders for the attack. A study of the map revealed three dominating land features. In the south, overlooking Cape Helles, was the great hump of Achi Baba. Inland from Suvla Bay was the tangled mass of cliffs, valleys and hills culminating in the peak of the Sari Bair system, which, from its height marked in feet, was afterwards known as "Hill 971." Lying further over near the Straits and protecting the fortress on the European side, was the mountain system known as the "Pasha Dagh" or Kilid Bahr Plateau. Both Achi Baba and Hill 971 had to be captured before attempting the plateau, which latter having fallen, we could take possession of the great fortresses of Kilid Bahr, and Chanak on the opposite shore. These two places in our hands, the passage of the fleet would be largely a matter of careful mine sweeping.

In order to mystify the enemy and to encourage him to disperse his forces, two subsidiary attacks were undertaken. Away up at Bulair a fleet of empty transports, accompanied by a few men-of-war, were to make a demonstration. Down on the Asiatic coast the French were to land, reduce Kum Kale and the forts in the neighbourhood, and then withdraw. The 29th and Royal Naval Divisions were to land on several beaches at the extremity of the Peninsula and push on towards Krithia and Achi Baba, being reinforced by the French Division after its withdrawal from Kum Kale. The Australian and New Zealand Army Corps was ordered to force a landing on the beach between Gaba Tepe and Fishremen's Hut. Hill 971 itself was to be avoided, the troops endeavouring to pass over its southern under-features to the road running from Boghali and Maidos. Mal Tepe was a hill specifically mentioned. "The capture of this position would threaten and perhaps cut the line of retreat of the enemy's troops on Kilid Bahr plateau, and have far-reaching results," said the operation order.

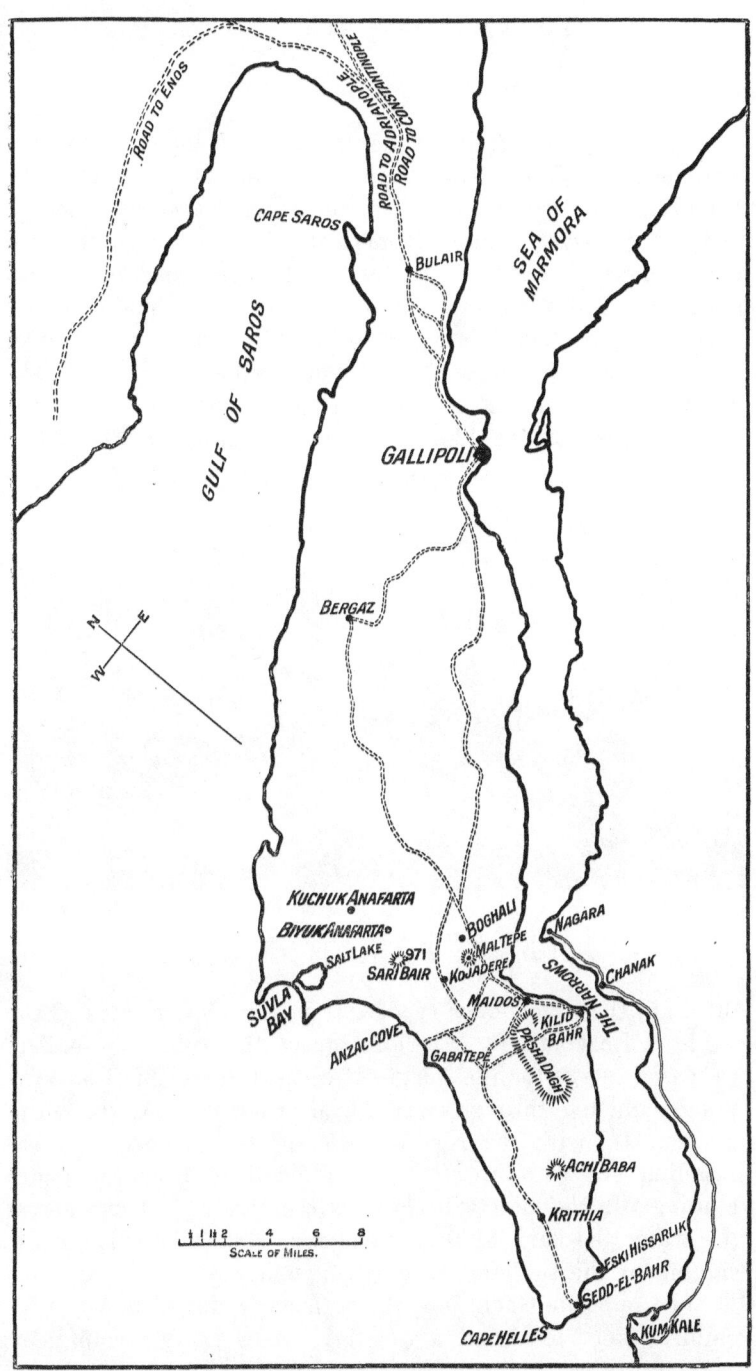

MAP OF GALLIPOLI PENINSULA.
Illustrating the projected landings at Cape Helles, Gaba Tepe, and Kum Kale.

Passing Cape Helles.

When morning fully broke the New Zealand transports were nearing Cape Helles. The big guns of the fleet were pounding the forts until the horizon seemed a mass of smoke and flame. Over against Kum Kale the French ships were hotly engaged; off Cape Helles the British stood close into the forts. Again we saw our old friend the "Askold"—now christened the "Packet of Woodbines," because of her five long funnels. The noise of the naval bombardment was truly extraordinary—the sharp crack of the lighter guns; the ear-splitting roar of the 12-inchers; and booming clearly above

[*Photo by Col. Hughes, C.M.G., D.S.O.*
A BATTLESHIP COVERING THE TRANSPORTS.
The old "London" steaming towards Anzac Cove.

them all, the tremendous reports from the 15-inch guns of the "Queen Elizabeth." Watching from the rail, the soldiers were very sorry for the Turk. It seemed impossible that anything could live through such a bombardment. At the morning service, with the reverberation of the incessant gunfire assailing our ears, we found it difficult to hear the padre reading "In the midst of life we are in death." From across the water the bark of the 6-inch guns struck harshly on the singing of the soldiers' favourite hymns.

Just opposite Gaba Tepe the transports slowed down. Like children kept inside on a wet day, we were very impatient.

A desire to be doing something possessed all ranks. The men broke up cases and split the wood for kindling fires ashore. Every man pushed seven or eight pieces through the straps on the back of his pack. Many seized the opportunity to write the letter that most thoughtful soldiers write at the beginning of a campaign—a letter to be carried in the breast pocket and only to be forwarded by the comrade that buries him—tender farewells, simply and beautifully written, as men always do write when they are face to face with the things that really matter.

[*Photo by the Author*
TRANSPORTS OFF ANZAC COVE ON APRIL 25.
The ship in the foreground has disembarked Echelon A and is steaming out to make room for the next transport.

In groups of four the transports, covered by the battleships, moved up to about a mile off shore, disembarked the troops of the first echelon, and then moved to the rear, letting the next four continue the manoeuvre. On our port side the old twin-funnelled "Majestic" belched a stream of 12-inch shells on the ridges; away to starboard, the four long funnels of the "Bacchante" were dimly discernible through a tremendous column of smoke. Southwards, as far as the eye could see, were transports innumerable, and closer in-shore, the angry, barking battleships.

Going Ashore.

The destroyers were taking their human freights as far in as they dared—and the average t.b.d. commander will dare a good deal. Over the side and down the swaying rope ladders we went for the last time. This was not a Mudros

Harbour practice. We felt uncommonly clumsy and three times our ordinary size. With our hob-nailed boots we clattered about the iron deck, until it was so crowded we had perforce to stand still.

Now the picket boat zone was reached. Off the destroyer and into a barge. Six barges made a tow. The little steamboat puffed and tugged, and off we swerved like a sinuous snake.

The 3rd Australian Brigade made the first landing about 5 in the morning, and had cleared the first ridges. New Zealand Headquarters landed at 10 a.m.; then there was a strange hitch, and the precious hours between 11 a.m. and 3 p.m. were wasted. By this time the Turk had in some measure made up his mind about the real attack and had concentrated his guns on the beach. He only had to fire at the water's edge, consequently he had no difficulty in ranging by the map. He knew that the Landing must be in a very circumscribed area, and his ranging was good. Shells plopped in the water all round as the tows set a course for the beach.

[Photo lent by Lieut. Moritzson, M.C., M.M.
GOING ASHORE.
A destroyer making ready to tow barges from the "Lutzow."

Boat after boat of wounded passed us going back to the transports they had left only a few hours before. They waved their blood-stained arms and cheered with feeble cheers. The encouragement was certainly welcome.

We were now well within range. Rifle and shrapnel fire was whipping the water round the boats. About 300 yards from the shore the barges were cast loose, and each, with a naval rating as coxswain, pulled vigorously for the beach. Casualties were frequent. As the boats grounded, the men tumbled out; many were hit in the water and were drowned A major, jumping from the bows—the water was about 2 feet deep—was hit in the knee. He fell into the surf, but was hauled on board again, and the picket boat towed him back to the transport he had just left. The survivors fell in and adjusted their heavy equipment under the protection of the sandy cliff.

Straight into the Battle.

Up in the maze of gullies our men were struggling with the Turks. As each company or platoon came ashore it was rushed up to the firing line. Casualties and the broken

[*Photo by Col. Hughes, C.M.G., D.S.O.*]
A GOOD TARGET FOR THE TURKS.
A tow going ashore about noon of April 25.

country made control very difficult, and up where the tide ebbed and flowed, the natural leaders of men, whether they happened to be officers or privates, led their little groups to the attack or stood stubbornly at bay among the scrub-clad hills.

The orders given to our Division on disembarkation were for the New Zealand Infantry Brigade to prolong the line to the left of the 1st Australian Division, and particularly to support the left of the Third Brigade, which had landed as the covering force to the Army Corps; the 4th Australian Infantry Brigade was to be held in reserve. The landing of the Auckland Battalion was completed at 12 noon. Walker's Ridge was given as its objective. By 12.30 p.m., two companies of the Canterbury Battalion were ashore, and were directed to support the Auckland Battalion.

"IN THE AIR."
A transport mule descending into a barge.

At 1 p.m., the Auckland Battalion was recalled from Walker's Ridge and brought more to the right, to occupy Plugge's Plateau, in order more directly to connect with the left of the covering brigade. The two Canterbury companies prolonged the left flank of the Auckland Battalion, in the direction of Walker's Ridge. Between 12.30 p.m. and 5 p.m. the Otago Battalion arrived and was sent up to Plugge's Plateau in support of the Auckland Battalion. When the remaining two companies of the Canterbury Battalion arrived they were sent to Walker's Ridge to prolong and reinforce the left flank.

Owing to the accuracy of the enemy big-gun fire, the transports with our field guns aboard were temporarily forced to retire. The Turkish gunners were punishing us severely, and we realized to the full the bitterness of not being able to effectively retaliate. But the Indian Mountain Batteries endeared themselves to all by their sacrificing efforts. Gallantly led, these matchless gunners, with their patient mules, wheedled their guns up to seemingly inaccessible vantage points; unlimbering, they would get in a dozen effective shots and be down in the gully and up to an alternate position before their opponents could sense the situation.

All along the beach, under the scanty shelter of the cliff, the wounded lay—some on stretchers, some on blankets, others on the shingle. The surgeons worked as they never had before. Wounded poured down from the hills incessantly. The picket boats towed their barges, crammed with troops, to the beach, and seemed to take away almost as many wounded.

The sun went down and the ships stood over against Samothrace silhouetted in the sunset. But with the night came no peace. The Turks attacked with renewed vigour—reinforcements had arrived for them. Blowing trumpets and shouting "Allah!" they surged forward. Our fellows ran to meet them, cursing in good round English and very bad Arabic. Up there in the tangled gullies many a strange duel was fought that night. When not actually fighting, men dug for their lives. Then on would come the Turks again, shovels would be dropped, and the attack repelled. One desperate rush was stemmed by a gallant band headed by a corporal with nothing more effective than a pick-handle.

A Desperate Night.

As the evening wore on, the beach became one long lane of suffering soldiers. The doctors could only attend to the most severe cases. Many a man, when asked if he was badly hurt, said, bravely enough, "Oh, no!" and died quietly in the night.

The stretcher bearers were magnificent. From the order, "Stretcher squads fall in" at the moment of landing, these

[*Photo by the Author*

AN EARLY VIEW OF ANZAC COVE.

The mule lines did not stay long unmolested. "Beachy Bill" ranged on them one day and caused awful havoc. They were then shifted up the deres for protection.

men slaved on the ridges and in those valleys of torment. A man without a load can dash from cover to cover, but the stretcher bearers, with their limp and white-faced burdens, must walk steadily on, ignoring sniper and hostile gunner. From the front line it took about two and a half hours to get a patient to the hospital on the beach. Hour after hour the work went on, until after twenty hours' stretcher bearing these unheeded heroes fell in their tracks from sheer exhaustion. Volunteers took up the work, but after a few hours' rest, the gallant souls were out again — medical officers, stretcher bearers and hospital orderlies literally working themselves to death in an endeavour to mitigate the awful anguish of the wounded men of Anzac. "I shall never forget that night," said a sergeant of the N.Z.M.C., "A twelve-stone

THE CROWDED BEACH.

weight on the stretcher, a dark night, a little drizzling rain, groping our way down a steep incline through prickly scrub, our wounded man crying with pain and begging for a drink every few yards, incessant rifle fire, and bullets whizzing all round us." Except those who lay so very quietly up in the scrub or on the shell-swept beach, no one rested that night. The firing line was gradually becoming a little defined as the tired soldiers on both sides became exhausted.

The units were inextricably mixed—Australian and New Zealand infantry clung doggedly to the hardly-won crest line. Approximately, the Australian 1st, 2nd, and 3rd Brigades held the right flank; the centre was in a state of flux, but the 4th Australian Brigade held the ridges at the

[Photo by the Author
THE SCORED CLIFFSIDES OF WALKER'S RIDGE.

A DESPERATE NIGHT.

head of Monash Gully; the Otago trenches grew up overlooking Monash Gully; the Aucklanders dug in along Plugge's Plateau; the Canterbury Battalion were desperately engaged on Walker's Ridge, where their gallant commander (Lieut.-Colonel Stewart) fell at the head of his men. The Wellingtons landed in the dark and went straight up to Plugge's Plateau. The gunners laboured all through the night pre-

[*Photo by the Author*

PLUGGE'S PLATEAU.
Taken from Howitzer Gully, showing the road cut round the cliffside.

paring for the eagerly expected howitzers; while the sappers hastily improvized a second line of defence along Plugge's Plateau down Maclagan's Ridge to the sea. Here the last stand would be made if the worst came, but the morning broke and the outer line was still intact; picks were laid aside and the indomitable men of Anzac again took up their rifles to face the trials of the day.

CHAPTER VII.

The First Week.

No one had slept during the night. Re-embarkation was suggested, but a conference was held and the Generals decided to hold on. The men made strenuous efforts. Those not actually fighting were employed making roads up Maclagan's Ridge in the centre, and up Walker's Ridge on the left, in order that the guns might be man-handled up to the positions selected by the artillery commanders.

[*Photo by the Author*

UNLOADING GUNS.
The stern of the horse boats dropped in the water makes an inclined plane down which the gun is manhandled. The country was too rough for horses, but fifty men on a rope can overcome most obstacles.

About midnight, three companies of the 15th Battalion, 4th Australian Infantry Brigade, arrived and were sent up to reinforce the 1st Australian Division away on the right. They had been hardly pressed just before sunset, and orders were given that all available troops were to support the covering force (the 3rd Australian Infantry Brigade) as they arrived, and to connect up with the New Zealand Infantry Brigade on the left. During the remainder of the night, platoons and companies of the Wellington Battalion of the New Zealand Infantry Brigade, and of the 13th, 15th, and 16th Battalions of the 4th Australian Infantry Brigade, were brought ashore.

The troops arrived in very irregular order—some from one ship and some from another. As each platoon or company came ashore, it was immediately despatched, under the senior officer present, to support the right flank, where the 1st Australian Division was most hotly engaged. The result was that units of both divisions became hopelessly mixed up, and it was several days before they could be disentangled.

By 3 a.m., the whole of the Australian 13th Battalion had arrived. The bulk of it was held temporarily in reserve. One and a half more companies of the Wellington Battalion now occupied Plugge's Plateau, above the beach, and half a company had been sent off to join the 1st Australian Division on the right. By 5 a.m., the remaining company of the Wellington Battalion had arrived, and by 6 a.m., a section of the New Zealand Howitzer Battery was brought ashore, and gladdened the heart of every infantryman as it came into action at the foot of Howitzer Gully. "Boom!" went the howitzer. "The guns, thank God! the guns!" murmured the tired soldiers.

Shrapnel Gully.

The Turk quickly realized that the valley running from behind Hell Spit deep into the centre of Anzac must be the channel of communication. His gunners were so assiduous that it was quickly christened Shrapnel Valley. The top of this valley was afterwards known as Monash Gully.

The glory of the spring was still on the Peninsula. Birds sang in the bushes and the fragrance of crushed wild thyme perfumed the morning air. Patches of red poppies glowed in the sheltered open places. Draped around the prickly scrub were festoons of wild honeysuckle. But down in the bottom of Shrapnel Valley was a dreadful sight. The moist earth in the old creek bed had been ploughed into mud by thousands of hurrying feet. Soldiers, in their eagerness to get forward, had thrown off their kits and equipment, and there the debris

THE FIRST DUGOUTS.

This picture was taken a few days after the landing, and shows the dugouts of the 4th Howitzer Battery and Divisional Engineers, near the foot of Howitzer Gully. The scrub is still uncut on the slopes of Maclagan's Ridge and Plugge's Plateau.

[*Photo by the Author*]

lay, punched and trampled into the mess. Dead mules were scattered about in helpless attitudes. Every few yards one met soldiers—their clothes torn by rock and scrub, their bodies mangled by bullet and bomb—stumbling down that Valley of Death to have their wounds dressed at the casualty clearing stations. A steady stream of stretcher bearers carried back limp forms; shrapnel burst high in the air; machine guns spluttered; mountain guns barked; the crash and rattle of musketry never ceased as the echoes rolled round the myriad hillsides. High over all, black specks up in the sky, but watchful as of old, the vultures gathered together, knowing full well that blood was being spilt.

The drumfire down at Helles boomed all day. The old battleships, with their big guns, raked the Turkish positions, while the big 15-inchers of the "Queen Elizabeth" roared loudly above the great roll of gunfire. The moral support afforded by this ship was incalculable. "Good old Lizzie," the soldiers shouted, as her great guns spoke. Optimistic always, the men looked continually for signs of the British and French advancing from Cape Helles. When the second day's battle was at its height, the cry was raised, "Cease fire! the English troops are here," but it was only a ruse of the Turks—and the musketry battle resumed its violence. Cries of "Cease fire" and "Retreat" shouted in English, caused at first a momentary wavering, but soon the Colonial soldiers realized the deceptions, and the would-be deceivers shouted commands in vain.

The End of the Second Day.

The second day crept to a close, and our lines were hourly being made secure. Units were inextricably mixed, but, roughly, the Australian Division held the line south of Courtney's Post, while the N.Z. and A. Division held Courtney's and all northwards of it.

No man thought of rest: to work was salvation.

On top of a big yellow mound at the head of Monash Gully there was a rough cross, inscribed, "Here lie buried twenty-nine soldiers of the King." Two of these men—one an Australian of the 14th Infantry Battalion, the other a sapper of the New Zealand Engineers—had been found just below the fatal crest of Courtney's Post, with their arms still clasped around each other's waists. As they lay among the scrub, those poor lifeless bodies seemed symbolical of the new spirit that had grown up on the Peninsula. While in Egypt, the Commonwealth and Dominion soldiers had their little differences; but the first two days on the Peninsula swept away all the little jealousies and the petty meannesses. Every man helped his neighbour. There was no question of corps, or rank, or colour. By common trials, a common suffering,

[*Lent by Col. J. G. Hughes, C.M.G., D.S.O.*
HEADQUARTERS OF THE N.Z. AND A. DIVISION.

and a common interest, Australian, Indian, and New Zealander realized they were brothers in fact, as in arms. These first two days made great things possible within the Empire. The experience of those sweet sensations of brotherhood will be cherished and handed down as one of the priceless gifts of Anzac.

The New Zealand machine gun sections experienced a particularly trying time. They were attached to individual battalions and were not fought as a unit. The Auckland guns were pushed forward with their battalion, and somewhere at the head of Monash Gully were so hard pressed that they had to abandon one gun, which was retrieved from its hiding place two days after. The Otagos also came under a very hot fire. They, too, abandoned a gun, but never regained it, as an Australian party found it and consistently refused to give it up! Right through the campaign the Otago Regiment were one gun short, fighting only three guns.

The Wellington gunners were heavily punished on April 27. They evidently pushed too far forward in their eagerness to get at the Turks, but snipers picked them off one by one, until the officer was killed and the whole of the personnel disabled, except one lad who was acting as ammunition carrier.

Gradually the field artillery got their guns from the barges, and with long ropes manhandled them to their almost inaccessible positions. Tracks were cut on the hillsides, rough jetties were improvised, and dugouts were constructed. Mostly these were holes in the ground big enough for a man and his mate to get nearly into. A waterproof sheet served as roof, and when it rained, as it did nearly every night, the waterproof sheet collected and deposited on the occupants whatever water had fallen in the catchment area.

Washing became a lost art. Mirrors were converted into periscopes. The previously spic-and-span New Zealand Army grew dirty-faced, unshaven, and ragged looking.

The rum ration was a boon at this time, as it engendered a little warmth, and enabled one, if off duty, to get a little sleep. "Stand-to" was at 4 o'clock, half an hour before dawn, when the entire force in the trenches and on the beach stood to arms in readiness for an attack.

The First Landing at Suvla.

The front line having been made fairly secure, attention had to be turned to the flanks. A glance at the map will show Nibrunesi Point, near Suvla Bay, about four miles to the north of Ari Burnu, and Gaba Tepe about two miles south. On both these promontories the Turks had look-outs, from which their observers spotted the effect of artillery fire. As with glasses they could see all that occurred in Anzac Cove, it was considered necessary to destroy both look-outs.

The First Trenches on the Cliff-edge near Russell's Top.

[*Photo by the Author*

The First Landing at Suvla.

For the Gaba Tepe cutting-out expedition Australians were detailed. Nibrunesi Point was assigned to the New Zealanders. Three officers and fifty men of the Canterbury Battalion (13th Westland Company) and an officer and two N.C.O.'s of the N.Z.E. were employed.

The party left Anzac Cove in the dark early one morning and steamed up the coast in a torpedo-boat destroyer. The plan was to land on the northern side of the Peninsula and work upwards to the highest point—Lala Baba. Two destroyers came close in and commanded each side of the Peninsula, whilst the old "Canopus" stood further out to sea and supported the whole. If the Turks at Anafarta behaved badly they would receive chastisement by the guns of His Majesty's Navy.

The observation post itself had some attention from the big ship the day before; but it was not known whether opposition would now be met with. The instructions were to destroy the station, get any prisoners for the Intelligence Officers, and to seek for and destroy a gun that the naval airmen had reason to suspect was being placed there.

The party got ashore without mishap. Day had now broken, and in three groups the attackers crept up the gullies towards the crest. It was a dewy morning, and the fresh, clean smell of the Turkish meadow flowers mingled with the scent of the wild thyme crushed with the soldiers' hobnailed boots.

The place seemed deserted. There was a traversed trench just below the crest. Most of the troops had jumped it, when —crack! crack! crack! broke on the morning silence. Down dropped the Westlanders; then rushed back to the trench, and there, in the sunlight, was the picture—the trench full of squirming Turks, and standing over them with threatening bayonets the gallant boys from Greymouth. Johnny Turk had been caught napping, and the initiative of the New Zealand private soldier had sealed his fate. It was then realized that the few Turkish phrases laboriously learned did not convey much to the terrified prisoners. They quickly decided that the proper thing to do was to throw all their arms out of the trench—and out they came, rifles, knives, and even safety razors. The poor Turkish wounded lay groaning in the bottom of the trench, while the unwounded, on their knees, murmured "Allah! Allah!" and passed their hands mechanically from their foreheads to their breasts and back again. A few men were left to get the wounded and prisoners down to the boat; the remainder scoured the Suvla flats in full view of the Turks on the Anafarta hills.

Three small houses proved to be empty, but in them were found the kits of the guard; in one, the cells of a telephone instrument, with which the garrison communicated with their headquarters at Anafarta. The wire was cut, and a slab of guncotton placed in each of the houses to demolish them.

[*Lent by Lieut. Moritzson, M.C., M.M., N.Z.E.*
THE EVENING HATE.
Shells falling among bathers off Hell Spit.

The gun position was located, but there was no gun mounted. The dead Turks were covered over in their own trench, the charges in the houses were fired, and the party, with captured papers and prisoners, re-embarked without mishap and returned at noon to Anzac.

Thus was the first landing at Suvla carried out successfully by New Zealanders without a single casualty.

The Australian attempt on Gaba Tepe was most unfortunate. The Turks at this place were not caught napping. As at Helles, barbed wire ran down into the water and machine guns enfiladed the landing place. After sustaining many casualties, the party withdrew, and the Turkish post on Gaba Tepe remained a thorn in the side of Anzac until the evacuation.

The Nerve-Centre of Anzac.

A walk along Anzac Cove was full of interest and incident. The little landing beach—a shelving strip of shingle, only twenty-five yards wide—was never safe, but in a measure it was protected from shrapnel by the height of Plugge's Plateau and the two ridges running down towards Hell Spit and Ari Burnu. The Cove became the nerve-centre of Anzac: nestling under the low cliffs on the beach were the Headquarters of the Army Corps, the hospital of the Field Ambulance, the Ordnance and Supply Depots.

General Birdwood had located his Army Corps Headquarters in the little gully debouching on to the centre of the beach. Close by were the naval shore parties with their wireless plant for maintaining communication with the fleet; the Headquarters of the Australian Division were tucked away a little further up the gully.

The southern extremity of Anzac Cove was christened Hell Spit. Jutting out into the water, this point got the benefit of fire from both of the flanks. Here were situated the engineers' stores of explosives and materials; working parties sent for wire, sandbags or timber, did not dwell too long in the vicinity. Close by, under the sandy cliff, the mule drivers of the Indian Supply and Transport had made their little dugouts—the waves of the Ægean lapping their very thresholds. At the foot of the track leading over the spur to Shrapnel Valley were the dressing stations of the Australian Ambulance, with their little Red Cross wharf from which the wounded were evacuated. Just opposite Army Headquarters some of the many stranded barges were made to serve as landing stages for great quantities of bully beef, jam and biscuits, which, placed in high stacks, gave some protection from the shells constantly arriving from the Olive Grove and Anafarta. Hereabout the water barge was also moored; the water being pumped ashore into tanks.

The New Zealand Sector.

The beach north of these stores was allotted to our Division. A little gully running up to the foot of Plugge's Plateau gave excellent cover for the New Zealand battery of 4.5 howitzers—the first New Zealand guns to get ashore, and the only howitzers at that time on the Peninsula. In those early days, infantry carrying parties were constrained to rest awhile in order to observe the shell pursue its lobbing course over Maclagan's Ridge towards the distant target.

[*Lent by Lieut. Moritzson, M.C., M.M., N.Z.E.*
MULES AT THE FOOT OF HOWITZER GULLY.

At the foot of Howitzer Gully were the New Zealand Ordnance Stores—for a time the most frequented place in Anzac. Fresh water was unobtainable for washing purposes. Continual washing of clothes in salt water made all undergarments very hard, so down to the Ordnance would the soldier go to procure new shirts and socks. Here, also, were piles of captured rifles and ammunition, and a pathetic heap of kits which had been thrown away during the first advance and since collected. A one-time famous old wrestler stood guard over these kits, and one had to establish an undeniable claim before the property was handed over. Very many of the kits were never claimed, being stained with the life-blood of those impetuous spirits who had established the Anzac line.

THE NEW ZEALAND SECTOR.

The mule lines of the Indian Transport Corps ran along the beach in front of Divisional Headquarters. Close by, the dressing station of the New Zealand No. 1 Field Ambulance caught the streams of wounded that flowed down Howitzer Gully and from Walker's Ridge. Out in front of the hospital squatted an Indian mule driver, who spent most of his time clipping mules. Between his bursts of singing in a minor key he would cry, "Hair cut, sixpence!" The soldier, who by this time realized that more than snipers took advantage of cover, would sit on the sandy bank and have his hair cut short by the mule clippers.

The northern extremity of Anzac Cove never received an English name, but was always known as Ari Burnu. The beach north of this point was unsafe for traffic in the daytime, as it was within easy range of Turkish snipers. A few hundred yards along this stretch of white sand were two or three stranded boats — boats that had run in there on the day of the landing, but were stove in and their crews killed by hostile fire. There they lay, a pitiful sight, out in the glare of the noonday sun. To avoid this piece of dangerous beach by day, a communication trench commenced in Anzac Cove along by the wireless station near Ari Burnu. This trench doubled back across the point, running out towards Mule Gully and Walker's Ridge, eventually becoming part of the "Big Sap" that led towards the extreme left flank.

[Lent by Col. Falla, C.M.G., D.S.O.
THE CEMETERY AT ARI BURNU.

Land was valuable at Anzac, particularly land that was safe. The parts that were exposed could not be used for dugouts or stores, so were set apart as cemeteries. Here, on the point of Ari Burnu, between the Big Sap and the sea, New Zealanders who were killed near Anzac Cove were carefully carried after dark and buried by loving comrades.

The Tragic Lack of Hospital Ships.

If there was one thing that showed our unpreparedness for war on a large scale, it was the neglect to anticipate accommodation for wounded. This did not apply only to the New Zealanders—British, French, Colonial and Indian suffered alike. The regimental medical officers and stretcher bearers did more than mortal men could be expected to do. But a man hit up on Walker's Ridge or at the head of Monash Gully, after receiving his field dressing at a sheltered corner of a trench or in the regimental aid post, had to be carried in the heat, down bullet-swept valleys and along the dangerous beach. Here the surgeons and orderlies of the Field Ambulances redressed the wounds, gave the men something to eat and drink, and placed them out of the sun, away from the torturing flies. Even in these Field Ambulance dressing stations men were not immune from the shrapnel which swept the beach. The Turk could not be blamed for this, as we had, of necessity, to place our hospitals wherever there was room. Streams of men constantly arrived, some walking, many on stretchers—Zionists with tears streaming down their faces, determined Colonials and pathetic-looking Indians— wounded in our cause, now separated from their fellows, and miserable because they could not understand the sahibs' language.

When night came, the picket boats would move into the little Red Cross wharves, and the wounded men were carried to the barges. When a tow was ready, the picket boat started on its journey for the hospital ship or transport. The high ground surrounding Anzac Cove ensured that bullets clearing the crest went many hundred yards out to sea. Some days, when Turkish firing was brisk, the sea was whipped into a white foaming line where the bullets splashed angrily into

[*Lent by Capt. Boxer, N.Z.M.C.*

THE TRAGEDY OF THE ANZAC WOUNDED.
Men, sick unto death, lying in the scuppers; tired, suffering, uncomplaining men with bloodstained kits and wounds that became septic before Alexandria was reached.

the water. Through this barrage of singing bullets the Red Cross barge must go. Picket boats or trawlers could not dodge from place to place like soldiers in Monash Gully, so they had to risk it, and take it in their course.

Outside the range of these "overs" were the waiting ships. The hospital ships proper had good appliances for handling wounded. A long box would be lowered over the side, the man and the stretcher placed bodily into it, and hauled up on to the deck, where he was seized by waiting

[*Lent by Capt. Boxer, N.Z.M.C.*

HOSPITAL SHIP AND HOSPITAL CARRIER IN MUDROS.

orderlies and whisked away to wards for a diagnosis, a hot bath, some very necessary insecticide, and a meal to suit his particular needs. But the hospital ships soon became overcrowded. Hundreds of men were accommodated on the decks without cots. They did not complain. They came to the war voluntarily, and took what was coming to them as a matter of course. Ask a sorely wounded man if he wanted anything, and if it was not a drink of water, it would be a laconic "Have you got a green?" He seemed more annoyed with the ration cigarettes than he was with the Turk.

Presently the cry would be, "Ship full!" and the next load would be taken to an ordinary transport, dirty, full of vermin, and entirely unsuited for handling wounded. But it had to be. Nothing better was offering. So the wounded men—tossing about on the barge, seasick, with their clothes stiff with blood and their heads burning with the fever resulting from wounds—were hauled up with the improvised tackle to the dirty decks of the transport. There were few medical officers. Some came from the overworked and understaffed field ambulances ashore, and laboured like galley slaves against the tremendous inrush of broken men. Naval surgeons and dressers left their battleships and toiled heroically among the wounded Colonials. But there were not enough doctors to do a tenth of the work. In the old British way, we were paying for unpreparedness with the flesh and blood of our willing young men. On one ship, the only man with any knowledge of medicine was the veterinary officer, who, assisted by clerks and grooms of the waiting Echelon B, saved dozens of lives by prompt and careful attention. So, with a score of men dying on each ship every night, the transports crept with their cargoes of human wreckage to the port of Alexandria—the hospital ships going on to Malta, Gibraltar, or even England. In Egypt, great emergency hospitals were opened, and everything possible was done to alleviate the dreadful suffering of the heroic and uncomplaining soldiers of the Mediterranean Expeditionary Force.

CHAPTER VIII.

At the Head of Monash Gully.

From the first the Turk held the high ground. Soldiers will realize what that meant. The Anzac army was as yet an untried one, and all new troops are apt to keep their heads down. This is but natural. It must not be forgotten that this was strange country to the newcomers, and that snipers lay concealed in every little dere.

The Turk as a soldier was never to be despised. Centuries of history studded with names such as Kossovo in olden times and Plevna in modern, show that the Turk is a good soldier even if he is a bad governor. The operations against Turkey in this war prove that in trenches the Turk is as good a

LOOKING TOWARDS BABY 700 FROM PLUGGE'S PLATEAU.
This very interesting picture shows the long white line, the limit of our furthest advance. The terraces of Quinn's can be seen perched on the side of the cliff.

soldier as he was of old. But the natural aptitude of the Colonial as a hunter soon asserted itself, and cunning marksmen proceeded to stalk the wily snipers. As the trench systems grew up, points of vantage, screened by branches, were occupied by the best shots, accompanied by an observer with a periscope. This gave an Australian corporal of engineers an idea that was instantly availed of—the application of a periscopic attachment to the ordinary service rifle.

The necessary glass for the mirrors was not available, but over on the horizon were a hundred transports waiting with

Below Pope's Hill: A Dressing Station of the N.Z. No. 1 Field Ambulance.

[Lent by Sergt. P. Tite, N.Z.E.

stores and horses. A fleet-sweeper with a working party went out one fine morning and called on each ship. From the ornate saloons and the cabins the mirrors were removed, lowered gently to the deck of the trawler, and hurried off to Anzac Cove. There the sappers cut the mirrors into little parallelograms and slipped the pieces into the wooden frames at the requisite angles. In a few weeks the new periscopic rifle was in use all along the line, and from that time the superiority of fire was ours, and it was the Turk's turn to keep his head down.

Straightening the Line.

At the end of the first week it was obvious that our defensive line could be much improved. Between Pope's and Walker's Ridge there was a deep canyon—one of the forks at the head of Monash Gully. The Turk held the high ground looking down the canyon, so that troops who were at Pope's, if they wanted to get around to Walker's, had to go away

A SHELL BURST ON STEEL'S POST.

down Monash Gully, along the beach, and up Walker's Ridge —a distance of nearly three miles, whereas the gap in the front line between Pope's and Walker's Ridge was only about 200 yards.

Again, between Pope's and Quinn's there was a ridge, so far unnamed. This ridge was practically "No Man's Land," and, if occupied by the Turks, would be a dangerous salient to us, as it looked into the back of Quinn's Post and down the head of Monash Valley.

So it was decided that if the left flank of our line—that is, from Quinn's to Walker's—was flung forward, a continuous front line could be obtained and communication within the Anzac area would be much simplified.

It was originally decided that this pushing forward of our line would be made on May 1, but a Turkish attack was launched that evening, and was heavily repulsed by machine guns and rifle fire from Pope's and Courtney's Posts, which enfiladed the attacking infantry. Our attack was postponed until the evening of May 2.

The Canterbury Infantry were to push forward from Walker's, the 4th Australian Infantry Brigade from the head of Monash Gully, while the Otago Infantry Regiment were to attack from Pope's and link up the Australians with the Canterburys who were to advance from Walker's Ridge. Two battalions of the Royal Naval Division were to be held in reserve below Quinn's and Courtney's. To get to their appointed place by 7 p.m., the Otago Infantry had to leave Walker's Ridge on their three-mile march early in the afternoon.

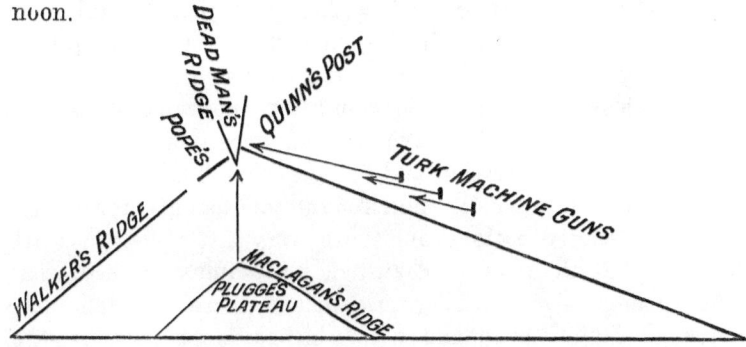

THE ATTACK ON DEAD MAN'S RIDGE.
It is obvious that the further an attack is pressed on Dead Man's Ridge, the better target is presented for the enemy gunner on the flank.

At 7 p.m. the attack was launched, but the Otago Regiment had suffered considerable checks on their march round the beach and up Monash Gully. This part of Anzac was so cut up and broken as to be almost unbelievable. The Otagos had to pull themselves up part of the way on a rope fastened on the steep slope of Pope's Hill.

The entire attack was carried out with great dash; but, owing to the darkness, our unfamiliarity with the country in front, and our misleading maps, we were brought to a standstill. The Canterburys found they could not get on from Walker's Ridge; some of our troops were beaten back, others, particularly the Otagos, hung on grimly through the long night. The Turk was plentifully supplied with cricket-ball hand-grenades, while we depended almost entirely on our rifles.

The Christening of Dead Man's Ridge.

As dawn approached, a message came back that the wounded were lying up in a gully between Pope's and Quinn's, and a party of New Zealand Engineers started to cut a track up an old watercourse to get the wounded out. They pushed on past the two battalions of the Naval Division, and asked them to use their entrenching tools on improving the track. The men, glad to do something to relieve the strain of waiting, set to work with a good will, knocking off the corners and hooking in the sides, until there was quite a passable track to get the wounded men away.

The scene at the top of that gully will never be obliterated from the minds of the survivors. Men were lying all over the place, in every depression and behind every bush. These men had landed on April 25, had fought unceasingly for over a week on scanty rations and with very little sleep. Little wonder that they were exhausted, but it must be said that, apart from the men who were delirious, there was little murmuring. Hollow-eyed and with pinched faces, these Australians and New Zealanders waited doggedly. There were no wild cries of "Stretcher bearer," or "Water," or "Reinforcements." These men realized that every available man was fighting; that the doctors and orderlies were overwhelmed with casualties; that water was scarce, and no one was available to carry it; and that reinforcements would come when they could be spared.

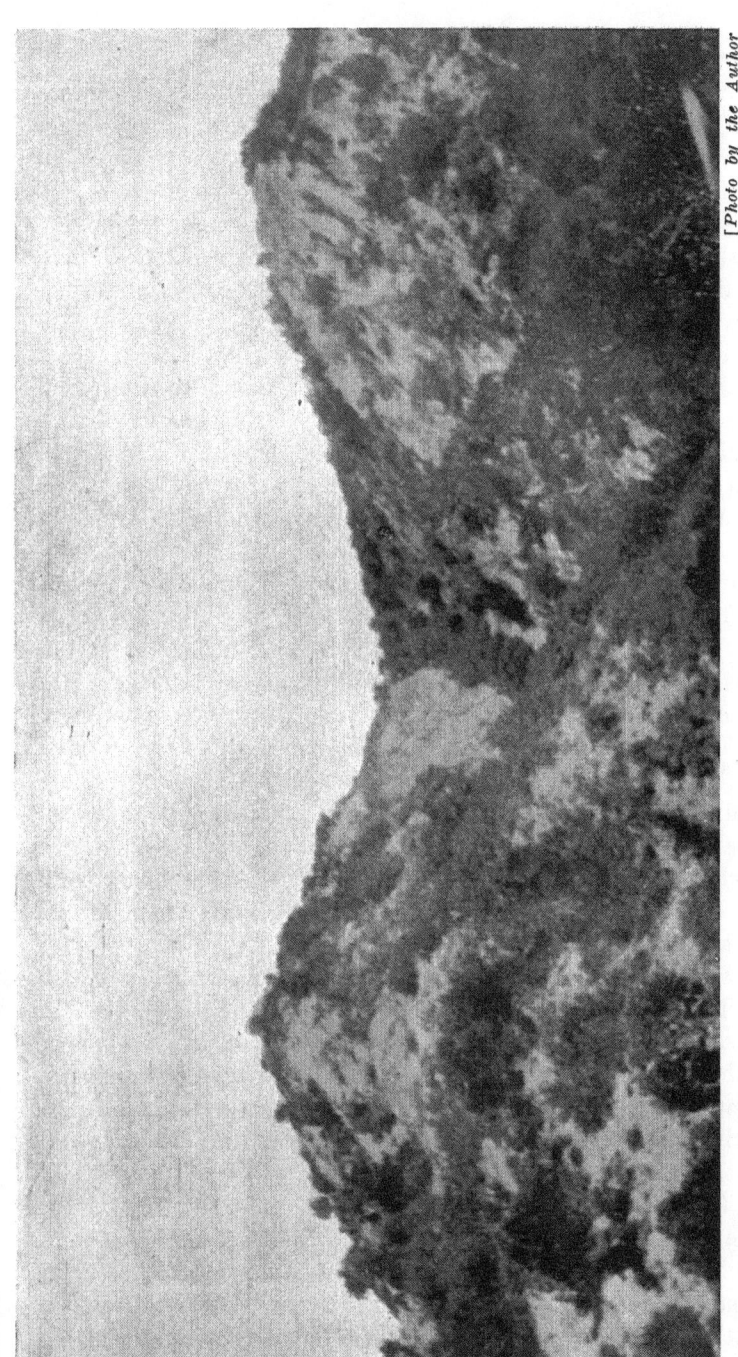

DEAD MAN'S RIDGE AND POPE'S HILL.

Taken before the scrub was cut away. Dead Man's Ridge is on the right. The first trenches can be seen growing up along the crest of Pope's.

[*Photo by the Author*

As grey dawn crept in, isolated parties—wild-eyed, clothes torn, and with blood-smeared bayonets—dashed back from No Man's Land to the security of the crest, where the Turk must be held should he counter-attack. One man, demented by suffering and loss of sleep, went mad and danced on the crest, cursing the Turk, defying him to come on, and then, in his madness, cursing his comrades taking cover in the improvized position of defence. One man was crying bitterly because he had lost his bayonet!

The Turk eventually did attack, but thanks to the defensive line hastily prepared and the imperturbable Anzac soldiery, only one Turk got through—an officer, who tumbled into our line with a revolver bullet in his forehead.

All this took place in No Man's Land, in that little gully to the left of Quinn's Post, and from that morning it was known as "Bloody Angle."

The units of the Naval Division were then directed to go up the ridge between Quinn's and Pope's, and their casualties were so heavy that the name, "Dead Man's Ridge," was instinctively applied to it by association.

The sorely tried Colonials could not but admit the bravery of the Royal Marine officers as they led their men up those scrub-covered slopes. They pressed straight up the goat track, and lined the ridge. As the ridge was a salient, the Turkish machine gunners from the trenches opposite our right flank opened fire, and caught the entire line of men in the back of the head. As fast as the men fell, others pressed forward to take their places. The officers suffered excessively as they encouraged their men. On occasions such as these, one realizes the devilish ingenuity of modern war—bullets streaming as from a hose, and cutting down everything in the line of fire—men and shrubs indiscriminately, until the clay slopes of Dead Man's Ridge were stained with British blood.

The troops holding the safe crestline just a little to the right were fascinated by the scene—the red and yellow of the hillside, the brave men steadily climbing up to the fatal crest, the burst of machine-gun fire as it caught the soldiers on the ridge; then the awful tumble down the slope until the

THE FIRST TRENCHES AT QUINN'S POST.
This picture was taken at the end of April, before the scrub was whittled into matchwood by the hail of bullets.

[Photo by the Author

maimed body came to rest at the foot of the gully among the sweet wild thyme.

The machine-gun fire was too deadly. The survivors reluctantly came back to the old line, leaving Dead Man's Ridge covered with dead—our own and the Turks'. Every night for weeks comrades risked their lives to get the bodies away, but the Turk gradually established himself on the ridge, and not until Armistice Day were the burials completed.

A party of the Otago Infantry had a most trying time. They did not fall back with their comrades during the darkness, and suffered severely all next day. They were hard pressed and given up for lost, but next evening managed to cut their way out through the exultant Turks.

The Evolution of the Anzac Line

The evolution of the Anzac front line was most interesting. Military text books lay down principles and often suggest their application to different situations. It is considered most necessary to get a good field of fire, so that the maximum loss may be inflicted on the enemy, and good communications assured for the passage of troops and the carriage of ammunition and food.

Consider for a moment what really does take place. The tide of battle sways backwards and forwards until at the end of a desperate day, those of the troops left alive on both sides sink exhausted behind any natural cover—it may be a clay bank, a bush, a big stone, a natural or artificial depression in the ground. Because these men have some protection while they are firing they often escape becoming casualties. These are the men who have really established the line. Other men have got into depressions and behind crests from which they cannot fire at the enemy at all. The energetic soldiers who have gone forward to exposed places have undoubtedly performed great service, but generally at the price of death. So it happens that when night comes, the men left alive increase the cover they have by digging in; thus the front line grows up—little "possies," as the soldier calls them, deepened and connected up with those on the right and left.

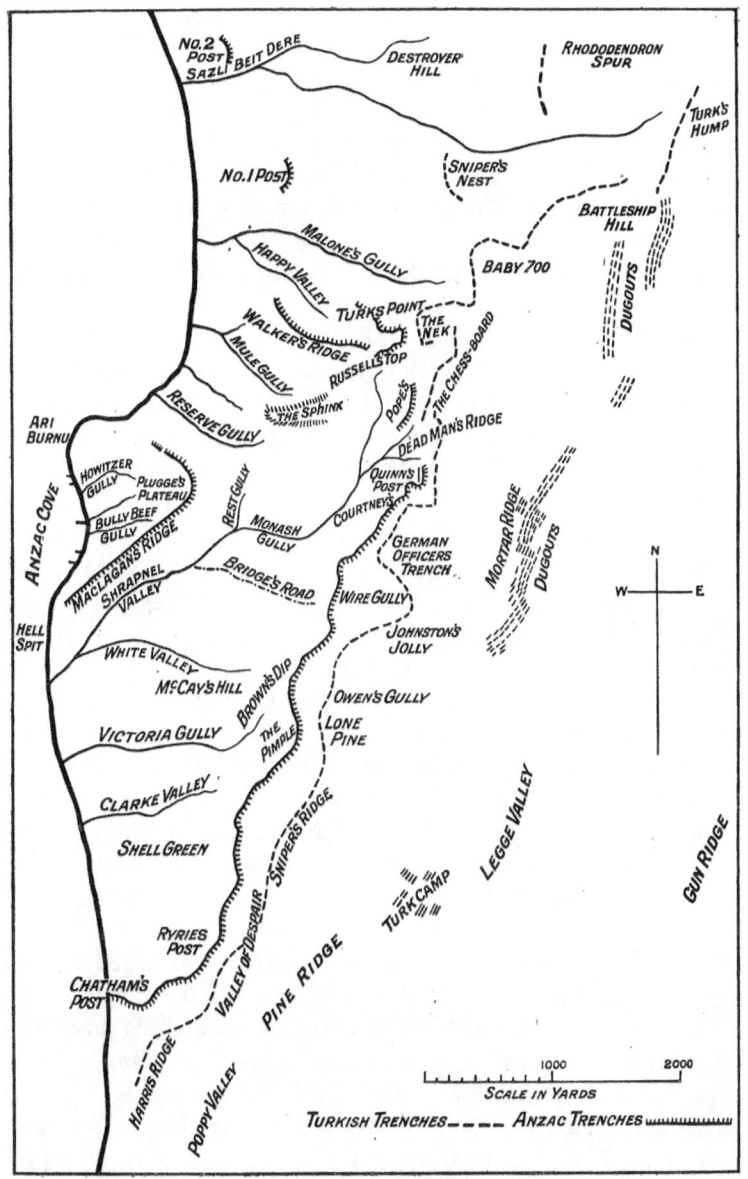

MAP OF THE ANZAC AREA.
Showing the inner and outer lines.

By daybreak a line has been constructed—not sited according to the book—it is probably in the main based on tactical strong points, but many portions of it are incorporated because of their safety—field of fire hardly being considered. Here it is that the tactical knowledge of ground is valuable, and trained officers and men are not slow to take advantage of it, thus avoiding much dangerous and laborious work later in sapping and tunnelling.

At the head of Monash Gully the valley forked into three steep gullies. The one to the left ran up behind Pope's Hill; the second between Pope's and Dead Man's Ridge; the third branched slightly to the right and culminated in the little ravine separating Dead Man's Ridge from Quinn's Post. Courtney's Post was just to the right of Quinn's, and was perched upon the side of a steep hill, in many places really a cliff. On this general line the fighting ebbed and flowed, and on the second day the troops began really to dig in. Harassed by snipers and bombers, the troops clung to the ground they had so pluckily won.

The Anzac area now consisted roughly of two lines. Taking the sea as a base, the inner line resembled a V, starting from Hell Spit, running up Maclagan's Ridge, around to Plugge's Plateau, and then down the face of the cliff to Ari Burnu, the northern limit of Anzac Cove. This was the inner line of defence, and was never really manned, except by field guns and a howitzer or two.

The outer line was shaped like a boomerang, with Quinn's Post as the apex. The fire trench started from a point about 1000 yards south of Hell Spit and ran up the crest of low ridges, thence to the hills overlooking Monash Gully to Steel's Post, Courtney's and Quinn's; next came Dead Man's Ridge and the post called Pope's Hill. Here the impassable ravine intervened, on the other side of which was the section later known as Russell's Top, whence the line took a right-angled bend down Walker's Ridge to the sea. There probably never existed a more tangled and confused line, consisting as it did of posts perched perilously on the brink of steep cliffs, often not even connected one to the other.

Quinn's Post.

Of all these posts, Quinn's became the most famous. It was the salient of the Anzac line and the nearest point to the Turk. Looking back, it is a marvel that the place ever held at all. If the enemy could have shelled it, Quinn's would not have lasted five minutes. It was first held, a ragged trench line just below the crest, by men of the 4th Australian Infantry Brigade, which formed part of the N.Z. and A. Division. Those famous battalions—the 13th, 14th, 15th, and 16th Australian Infantry—established themselves on the night of April 25 at the head of the gully named after their well-

HEADQUARTERS OF QUINN'S.
The three officers are Colonel Johnston, N.Z.I.B.; Lieut.·Col. Malone, Post Commander; and Major Ferguson, R.E., Engineer Staff Officer for No. 3 Defence Section.

known Brigadier. The Turk seemed determined to regain possession of Quinn's—this would have imperilled the whole Anzac line, for the holding of Quinn's alone ensured the communications by way of Shrapnel Valley and Monash Gully. Because holding Quinn's meant holding Anzac, no labour was too great to be expended on it. Men in the bomb factory, having completed a long day's work, turned to again when it was made known that "Quinn's was short of bombs," and pathetic it was to see these hard-swearing Australian and New Zealand sappers nodding their heads and dropping off to sleep with a detonator in one hand and a piece of fuse in the other, only to wake with a start and, in the small hours of the morning, carry the product of their toil up to their beloved Quinn's—a journey of over a mile in the dark with a box of high explosives!

A party of New Zealand Engineers was established in Quinn's and Pope's from the second day, and their duty was to sap forward with a deep trench through the crest, and then put T ends on the ends of the saps, thus making farther towards the Turk a new firing line which gave a better field of fire. This most dangerous work was much hindered by the enemy dropping grenades in the head of the sap. Men often had bullet holes drilled through their long-handled shovels, but despite the casualties, the work went on.

To the right of Quinn's it was necessary to dig a sap through to join up with Courtney's, and after much labour and loss this work was accomplished. To the left of Quinn's was the hotly-contested Dead Man's Ridge, which, after the morning of May 3, rested in the hands of the Turk. This vantage point almost looked into the back of Quinn's, and a work of great magnitude was the construction of a sandbag wall to protect the tracks to Quinn's from the Turkish machine guns on Dead Man's Ridge.

It was foreseen that if the enemy commenced mining in earnest, a fair-sized charge might blow the post off the hillside into Monash Gully. So counter-mining was decided on. There were no tunnelling companies then in the Mediterranean Expeditionary Force, and the sapper field companies were too reduced by casualties to do the work. But all through the Colonial armies were miners and tunnellers— these men from Broken Hill, Coolgardie, Waihi, Westport, and other places where coal and gold are won, were formed into companies under experienced officers, and in a large measure the strenuous labours of these improvized units at Courtney's, Quinn's and Pope's saved Anzac to the British.

Right through the twenty-four hours the miners sweated at the tunnel face, interested in only one thing: how far the man just relieved had driven in his last shift. There was no talk of limiting the output or of striking in Anzac, for here there was a great community of interest—each one was prepared to labour and, if needs be, to sacrifice himself in the interests of the common weal.

COURTNEY'S POST.

One of the best photographs taken of an Anzac trench system. The front line is just over the crest; the reserve trenches are near the top left hand corner; the white earth spilled down the cliffside is from the mines running out to the front; the zig-zag track up the steep cliff is cleary shown.

[*Lent by Sergt. P. Tite, N.Z.E.*

Aeroplanes.

Our flying men had their headquarters in Mudros Harbour. Daily they flew up and down the Peninsula, but they were sadly overworked. Mostly they were seaplanes belonging to the Navy. This was a sad handicap to our artillery ashore, for guns without aeroplanes spotting for them are almost as ineffective as a blind pugilist.

Every day out to sea the "sausage ship" could be seen with her big captive balloon observing for the naval gunners. For the first week no enemy planes were seen, but one day this new sensation appeared. Eyes were turned skyward,

ON THE RIGHT FLANK.
Notice the deep communication trenches through the crest to the firing line, and the 25 graves in the little cemetery.

watching the machine, when someone cried out, "It's a German." There, sure enough, were the big black crosses instead of the familiar red, white and blue circles. A rather amusing feeling of "What do we do now?" pervaded the onlookers. It seemed to be little use going into the dugout with a waterproof sheet for a roof! But this time he was only spying out the land, and sailed away without molesting anyone. Next day he was back with a sting. As necks were craned upwards, something was seen to leave the machine, and with a succession of "Whoo! whoo! whoo!" came rapidly to earth, or rather, to water, for splash it went into the sea 200 yards from Walker's Pier. "Splash!" came another, and still another, whereupon the plane wheeled back over the

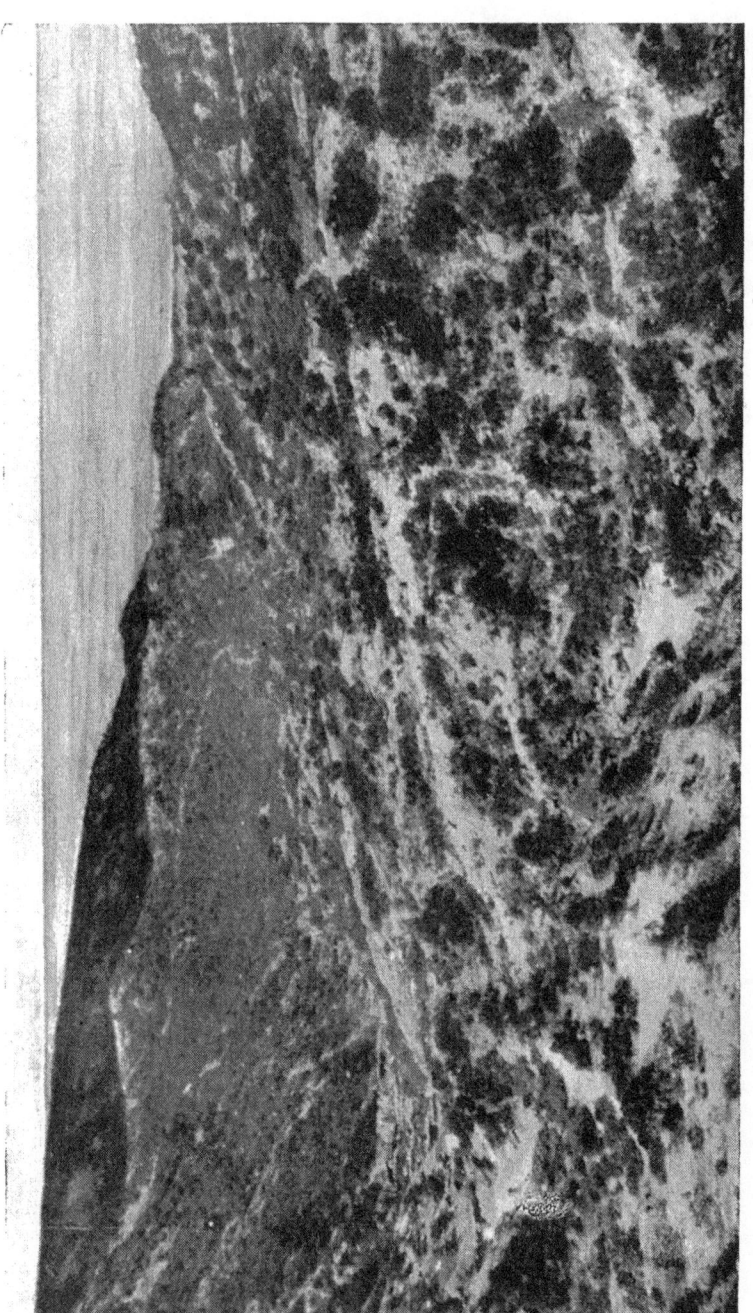

LOOKING DOWN MONASH GULLY.

[Lent by Sergt. P. Tite, N.Z.E.

Peninsula and off home. Daily the machines flew over and dropped their three bombs each, but never was any material damage done.

At the head of Monash Gully showers of steel darts, about the size of a lead pencil, were sometimes dropped, and at intervals the airman wasted his energies in the distribution of leaflets intimating that "As the English are in desperate straits, you will be well treated if you surrender soon." This was sometimes varied by a sheet on which was a picture of soldiers alleged to be Mohammedan deserters from our Indian troops, telling of the good time they were having with their co-religionists. These papers were greatly treasured by the troops as souvenirs.

One of the most beautiful sights in the campaign was witnessed when one of our seaplanes was attacked by a Turkish anti-aircraft. Standing on the hillside and looking out over the blue Ægean Sea, the eye would pick up, sailing through the azure of the Mediterranean sky, the naval planes with the sun shining on its oiled-silk wings like those of a great dragon fly. Suddenly, below it, a puff of pure white smoke would open out as a silk handkerchief does when released from a closed hand. On would sail the plane, and above it would open another puff of smoke. So, with unders and overs, the picture would be limned in, until the eye got tired of watching, and the plane climbed out of range.

CHAPTER IX.

The Battle of Krithia.

Bitter as had been the struggle at Anzac, the fight at the southern end of the peninsula was even more bloody. To the most honourable traditions of the British Army and Navy was added a further lustre. The story of the "River Clyde" and the "Lancashire Landing" are amongst the most tragic and glorious in the history of the British race.

But the advance towards Achi Baba was held up some distance from the village of Krithia, and General Sir Ian Hamilton made up his mind to undertake one big final assault before the Turks could receive their reinforcements.

On the night of Wednesday, May 5, the New Zealand Infantry Brigade and the 2nd Australian Infantry Brigade, were assembled on the bullet-swept Anzac beach, placed in destroyers and barges and landed just east of Cape Helles early next morning. Here was the battered "River Clyde," and on the cliff to the right Sedd-el-Bahr fort, completely wrecked by the naval guns.

NEARING "V" BEACH, CAPE HELLES.

As the troops moved from the landing place, they saw deep Turkish trenches and formidable barbed-wire entanglements. The landscape was vastly different from the hungry hills of Anzac. This was fairly easy rolling country, intersected with sod walls, through which gaps had been worn by passing troops; most of the land was cultivated, and dotted here and there with clumps of fir trees, from behind which the French 75's and British 18-prs. threw their hail of shrapnel. Among the 18-prs. was the 3rd Battery of New Zealand Field Artillery that had lain off Anzac, but was not disembarked until landed here at Helles on May 4. This battery stayed at Helles until the middle of August.

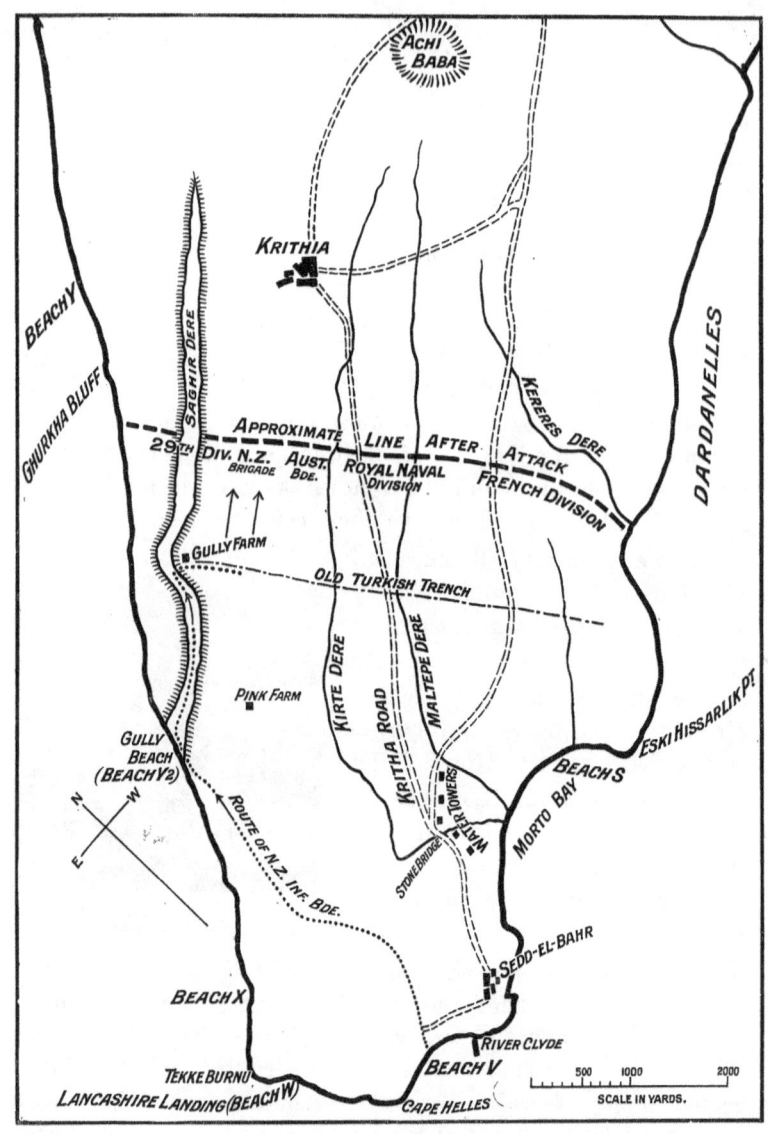

MAP OF CAPE HELLES SECTOR.

This map shows the route taken by the New Zealand Infantry Brigade on May 6-7.

On April 25, a landing at "Y2" or Gully Beach was not attempted. The troops that landed at "Y" Beach were consequently isolated and eventually withdrawn. The landing at "X" Beach was very successful and is some times spoken of as the "Implacable Landing." "W" Beach, afterwards called "Lancashire Landing," and "V" Beach, made famous by the "River Clyde," were the two most costly landings. The landing at "S" Beach in Morto Bay was successfully carried out by the 2nd South Wales Borderers, covered by the "Cornwallis" and the "Lord Nelson."

The Battle of Krithia.

Having climbed the heights from the beach, the eye took in at once the great hump of Achi Baba, the crest just five miles away. Two ridges, like sprawling arms, ran down to the sea—one towards the Narrows, the other to the Gulf of Saros. From Sedd-el-Bahr a road traverses the centre of the Peninsula, running through the village of Krithia, which is four miles from Sedd-el-Bahr; it skirts the lower slopes to the left of Achi Baba, rounds the northern shoulder of the Kilid Bahr Plateau, and so to Maidos, on the shores of the Narrows, thirteen miles in a direct line from Sedd-el-Bahr. At Krithia, for which village most of the subsequent desperate fighting took place, the Peninsula is about three and a half miles across.

Let the reader take any railway guide and select two stations four miles apart. It is hard to realize that troops like the French, the 29th Division, the Australians, the New Zealanders and the Indians should be held in such narrow limits for so many months. But with the sea on the flanks and the enemy holding the high ground, the defence of a natural fortress like Achi Baba was comparatively easy.

Following on the landings of April 25, the British held the left of the line, with the French (withdrawn from Kum Kale) on the right. Coming from the cramped confines of Anzac, the New Zealanders marvelled to see French officers in blue and red riding up and down the road, and motor cyclists dashing about with signal messages. Poor Anzac could not boast of a road on which to run even a bicycle. As a relief from our inevitable khaki, the French Senegalese with their dark blue uniforms, the Zouaves with their red baggy trousers, and the French Territorials with their light blue, imparted quite a dash of colour to the scene, On May 6, the French away on the right attacked all day, while the Royal Naval Division moved a little down both sides of the Krithia Road.

In the reconstitution of the British forces for the renewed assault on Krithia, a new composite division, to be used as a general reserve, was formed of the 2nd Australian Brigade, the New Zealand Brigade, and a Naval Brigade consisting of the Plymouth and Drake Battalions.

[British Official Photograph.

THE "RIVER CLYDE" ASHORE AT "V" BEACH.

This was a most daring enterprise. The old ship was specially fitted to run ashore, when troops were to pour out of the big doors cut in her sides and fill a string of lighters towed alongside, and so to the shore to form a bridge. But the 1st Munster Fusiliers, the 2nd Hampshires and a company of the Dublin Fusiliers were subjected to a murderous fire and did not get ashore till darkness intervened. Their endurance and gallantry was a fitting complement to the bravery and devotion shown by the officers and men of the Royal Navy.

The New Zealand Brigade in Reserve.

After leaving the congested beach the New Zealand Brigade pushed across country. The men were much interested in the first sight of the French 75's. Coming to rest in some fairly level fields, rough shelter trenches were dug in the moist earth. Shells flew backwards and forwards all that night, and very few men could sleep owing to the wet trenches. Everybody was a little hurt because the Australians were served with Machonochies, whereas the New Zealanders got the usual bully beef; but a few gay spirits refused to be depressed, and lustily sang "There's something in the seaside air," which was unfortunately true.

On the morning of the 7th, extra ammunition and entrenching tools were issued, and the brigade started on a long trek in a north-westerly direction, eventually coming down to Gully Beach on the Gulf of Saros. After a short rest, the march was resumed. The leading files struck back again up the hill and met many Lancashires coming back wounded. Everywhere equipment was scattered. Many of our men secured sun helmets, which later were the envy of Anzac. When word came to rest for the night and dig in, the brigade pulled off the track to the sides of the valley, posted outpost groups, and endeavoured to rest for the night. But there was a good deal of confusion and noise, Ghurkas and other troops were moving up and down, and presently word came to move further up the gully. On the weary men stumbled, past a trench held by the King's Own Scottish Borderers, and evenutally arrived near a small stone farmhouse on the right hand side of the gully. On both sides of the road were some old Turkish trenches, in a filthy condition. Sticking up in the parapet was a dead man's hand, like a stop sign, seeming to indicate "this far and no farther." Backwards and forwards, this way and that, men wandered in the search for a comfortable resting place. Here the brigade passed the night, acting as a reserve to the 87th and 88th Brigades of the 29th Division, but the morning came without our men being called on.

The shelter of a ruined building was seized upon for a dressing station. Near by was a large fig tree, which later

[*British Official Photograph.*

LANCASHIRE LANDING AT "W" BEACH.

Here the 1st Lancashire Fusiliers added fresh glory to their illustrious record. The barbed wire was placed down to the water's edge and in the water. But the gallant Lancashires were not to be denied and performed prodigies of valour.

served as a landmark for the last resting-place of many New Zealand soldiers. From this dressing station the wounded were carried by the stretcher-bearers some distance to the rear to the Pink Farm, whence the mule ambulances carried the suffering men over the well-worn roads to the beaches.

On the morning of May 8, the New Zealand Brigade was ordered to the support of the 29th Division. We were to go through the 88th Brigade, and with the 87th Brigade on our left, renew the attack on Krithia at 10.30 a.m. The advance was made in a succession of waves; the Wellingtons were on the left, the Aucklands in the centre, and the Canterburys on the right; the Otago Battalion was in reserve. After an intense bombardment by our ship's guns and field artillery, the brigade advanced from the reserve trenches at 10.30 a.m. The ground was broken, and this hindered the pace. Many were lost who might have been saved if this advance had been made before daylight. The troops pressed on despite the casualties. When the officers ordered a breather, the tired men fell down flat right out in the open. Past the Hants' trenches and the Essex trench they went steadily forward until they came to the big front-line trench held by the 29th Division. From here it was about 800 yards to the enemy main line trench, but scattered in front of his line, in every depression and behind every clump of bush, were machine guns and hosts of enemy snipers.

The Daisy Patch.

From this front-line trench the Regulars had advanced the day before, but had been driven back. Presently the word was passed along that the New Zealanders would prepare to charge. When some Munsters and Essex saw the preparations, they shouted, "You're not going to charge across the daisy patch, are you?" "Of course we are," the Aucklanders answered. "God help you," they said, and watched with admiration as the New Zealanders flung themselves over the top.

The converging machine-gun fire from the clumps of fir trees swept the ground like a hose. This famous "daisy patch" was situated just to the left of a dry creek-bed running from near the village of Krithia down the centre of the Peninsula towards the Cape—a piece of ground about 100 yards across, absolutely devoid of cover; apparently it had once been sown with some crop, but was now overgrown with the common red poppy of the field and countless long-stemmed daisies comparable to the dog daisy of England and New Zealand. The bank of the creek afforded good cover, and the Turkish snipers took full toll of our men.

[*Lent by Sergt. P. Tite, N.Z.E.*]
THE NEW ZEALAND INFANTRY BRIGADE STAFF.
Taken just before the "Daisy Patch" attack. The officer standing is Colonel E. F. Johnston. Major Temperly (to whom much credit is due for the good work of the Brigade) is sitting on a box, facing this way.

The troops had hardly got a quarter of the way across the patch when there burst a further terrific storm of machine-gun and rifle fire. Heavily laden with entrenching tools and equipment, the troops were exhausted and could go no farther. By 3 p.m. the thin line was digging itself in.

Canterbury had advanced about 250 yards, Auckland had two companies about the same distance, but the right company had fallen back owing to heavy cross machine-gun fire from a clump of fir trees. Wellington had made good about 300 yards, but were under very heavy fire from a Turkish trench on our left front. Two companies of the Otago Regiment were sent in to help Auckland, who had lost heavily and were somewhat shaken.

A squadron of armoured cars advanced in fine style up the Krithia Road, but a few Turkish trenches dug across the road damped their ardour, and they disconsolately returned to the rear.

All that afternoon our men hung on under a withering fire. The wounded lying out in the open were hit again and again. Away on the right, the French could be seen pressing vigorously forward towards the crest, but were ever beaten back. Times without number they surged forward, but could not hold the ground so hardly won. Again and again that awful afternoon did the British, French, Indian, and Colonial soldiers hurl themselves forward towards the Turk. But the enemy machine guns were not to be denied; from end to end of the line the attack was undoubtedly held up.

It was resolved to make one final effort before nightfall. The remaining two companies of the Otago Battalion were pushed up to support Wellington's right and Auckland's left, and a newly arrived draft of New Zealand Reinforcements was moved up into reserve. At 5 p.m., every available gun ashore and afloat opened on the Turkish lines. Never before had the troops heard such an awesome uproar—the spiteful French 75's vied with the 15-in. monsters of the Queen Elizabeth in heaping metal on the Turk. Half an hour later the whole line advanced against the Turkish lines, but it was more than flesh and blood could do to make a permanent advance. Everywhere ground was gained, but at a tremendous price. The thinned-out ranks were not strong enough to hold what had been gained.

This effort had spent itself before 7 p.m. The Canterburys had gone forward some 400 yards. The Aucklands went well ahead, but lost very heavily in officers. They fell back almost to their original line. Wellington made a substantial advance, but were held up by the enemy machine

A GUN OF THE 3RD BATTERY, N.Z.F.A. AT CAPE HELLES.
After our experience of cover in France, the sheet of galvanized iron and row of sandbags

[*Lent by Capt. Farr, D.S.O., M.C.*

guns, which before had proved troublesome. These guns were difficult to get at, as a deep nullah lay between these guns and the New Zealanders, and could only be assaulted by the 87th Brigade.

Away on the left a fire broke out among the gorse and scrub. The Sikh wounded fared very badly in the flames.

After dark it was found that the Canterburys were in direct touch with the 2nd Australian Brigade on the right. Canterbury's left was not in touch with anyone, but a second line some distance to the rear filled the gap. Our line from Wellington's right was also not in touch, but was protected by trenches of the 87th Brigade echeloned in rear.

[*Lent by Sergt. P. Tite, N.Z.E.*
FRENCH TERRITORIALS BEFORE THE ADVANCE.

During the night the position gained was consolidated. The Auckland Battalion was much disorganized and split up, so was withdrawn to the reserve trenches. The casualties had been very heavy. Large numbers of wounded had to spend the night on the battlefield, as their evacuation was difficult.

At 3.53 p.m. on May 9, an order was received to take over the section from our left to the Krithia Nullah. The 87th Brigade was to go into support, the line being held by the Wellingtons, Otagos, and Canterburys. Part of the 88th Brigade was also retired. The marksmen of the Canterburys took the enemy snipers by surprise, and established a moral superiority over them.

The Relief of our Brigade.

During the next few days the weather was good, but the nights were very cold. The Turks attacked intermittently, but were definitely held. On the night of May 11, the New Zealanders were relieved by units of the East Lancashire Division, recently arrived from Egypt. This was achieved by 3 a.m. on May 12, without much confusion, whereupon the brigade moved back to its bivouac near the stone bridge on the Krithia road. Just after arriving there was a heavy fall of rain, which converted the surroundings into an absolute quagmire. The following days, however, were beautifully fine, and the men had a much-needed rest. In the reorganization it was found that the brigade had suffered a

TROOPS GATHERING FIREWOOD AT SEDD-EL-BAHR.

total of 771 casualties at Helles, but all ranks were greatly cheered by the appreciative comments passed by the Regular Army officers, and especially by Sir Ian Hamilton's official message: "May I, speaking out of a full heart, be permitted to say how gloriously the Australians and New Zealanders have upheld the finest traditions of our race during this struggle still in progress; at first with audacity and dash, since then with sleepless valour and untiring resource. They have already created for their countries an imperishable record of military virtue.''

Several days of welcome relief from the front line ensued. Men wandered through the battered forts of Sedd-el-Bahr, and marvelled at the dismantled guns and twisted ironwork. Others strolled around the fertile countryside, which was smothered with a profusion of red poppies, white daisies and blue larkspurs, as if to honour the French and British occupation.

After dark on the evening of May 19, the brigade again embarked from V Beach to return to Anzac Cove, where they arrived at dawn next morning. During the disembarkation a very sad incident occurred in the Auckland Battalion, which lost another officer, he being the twenty-seventh officer incapacitated out of the original twenty-nine combatants.

CHAPTER X.

The Arrival of the Mounteds.

During the first few days the troops were exhorted to hold on. There was no option. The line could not go forward, and it dare not go back. First it was rumoured that the East Lancashire Division, associated with us in Egypt, was coming to Anzac; then the 29th Indian Infantry Brigade

[*Lent by Sergt. P. Tite, N.Z.E.*
THE TANGLED SLOPES OF MULE GULLY.

from the Suez Canal; but Helles absorbed these. Worst still! On May 5 the New Zealand Infantry Brigade and the 2nd Australian Brigade were taken out of Anzac to assist in the thrust towards Krithia. On the left flank of Anzac, two weak battalions of the Royal Naval Division took over the line the New Zealand Brigade had vacated.

The Anzac position was now reorganized in four defence sections numbered from right to left. General Bridges, with the 1st Australian Division, held Sections 1 and 2—that is, from Chatham's Post on the sea up to, but not including, Courtney's Post. General Godley, with the N.Z. and A. Division, was responsible for the rest of the line. No. 3 Defence Section contained the three famous posts at the head of Monash Gully—Courtney's, Quinn's, and Pope's. Russell's Top, Walker's Ridge, No. 1 and No. 2 Posts made up No. 4 Section. General Birdwood, the Army Corps General, was at his headquarters in Anzac Cove, and each Divisional General was in charge of half the defensive line.

The sections were held as follow:—

No. 1 Section (Colonel Sinclair-Maclagan)—3rd Australian Infantry Brigade.

No. 2 Section (Brigadier-General Walker)—1st Australian Infantry Brigade.

No. 3 Section (Brigadier-General Trotman, R.M.L.I.)— 4th Australian Infantry Brigade; Royal Marine Brigade (Chatham and Portsmouth Battalions); 3 sections No. 1 Field Company, N.Z.E

No. 4 Section (Brigadier-General Mercer, R.M.L.I.)— Royal Naval Brigade (Nelson and Deal Battalions); 1 section No. 1 Field Company, N.Z.E.

We, as a nation, are prone to underrate our efforts and laud those of our adversaries. Before and during the war it was loudly asserted that the German Secret Service and German diplomacy always outwitted the British. To-day the world knows the truth of the matter. Likewise, it was contended that the Turkish Intelligence Department was superior to ours. "Look how they always know what we are about to do," said the critics. Truly, anything planned in Egypt was bound to leak out if it had to be printed or circulated, as Egypt was always a cosmopolitan place, where it was unsafe to trust a stranger. But if the Turks knew so much, why did they not attack Walker's Ridge that anxious week in May? Any attack must have succeeded, and the thin line of single trenches once broken, Anzac must have crumpled.

The enemy did nothing serious, and on May 12 the joy at Anzac was unbounded. The Mounteds had arrived! Every face on the beach was wreathed in smiles. Here they all were—without their horses, but keen, and spoiling for a fight—the Australian Light Horse; the New Zealand Mounted Rifles Brigade, consisting of the Auckland, Wellington, and Canterbury Regiments; the field troop to reinforce the overworked 1st Field Company in its sapping and mining; the signal troop, to help with the telephone and buzzers; and the mounted field ambulance, to assist their overworked confreres with the wounded.

Whatever the trudging infantry men had thought in Egypt as the mounted men swept by, to-day there was nothing but

THE BEACH SWEEPING TOWARDS NIBRUNESI POINT.

the good humoured banter of "Where's your horses?" As the eager troopers climbed the goat tracks of Walker's Ridge a great sigh of relief was heaved by the sorely tried garrison of Anzac. Never were troops more welcome.

The same day, Colonel Chauvel, with the 1st Australian Light Horse Brigade, took over No. 3 Defence Section from Brigadier-General Trotman, who embarked with the Chatham and Portsmouth Battalions that night for Cape Helles.

Brigadier-General Russell relieved Brigadier-General Mercer on Walker's Ridge. The New Zealand Mounted Rifles Brigade took over the line from the Nelson and Deal Battalions, who also left Anzac to rejoin the Royal Naval Division at Cape Helles.

The highest part of Walker's Ridge became known as Russell's Top, because, close at hand, practically in the firing line, the commander of the N.Z. Mounted Rifles Brigade established his headquarters. Hereabouts No Man's Land was very narrow. Away to the right ran the deep gully, which, passing behind the back of Pope's Hill, became Monash Gully. So far, Pope's and Russell's Top were unconnected, the Turks holding the head of this gully, which made their sniping of Monash Gully so effective. It was from here, on May 15, that a Turkish sniper mortally wounded General Bridges, as he was proceeding up Shrapnel Gully. At that time no place in the Anzac area could be considered safe.

THE SPHINX.
Owing to the steep cliffsides, the bullets could not reach the dug-outs on the slope.

To the left was another gully running down and losing itself in the ramifications of the outlying spurs of Walker's Ridge. The little flat watershed separating these two gullies ran like an isthmus across No Man's Land, and connected Russell's Top with that part of the main Turkish position known as "Baby 700" and "The Chessboard." This connecting link was known as "The Nek." Only a few yards behind our main fire trench were precipitous cliffs, which, running round to the right, culminated in a remarkable knife-edged cliff eventually known as the "Sphinx"; while to the extreme left flank these cliffs, scored with the torrential winter rains, eventually resolved themselves into broken under-features of Walker's Ridge, sprawling out and forming one side of the Sazli Beit Dere. Near the bottom of this dry watercourse was the little Fishermen's Hut, so often used as a landmark. Just south of these huts was No. 1 Post, and a few hundred yards past the valley and on the coast was the little knoll eventually to become famous as No. 2 Post.

No. 2 Post.

This No. 2 Post was the northern extremity of our line. Measured on the map, it was a distance of 3600 yards—just two miles—from Chatham's Post on the extreme right. As Quinn's Post was about 1000 yards from the sea, a rough calculation will show that the area of Anzac was approximately 750 acres. Seven hundred and fifty acres of prickly scrub and yellow clay, stony water-courses, sandy cliffs and rocky hill tops, land that would not support one family in comfort, yet for eight long months, men of divers races lived a Spartan life there, studding the hillsides so thickly with their rude dugouts that a Turkish shell seldom failed to find a victim.

No time was lost after taking over this No. 4 Sector. The engineers had made a track for guns and mules up to Russell's Top. This road was regraded and improved in parts; trenches were deepened and made more habitable;

saps were pushed out wherever the field of fire required improvement. The line from "the Top" to No. 2 Outpost was very broken, with many rough gullies intervening; secret saps were dug, and machine guns placed to cover this "dead" ground, up and down which the scouts of both sides roamed as soon as it was dark.

The panorama from Walker's Ridge was magnificent. Looking across the yellow clay hills, decorated in patches with green scrub oak and prickly undergrowth, red poppies and purple rock roses, one saw the beautiful beach sweeping up towards the Suvla Flats; the Ægean Sea was generally as calm as a mill pond, dotted all over with leisurely trawlers, barges, and restless destroyers; the white hospital ships, with their green bands and red crosses, lay a few miles out to sea; over in the distance the storied isles of Imbros and Samothrace stood out in all the glory of their everchanging tints. The men of the Wellington regiments recognized a strong

THE SUVLA FLATS FROM WALKER'S RIDGE.

resemblance to the view from the Paekakariki Hill, looking out towards Kapiti and the long white stretch of the Otaki beach.

Later in the month the Otago Mounted Rifles were stationed down at No. 2 Post. Between the post and the sea was a delightful little strip of level ground, ablaze with poppies and other wild flowers, but under the eye, and within the range of the enemy. Near this outpost was discovered an old Turkish well. Elsewhere men searched for water, and sometimes found it, but when pumps were applied the flow ceased after a day or so. This, on the contrary, was a most reliable well, a godsend to the thirsty men and mules, and a most welcome addition to the scanty supply procured from the barges. Soldiers came from far and near to draw the precious water.

Owing to its visibility to the snipers on the Turkish right flank, the beach between Ari Burnu and Fishermen's Hut could not be used during the day. Almost under the shadow of the Sphinx a group of boats and barges lay stranded on the beach. Late one night a party of mounteds went down and buried the remains of forty Australian infantrymen who had been killed at the April landing.

The Mounted Rifles repulse a determined Attack.

About the middle of May, the Turks decided that one determined effort would drive the men of Anzac into the sea. These people perched on the hillside annoyed him enormously. Never did he make an attack in the southern zone but these Colonials threatened to advance towards Maidos. News was gleaned of the withdrawal of troops from Helles and the arrival of reinforcements from Constantinople.

On May 17, the "Lord Nelson" delighted all beholders by turning her big guns on to the village of Kuchuk Anafarta. All along the coast line the ships joined in, until every village behind the line, and every road running towards Helles and Anzac, was swathed in dust and flame. The Turk retaliated with guns ranging from 11in. down to .77. Their shooting was good—one Australian 18-pr. was put out of action by a direct hit. The enemy reinforcements were delayed, but with the darkness, on they came again.

Next day was fairly quiet, but the sentries were warned to prepare for an attack, and during the night the reliefs slumbered behind the line with their clothes on, their rifles loaded, and their bayonets fixed. Sure enough, just after midnight, firing commenced from Chatham's Post along to No. 2 Post. Thousands of cricket-ball hand-grenades were hurled into Quinn's and other critical places. The big guns on both sides renewed their efforts. The bursts of shells in

PENINSULA PRESS.

No. 44   SATURDAY, JULY 3rd 1915.   Official News.

The Attack that Failed.

Further details have now been received of the attack made by the Turks on the night of the 29th-30th ult. At about 2 o'clock on Wednesday morning the searchlights of H.M.S. "Scorpion" discovered half a Turkish battalion advancing near the sea, North-west of Krithia. The "Scorpion" opened fire and few of the enemy got away. Simultaneously, the enemy attacked the knoll we had captured due West of Krithia, advancing from the nullah in close formation in several lines. The attack came under artillery and enfilade rifle fire and the enemy lost heavily. The foremost Turks got within 40 yards of the parapet, but only a few returned.

The Turks made several heavy bomb attacks during the night, our troops being twice driven back a short distance. In the early morning we regained these trenches by bayonet attack and they have since been strengthened. At 5.30 a.m. 2,000 Turks moving from Krithia into the ravine were scattered by machine gun fire. The operations reflect great credit on the vigilance and the accurate shooting of H.M.S. "Scorpion." The Turkish losses in the nullah and ravine are estimated at from 1,500 to 2,000 dead. At about 10 p.m. on Wednesday the Turks again attacked with bombs a portion of the most northerly trench captured by us on the 29th.

An officer of the Gurkas being wounded (not dangerously as it turned out) the men became infuriated; flung all their bombs at the enemy, and then charging down out of the trench, used their kukris with great effect. About dawn the Turks once more attempted an attack over the open but nearly the whole of these attacking forces, about half a battalion, were shot down; and a final bomb attack, though commenced, failed utterly.

A further report from Anzac of the enemy's attack on Tuesday and Wednesday last, on our right flank states that the action commenced with very heavy fire from midnight till 1.30 a.m. to which our men replied only by a series of cheers. The Turks then launched their attack and came right on with bayonet and bombs. Those who succeeded in getting into our saps were instantly killed, the remainder being dealt with by bomb and rifle fire from the 7th and 8th Light Horse. By 2 a.m. the enemy broke and many were killed while withdrawing. The enemy's attack was strongest on his right. They were completely taken aback by a concealed sap constructed well ahead of our main line, and their dead are lying thickly in front of this. Some got into the sap and several got across it, and all these were wiped out by fire from the main parapet farther back. Following the defeat of this attack, the enemy attacked at 3 a.m. on our left and 80 men came over the parapets in front of the right of Quinn's Post. These were duly polished off.

Prisoners brought in state that three fresh battalions were employed in the main attack which was made by the personal order of Enver Pasha who, as they definitely assert, was present in the trenches on Tuesday the 29th ult.

Wednesday was very quiet at Anzac, except for heavy musketry fire along our left and centre during the storm in the evening. Latest report of enemy casualties on 29th, estimates them at between 400 and 500 actually seen to fall on those areas alone that are exposed to view and exclusive of any loss inflicted by our bombardments of reverse slopes and gullies in which reserves are known to be collecting.

It is manifest with what apprehension the Turks regard our latest gains and how bravely they have tried to neutralize them and at what cost.

On the West Front.

Paris, July 2nd.

After a continuous bombardment which lasted three days, the Germans attacked the French positions in the Argonne, between the road from Binarville and the Four-de-Paris. Twice driven back, they eventually succeeded, after a third attempt, in setting foot in some parts of the French lines near Bagatelle, and were repulsed everywhere else after a very fierce struggle. Two fresh attacks against the trenches to the East of the road from Binarville were defeated. A violent attack in the neighbourhood of Metzeral was completely repulsed, the Germans suffering heavy losses.

(Official Report by wireless).

Letters to a Turkish Soldier at the Front.

The following characteristic letters, written to a Turkish soldier at the front, will be read with interest:—

"To my dear son-in-law, Hussein Aga. First, I send you my best salaams and I kiss your eyes. Your mother Atrf also kisses your eyes. Mustafa also kisses your eyes and Mrs. Kerim also sends her salaams. Your daughter Ayesha kisses your eyes. Should you inquire after our health, thank God I can tell you we are all in health, and I pray God we may continue to be so. Your letter of the 4th February we have received.

Your mother kisses your eyes and Abdullah kisses both your hands. Your brother, Bairham's wife, has died—may your own life be long—but before dying she brought into the world a child. The child also has died.

What can I say about the decrees of God? Your brother Bairham has also been taken as a soldier. We pray God that his health may be preserved. The money you sent has arrived. Thank God for it, for money is scarce these days. Everybody sends salaams; everybody kisses your hands and your feet. God keep you from danger."

Your father,

Faik.

———

To my dear husband, Hussein Aga. I humbly beg to inquire after your blessed health. Your daughter sends her special salaams and kisses your hands. Since you left I have seen no one. Since your departure I have no peace. Your mother has not ceased to weep since you left. Your daughter declares that she is enceinte and weeps all day. We are all in a bad way. Your wife says to herself "While my husband was here we had some means." Since your departure we have received nothing at all. Please write quickly and send what money you can. All your friends kiss your hands and your feet. May God keep you and save us from the disasters of this war.

Your wife,

Fatima.

R.E. Printing Section, G.H.Q., M.E.F.

"THE PENINSULA PRESS."
Printed by the R.E. Printing Section at Imbros.

mid-air momentarily lit up the scene, intensifying the blackness of the night. But this was only the enemy's preliminary bombardment, for about 3 a.m., the watchful sentries detected forms moving cautiously in No Man's Land. Soon the attack was made in earnest at the junction of No. 2 and No. 3 Defence Sections. Then it burst in its fury on Quinn's and Russell's Top.

The machine guns sprayed the front with a shower of lead, and for an interval the attack seemed held up, but in the grey dawn the mass advanced again. Crying on their God—"Allah! Allah! Allah!"—they surged forward in tremendous strength. From their trenches opposite Russell's Top and Turk's Point on Walker's Ridge they sallied forth in thousands. This was the first real test of the New Zealand Mounted Rifles. The Turks flung themselves against the trenches held by the Auckland Mounted Regiment; but with rifle and machine-gun fire the troopers beat them off, hardly a Turk reaching the trench.

This was a field day for the machine guns posted in No. 4 Section. Carefully trained by some of the greatest experts in the world, who were not slow to recognize their golden opportunities, these excellently placed weapons carried disaster into the enemy's attacks, enfilading them time and again. To the intense delight of the gunners, the Turks advanced in lines that presented ideal machine-gun targets. As the enemy had treated the Royal Naval Battalions on Dead Man's Ridge, so the Turk was now treated in return.

Again and again the foe came on—by their French-grey overcoats they were identified as new picked troops from Asia. Again and again they advanced, but, caught by the loosely-strewn barb wire, they dropped like flies and were beaten to the earth by the machine guns. The din was indescribable. Above the rattle of the musketry combat and between the boom of the guns could be heard the Turk, crying on his Maker as he advanced, yelling and squealing as he retired to the Colonial shouts of "Imshi Yallah!" and the glorious battle chorus of "Ake, Ake, Kia Kaha!"

Down the gullies on the left flank the enemy came in the dark. A determined attack about the Fishermen's Hut would cut off No. 2 Post and let the Turkish hordes surge along the flat beach and low ground into the heart of Anzac. The anxious garrisons detected sounds of men scrambling down the gully. Around the posts alert ears heard the undertone of voices. It was some time before the listeners could determine the mutterings as undoubtedly Turkish. Into the mysteries of the scrub volley after volley was poured. The attackers, feeling that they were "in the air," squealed and disappeared in the direction of the Suvla Flats. When the sun was well up, from No. 2 Post Turkish reinforcements were discernible in the trenches opposite Walker's Ridge. A machine gun of the Canterbury Regiment was posted to

[Lent by Capt. Boxer, N.Z.M.C.

ON WALKER'S RIDGE.
The Field Troop, N.Z.E., regrading the road to Russell's Top.

enfilade them. The rifles of the 10th Nelson Squadron, assisted by the machine gun, brought a devastating fire to bear on a grey-coated battalion of the enemy lying in the trenches and in the depressions, evidently preparing for an advance. For a few minutes a stream of lead played up and down their ranks, causing awful havoc. The mass heaved and swayed convulsively, then broke and stampeded to the rear, assisted in their flight by the ever-watchful guns of the torpedo-boat destroyers, while the machine guns from Steel's, Courtney's, Quinn's, Pope's and Walker's, emptied belt after belt into the enemy reserves. Now was the opportunity of the field gunners. From Howitzer Gully, from Plugge's Plateau, from Walker's Ridge, the New Zealand Field Artillery shells were pumped in streams. The No. 2 Battery, N.Z.F.A., though only able to get two guns to bear, fired 598 rounds almost without intermission. The ships were having a day out, perfect targets presenting themselves all along the line.

Right along the two and a third miles of front the attacks melted away—nowhere was the Anzac line penetrated. The great attempt to drive the infidel into the sea had miserably failed. Everywhere along the line Turks lay dead in heaps. The mounted men—Australians and New Zealanders alike—had demonstrated that southern-bred soldiers were as dogged in defence as they were brilliant in attack.

The night was fairly quiet, but on the 20th the attack was resumed, when the machine gunners had it all their own way. Perhaps the enemy remembered the tragedy of the preceding day, for when the machine guns spluttered, the attackers broke and fled.

In the afternoon a dramatic episode occurred. At different points in the Turkish trenches small white flags appeared. Linguists in the enemy's ranks made known their desire for a truce to bury their dead. At many parts in the line, particularly opposite the Auckland Mounted trenches on Walker's Ridge, some conversation was carried on in German. But observers noticed men crowding in the front line and the communication trenches. It seemed that the white flag incident was a ruse to launch a surprise attack. The white flag parties were given two minutes to get down out of sight. Down they scurried, and once more the musketry battle resumed its violence. As night came the searchlight from the warships played around the Turkish trenches and brilliantly illuminated the gullies on the flanks. Some desultory firing took place, but the Turk had no stomach for more infidel driving.

Burying the Dead on Armistice Day.

Next morning, the look-out on the destroyer guarding our right flank was mystified by a Turk waving a big white flag on Gaba Tepe, previous to coming out right into the open, and well within range. After the tremendous losses a few days previously, some of us thought that here at last was the long-looked-for peace. After a certain amount of justifiable hesitation on our part, a patrol went out to meet the white flag party. The groups met along the seashore, and finally, a Turkish officer, blindfolded, was escorted through the lines, past Hell Spit, and along the beach to Army Corps Headquarters. He carried no proposals for a surrender, but only for a truce to bury the dead. In the interests of both armies this was desirable, but extremely difficult to carry out. No

An Indian Doctor Searching for Wounded on Armistice Day.

Man's Land was very narrow, especially opposite Quinn's and the Nek, and we, for our part, did not care to have inquisitive soldiers poking about, ostensibly burying dead, but with an eagle eye upon our front line trenches.

It took some days to work out the rules to be observed. They ran into many typewritten pages, but briefly they were as follow:—

1. The suspension of arms was to be from 7.30 a.m. to 4.30 p.m., on May 24.
2. A line was to be pegged out down the centre of No Man's Land—the Turkish burying parties to work their side of the line, while we worked on our side.

3. Any dead belonging to the Turks on our side of the line were to be carried on stretchers to the centre line. The enemy was to do the same for us, so that each side would bury its own dead, and so identify them.
4. Rifles found on No Man's Land were to be collected, and immediately placed on stretchers. No man was to carry a rifle in his hand. Each side was to carry off its own rifles found in its burying area. Enemy rifles were to have the bolts removed, and were to be then carried on stretchers, and handed over to the original owners.

The morning of "Armistice Day" broke with a steady drizzle. At the appointed hour fifty Turks, with Red Crescents on their arms, and fifty Australians and New Zealanders with Red Cross armlets, met on the extreme right. Each party had a staff officer and a medical officer. The men carried short stakes with little white strips of calico on the top, and, headed by the staff officers, who each walked near his own front-line trench, the party went right down the centre of No Man's Land, sticking in their little white flags.

By about 10 o'clock the demarcation was complete. As the party had moved down No Man's Land, heads appeared over both parapets, and, cautiously first, and then quite boldly, the soldiers on both sides scrambled up on the parapets and experienced the uncanny sensation of safety.

The burying parties struggled up the greasy clay tracks, marched out with their shovels and their stretchers, and the day's work began in earnest. And what a work! In some sectors the dead lay in heaps. In one area of about an acre, three hundred bodies were tallied—mostly Turks. "They are lying just as thick as sheep in a yard," said a Hawke's Bay boy in the demarcation party. It was soon realized that proper burials were out of the question, and that it was impossible to carry the enemy's dead to the centre line. A mutual agreement was made to cover up friend and foe, the Turk on his side and we on ours. So the Anzac dead in the Turkish area were not identified by us; these are the men who eventually were described as "Missing, believed killed" by the Court of Enquiry.

ARMISTICE DAY, MAY 24, 1915.

These two pictures were taken by Brig.-General Ryan, of the Australian Medical Corps. The top one shows the Turkish Staff Officer who brought in the flag of truce. While going through our lines he was blindfolded, according to custom, and escorted by a British Staff Officer.

The bottom picture shows the burying parties at work in No Man's Land.

Away in the tangled gullies on our left flank, several wounded Turks were discovered in desperate straits. These men were evidently snipers who had been hit while crawling round in the prickly scrub past Walker's Ridge. One man was picked up, and as he made gestures asking for water, an N.Z.M.C. orderly lifted his head up and discovered that his bottom jaw was almost shot away. Another wounded Turk was carried in a distance of two miles, and most inconsiderately died as the hospital was reached.

Very few New Zealanders were found unburied, but there was evidence that they died game. One Aucklander was found still grasping his rifle, which was—barrel and bayonet—firmly embedded in the body of his dead opponent.

By midday, the heat was tropical, and the Anzac beaches were crowded with the battalions from the trenches. The Turk was wont to boast that he would drive us into the sea. What Enver Pasha failed to do, the lice achieved, and the unique opportunity to get a safe wash was fully appreciated.

Up on the hillsides the burial parties were hard at work. The chaplains never had a busier day, searching for identity discs, and reading the burial service. In some parts of the line the men mingled freely with Johnny Turk. A Melbourne medico was an object of great interest to the Turkish soldiery, as he wore the ribbons of the Medjidie and the Osmanieh, gained in a previous war when the Turk and we were allies. A German doctor in Turkish uniform asked for news of his whilom friends in Sydney. The Turks had a supply of brown bread, and many exchanges were made with the Colonials, who were very pleased to barter their flint-like biscuits for something that would not torture their tender gums.

The afternoon wore on, and as 3 o'clock came, we realized that our work was nearly done—over 3000 Turks buried. By 4 p.m., everybody had returned to the trenches, and for the next half-hour deathly silence reigned. To all appearances the truce had been honourably kept. At 4.30, both sides delivered tremendous volleys at nothing in particular, and settled down quietly for the night. Thus ended one of the strangest days in the history of the campaign.

During the day we had been requested not to use binoculars, but all along the line it was noticed that Turkish and German officers were taking the bearings of our trenches and emplacements. From the Turkish trenches on the Chessboard, officers were quite obviously marking down our machine gun emplacements commanding the Nek and Russell's Top. But the New Zealand machine gun officers were equal to the Turks in cunning. During the night all the machine guns were taken down and the crews took cover. With the dawn

RENOVATING GRAVES ON TURK'S POINT.

came the searching shells of the Turkish Field Artillery. The empty emplacements were badly damaged, but as soon as the guns switched on to another target, the New Zealand gunners rebuilt their emplacements and were again ready to fire within twenty minutes of the bombardment.

The Sinking of the "Triumph."

In war man is often made to feel his impotence. An illustration of this occurred the day following the armistice. About midday the workers on the beach heard "Picket boat" cried in those anxious, agonized accents that characterize the cries of "Stretcher bearer" or "Wire," cries that send a shiver down the spine of the most hardened. Looking out to sea, a great column of smoke welled up from the side of the "Triumph," lying about a mile off shore from Gaba Tepe. It was obvious she was hit, for at once she commenced to heel over. Glasses revealed her decks crowded with men, her crew falling in at their stations. Swiftly from every point of the compass came the torpedo-boat destroyers—from Nibrunesi Point, Imbros and Helles. Our old friend the "Chelmer" nosed into the flank of the stricken ship, and orderly, as if on parade, the bluejackets commenced marching off. More and more boats crowded alongside to take off the crew. Steadily the vessel heeled until her masts were almost parallel with the water, her port guns sticking aimlessly into the air. Suddenly she quivered from stem to stern. Her attendants drew back quickly, as she turned completely over amidst a cloud of spray and steam, which, clearing away, revealed her red keel shining brightly against the

THE SINKING OF THE "TRIUMPH."
The old ship, surrounded by small craft, is near the horizon on the left of the picture.

blue Ægean Sea. Once again the destroyers and trawlers closed in to pick up the men in the water. Other destroyers, working in ever-increasing circles, engaged in a hunt for the submarine. Presently the old craft commenced to settle at the bows. Slowly and gracefully she slid into the depths, and the watchers on the Anzac hills heaved a heartfelt sigh. But out there in the blue, the gallant sailormen gave three hearty cheers as the old ship disappeared. An irrepressible cried, "Are we downhearted?" "No," roared the crew of the sunken ship, and a great volume of cheering rose from the vessels gathered round.

This disaster cast a gloom over Anzac. To see one's friends in peril and be powerless to help caused the Colonial soldiers more pain than any previous experience. This old ship had been such a trusty friend, and now, in a short twenty minutes, she was gone! Men sat up on the hill that night, cursing the Hun and all his allies!

The Taking and Losing of "Old No. 3 Post."

Between the ridge of Chunuk Bair, held by the Turk, and our No. 2 Post, there were three other conspicuous pieces of high ground bounded on the north by Chailak Dere, and on the south by the Sazli Beit Dere. The highest of these was Rhododendron Ridge; the next was a little plateau appropriately named Table Top, and nearest to No. 2, really a higher peak of the same spur, was a Turkish post from which most of the deadliest sniping was carried on. It was thought advisable to occupy this ridge and deny it to the enemy. It was a hopeless position for us—away out in a salient—and should never have been attempted. On the night of May 28, a squadron of the Canterbury Mounted Rifles crept up the dere and took this sniping post by surprise at the point of the bayonet. They, in their turn, handed over to a squadron of the Wellington Mounted Regiment, who proceeded to put the post into a state of defence by entrenching it. The garrison was again relieved by a squadron of the Wellingtons (9th Wellington East Coast) on the night of May 30. Getting in about 8 o'clock at night, the men were hardly distributed along the meagre trenches when sounds of movement were heard. Presently, showers of hand-grenades descended on the post. Calling on "Allah," the enemy, numbering many hundreds, surrounded the post. The Wellingtons had no hand-grenades (the shortage of these weapons at Anzac was deplorable), so had to depend upon their rifles. Rushing up to the parapet and yelling their eerie cries, but never daring to press the attack home, throwing hand-grenades and then retreating, the Turks let the precious hours of darkness slip by.

The garrison decided to make the Turks pay a big price for the post. The strain of hanging on through that awful night was tremendous. But with the welcome dawn came fresh hope. All that day the garrison lay in their trenches waiting for the final assault.

The guns from the "W" Hills broke in parts of the parapet; the telephone wire to No. 2 Post was cut, and the Turk actually penetrated a section of the trench, but was driven out. Things becoming desperate—water and ammunition both running short—a message was semaphored back to Walker's Ridge, and it was decided to attempt the relief of the post at dusk.

Two Wellington squadrons went out, but were held up. Later—this was the night of May 31—two troops of the 8th (South Canterbury) Squadron and the 10th (Nelson) Squadron proceeded to fight their way from No. 2 Outpost up to this new ill-starred outpost, now known as No. 3. They joined forces with two Wellington squadrons, and with Turkish hand-grenades lighting the gully, the relief party pushed aside all opposition, got into the post, and relieved

A VIEW FROM THE LEFT FLANK.

On the left is the Sphinx; the next high ground is Plugge's Plateau, which running down to the sea resolves itself into the point of Ari Burnu.

the Wellingtons. There was to be no rest for the unlucky garrison of No. 3. On came the Turks again, and the performance of the night before was repeated almost without variation, the throwing of hand-grenades, calling on "Allah!" and rushing up to the parapet, but never daring the final assault. For some hours the inferno continued. About midnight word came through from Headquarters that the post might be abandoned. The task of removing the wounded presented no small difficulties, but they having been removed down the dere, the perilous retirement commenced. In the faint moonlight, the Turks could be seen flitting hither and thither. Now that our retirement was commencing, their exultant yelling and squealing burst out afresh. Down the dere slowly came the rearguard, calmly and methodically picking off any too adventurous enemy. When the troopers reached the "Big Sap" running out past No. 1 and 2, they lined the two sides of the gully and the trench and waited for the Turk. A squadron of the Auckland Mounteds now arrived, and based on No. 2 Post and the Fishermen's Hut, the whole party made a determined stand, and enabled the 9th Squadron, who had been fighting for forty-eight hours, to be withdrawn.

To the highly-strung men, many of whom had not slept for three days, the yelling of the Turks, the ghostlike sea

[Photo by the Author
THE BIG SAP RUNNING PAST NO. 2 POST.

lapping on the beach in the background, and the enemy jumping from bush to bush in the moonlight, the whole business resembled a frightful nightmare. Gradually the Turks grew tired of yelling, and retired to occupy "Old No. 3," while the weary troopers trudged along the dusty sap to their much-needed bivouac, leaving the squadron of the Auckland Mounted Rifles out watching the position until daylight.

A new No. 3 Post was established by the Otago Mounted Rifles on rising ground about 200 yards north of No. 2 Post. This became the extreme right flank of the Anzac position until the great advance in August.

CHAPTER XI.

Supplying the Needs of the Army.

The Germans selecting their time for opening the World War, it was not surprising that Britain was sadly handicapped as regards munitions and material generally. As yet the organization by the Ministry of Munitions was a thing undreamt of, and seeing that the Gallipoli campaign was considered a subsidiary one, and that all supplies available were not sufficient for the needs of the army in France, was it surprising that comparatively little attention was given to our operations in what was assumed to be a minor theatre of war?

It is easy at this stage to find fault, but the fault lies not only with the lack of preparation of the Government and

[Lent by Sergt. P. Tite, N.Z.E.
THE A.S.C. DEPOT IN MONASH GULLY.

people of Britain, but also in a less degree with the Governments and people of the Dominions beyond the seas. We cannot be blind to the fact that democracies are short sighted, and must educate themselves to acquire long and wide vision, if they are to hold their own and exist peacefully among ambitious and designing peoples. But we must not moralize, for this narrative deals with facts, though it is just as well to remember that even now, in the days of Peace, we are making history, and at times we may be allowed to peer into the future and see visions of the Pacific in which the people of Australia and New Zealand will surely be called upon to play an important part.

Academic inquiry into our unpreparedness and the causes of the shortage of supplies was of little value to the soldiers trying to defeat the enemy. The men of Anzac had often to procure their stores in a manner not strictly orthodox.

The principal requirements of the army at Anzac were food and water to sustain life; ammunition—big-gun, field-gun, small-arm, and hand-grenades; while to provide some measure of shelter from the adversary and from the weather, timber and sandbags became primal necessaries. There was no hinterland from which these supplies could be drawn. Mudros, the nearest safe anchorage, was fifty miles away; Alexandria, the chief port from which most supplies must come, was distant over 500 miles. The area occupied by the troops produced no food, no timber, and only a very little hardly-won water. Few have any conception of the difficulties that had to be overcome.

The difficulties were chiefly the scarcity of essential articles, but a further obstacle was the matter of transport. It was comparatively easy to get goods as far as Alexandria, to which, situated as it is on the ocean highway to the East, the largest ships brought produce from the ends of the earth. The next stage, to Lemnos, was off the beaten track, and smaller vessels were employed. At Mudros, the goods were transhipped to vessels that again had shrunk in size and were fewer in number. Here the greatest difficulty of all arose, for ships could not come within a mile of the shore. The enemy big guns ranged well out to sea, and at the Anzac piers, nothing as large as even a trawler could lie owing to the shallowness of water. The stores that had started from England or New Zealand in ocean liners, continued their long journey in trawlers manned by hardy North Sea fisherfolk; and made the final stage of all in barges towed by five small picket boats from the ships of His Majesty's Navy.

DRAWING THE WATER RATION AT MULE GULLY.

This was the principal supply for the Units on Walker's Ridge and Russell's Top. In the picture are Maori and Pakeha New Zealanders, Australians, Englishmen,

[Photo by the Author

Think of it, those five small steam boats, officered by fifteen-year-old boys and manned by half a dozen gallant sailormen, were the slender link connecting the army ashore with the world overseas. All through those strenuous months, during fair weather and foul, splashed with the spindrift of the Ægean gales, drenched with the spray from the hissing shells, the daring crews of those stout trawlers and trim picket boats, from the first tow of the landing to the last of the evacuation, made Anzac possible.

The Utter Dependence on the Imperial Navy.

The Gallipoli campaign, perhaps more noticeably than any other phase of the war, demonstrated the utter dependence of the Dominions Overseas on the supreme Imperial Navy. Of what use are mighty armies if they cannot be concentrated

[*British Official Photograph.*
The "Albion" ashore off Gaba Tepe.
The "Cornwallis" is towing her off.

at the decisive point at the right moment? Every New Zealander who was on Gallipoli fully recognized that without the Navy we could not have got ashore, we could not have had our daily beef and biscuits, and worse still, we could never have got safely away. How the admiration of the soldiers for the sailors was reciprocated! What a galaxy of glorious memories—the old "Majestic" and gallant "Bacchante" enveloping Walker's Ridge and Gaba Tepe in clouds of smoke and dust on the day of the landing; the dear old "Albion" ashore that momentous morning off Gaba Tepe, when the destroyers and the "Cornwallis" tugged and tugged while the old ship spat broadside after broadside at the Turkish guns on the ridge; the sleepless destroyers, with their searchlights on the flanks — the "Chelmer," the "Pincher," the "Colne," the "Usk," and a dozen others—men up and down New Zealand to-day recall those magic names and remember the hot cocoa, the new bread, the warm welcomes and the cheery freemasonry of the sea. The service of the Navy was a very personal thing, and meant more to the men of Anzac than feeble words can tell.

[Photo by the Author
AMMUNITION FROM EVERY ARSENAL IN INDIA.

The ammunition problem was an acute one. Fortunately for the supply arrangements, the big guns of the Gallipoli armies were on the warships, but the howitzers and the field guns ashore were often sadly supplied. At one time the howitzers were restricted to two shells daily. Everything had to be saved for the days on which the Turk decided to "drive the infidels into the sea."

Small arm ammunition was always plentiful, and the machine gunners, thanks to the Navy, never had to go short. As far as rifles and machine guns were concerned, many of the outlying parts of the Empire were called on, and at one time Anzac Cove was inundated with thousands of small arm ammunition cases, on which were inscribed the signs of all the famous arsenals of India.

When "jams"—those bugbears of machine gunners—were at first much too frequent, we overcame these difficulties by using only New Zealand-made ammunition, which proved to be less variable and more reliable than the ordinary issue.

The Bomb Factory.

The hand-grenade position was often desperate. For the first few months no grenades were available, and the supply had to be improvized on shore. A "bomb" factory was instituted, and here, day and night, men toiled to make the weapon so effective in the short-range fights that burst with such fury around the devoted posts of Quinn's and Courtney's. The Turk had a plentiful supply of a round, cricket-ball hand-grenade, with a patent match-head ignition, and these he literally showered on Quinn's.

The Anzac factory retorted with several brands, but the most favoured one was made out of the green fuse tin from the 18-pr. guns. These tins were stout, and of the size of a condensed milk tin. Two holes were punched in the bottom for a wire to go through, and three holes in the lid—two for the wire and a larger one for the fuse. The wire came from hawsers salved from the wreckage of the trawlers off the beach. Into the centre of the tin was placed a dry gun-cotton primer or half a stick of gelignite, the detonator and a five-seconds fuse was fitted, and the remaining space packed with unexploded Turkish cartridges with the bullets cut off to let the lid close, after which the whole was secured across the top by joining the two ends of the wires. So, from the cast-off tins and wires, captured ammunition, and the engineers' stores of explosives, these grenades were manufactured to repel the apparently rejuvenated "Sick Man of Europe."

A time came when the guncotton and gelignite got scarce, and a powder explosive called ammonal had to be used. This presented a difficulty, as the stuff had to be packeted. But an active brain came to the rescue with a suggestion that cloth might be used for the packet. It so happened that about this time a large consignment of shirts had been opened up, all cut out and in the multitude of parts that go to make a shirt, but no two parts stitched together! This material was requisitioned, cut into squares, and the explosives packed like little bags of washing blue, with the detonator and fuse inside. Another time, tins ran out. The little mountain battery fuse tin was used as a stopgap, and then, luckily for

[Lent by Capt. Boxer, N.Z.M.C
CARRYING STORES UP WALKER'S RIDGE.

Quinn's, another rascally manufacturer sent a shipment of mildewed tobacco to Anzac. The stuff was condemned, and before the day was done the empty tins lay in the bin of the bomb factory. Thus, though they did not intend it, did the careless London shirt inspector and the bad tobacco specialist help to keep the front line of the Anzac area.

The Scarcity of Building Materials.

It is questionable if any army in the field ever had too many sandbags. To keep earth walls standing at as steep a slope as possible is the object of all builders of trenches, for the steeper a wall the safer it is. "It is difficult to make war safe," says the soldier, who, being wise, does not attempt the

The Scarcity of Building Materials.   159

impossible. But the same soldier takes few chances, and wherever he can build a wall or put on a roof that gives him real or fancied protection, nothing will stop him from collecting from somewhere the necessary material.

The scrub did not run to the size of trees, and apart from a little firewood nothing was obtainable on shore. The much-talked-of "Olive Groves" always seemed to be in the hands of the enemy. All the timber for building purposes, for the timbering of well shafts, and the casing of mining galleries, had to be brought ashore on barges. It was carried to the engineers' store yard on Hell Spit and guarded like the Bank of England, for everybody wanted two or three pieces and a few sheets of corrugated iron for the roof of a dugout. If a staved-in boat or a shattered barge stranded on the beach, it was quickly pounced upon and carried off.

A Maori on Sentry at the Water Tanks in Mule Gully.

One benefactor conceived the idea of tearing timber out of the fittings of the transports, and for some time working parties gathered in much spoil. If these ships had stayed much longer they would have been torn to pieces by the energetic builders of dugouts and "hospitals." The decree had gone forth that timber and sandbags could only be issued for the front line and hospitals, with the natural result—every requisition was marked "for hospital" and initialled by some strange hand, the owner of which was most likely of the humble rank of private.

The man who invented barbed wire is as heartily cursed by soldiers as by dairy farmers. The sudden cry of "wire" sends a shiver down the spine of the most seasoned. For wherever wire is, machine guns are placed to enfilade it. The Turk was a great believer in wire. It was of German manufacture, and very skilfully and strongly placed. In order to make it effective, it must be made very secure. Only in positions previously prepared can the requisite work be put in. In preparing for the Gallipoli landings the Turk put it well out in the water, whereby, it being concealed, many casualties occurred.

As our No Man's Land was so narrow, it was difficult to put out the ordinary high wire entanglement, the noise of driving the stakes alone putting it outside the pale of practicability. At the time the new screw-picket wiring system had not been evolved. But as something had to be done, in the workshop on the beach many "knife-rest" obstacles were made by constructing two stout wooden X's about 3 feet high, joining them by 3 x 2 distance pieces of 12 feet long, and wrapping the whole round and round and diagonally with wire. These fearsome arrangements, with much profanity from the unfortunate working party, were carried up the communication trenches—no easy task on a hot day, with a traverse to negotiate every few yards. The front line at last reached, the awkward obstacles were pushed unceremoniously over the parapet and levered out as far as possible by long props under cover of darkness.

The Water Supply.

Though the scored cliffsides of Gallipoli give indications of a torrential rainfall during winter, water was difficult to obtain even in April and May. Wells were sunk in all likely places and water diviners plied their uncanny calling with some success. The wells, however, did not last long, except the one near No. 2 Outpost. Greek tank steamers brought the bulk of the water from Egypt, and over by Imbros pumped it into water barges, which were towed in by the picket boats or a tug. By a manual, the water was forced into tanks on the beach, to which day and night came a stream of thirsty men with water bottles. Sometimes the barge would be holed by shellfire and the valuable load lost, or again a leak might turn the precious water brackish. Two quarts a day was often the ration—this had to be used for all purposes. Mostly it was drunk in the form of tea. Any tea left over was not wasted, but used for shaving!

A PUMPING FATIGUE ON THE WATER BARGE

The men in the front line had great difficulty in getting water as the carrying fatigue was often shot as it dodged up Monash Gully or the track to Walker's Ridge. Whatever the men on the beach got, those in the trenches were always desperately short.

From a hygienic point of view, the sea was the salvation of the men. Everyone near the beach bathed twice a day even at the risk of "stopping one," while the men from the hills came down whenever the reliefs took over.

Bully Beef and Biscuits.

Food was always plentiful (except just after the Great Blizzard in November when stocks ran very low). Tinned meat, jam and hard biscuits and a mug of tea provided 99 per cent. of the meals. Thoreau once suggested that we could make ourselves rich by making our wants few. On Gallipoli this did not mean a very great effort on the part of the will, but sore gums and rebellious stomachs were the price of getting wealthy. The army biscuits can never be forgotten—their hardness was beyond belief. When made for long journeys on sailing ships, it probably was necessary to make them so that they would keep, but surely in war time the soldier could get a softer one? The white ones taken from New Zealand were quite easy and pleasant to eat, while the oatmeal ones, grated on a piece of kerosene tin, made a tolerable porridge for the mornings! But the ordinary white biscuit as supplied by the A.S.C., while it may have been full of nourishment, was so hard that it was nibbled round the edges and then tossed into No Man's Land. After a month or two, a little bread arrived periodically, and many a penitent soldier vowed he would never waste a crust again.

But the perversity of the man who packed the jam! Why the cases did not come assorted no one knew. As it was, each area seemed to get its one particular variety right

[*Photo by the Author*

"BREAD AND JAM."
Two Signallers outside the Divisional Signal Office.

through a campaign. The familiar plum and apple, and the fruit of the golden apricot should never be placed before the Anzac soldier.

Fresh beef was also tried, but, considering the heat and flies, there is little wonder that the soldier suspected it of causing not a little of his internal disturbances. An article in great request was "Maconochies," a line of meat goods packed with a few slices of potatoes, carrots and beans. The tins were boiled in a petrol tin of sea water, and when turned out made a steaming mess considered far superior to the traditional "dainty dish" that was set before the king. Tinned meat is very good picnic fare, but when the meat is not a New Zealand brand but comes from somewhere in the Argentine; when it is served up for breakfast, dinner, and tea; curried or "hashed with broken biscuits"—it is apt to lose its savour, and the nominal pound (really 12 ounces) becomes more than the constitution of a New Zealander can stand.

Vegetables were always scarce — here the tinned concoction known as "Julienne" filled a gap. The mixture seemed to be all manner of vegetables flaked and dried so that they resembled multi-coloured shavings. On the principle that what does not fatten will fill, large quantities of this dried vegetable were consumed in the early days when men were strong enough to stand it.

A SIKH WATER CARRIER.

Newcomers from Egypt sometimes brought a little fruit, while scouts were always out among the sailors to induce them to bring back delicacies from the canteens of the warships off the coast. Any excuse was better than none to get alongside a hospital ship, not only for the meal that the insinuating soldier was bound to get, but for the chance of buying a loaf or a tin of milk from the canteen or the commercial-minded baker! People going to Mudros or Imbros were loaded with commissions and made the Greek traders rich by buying tinned figs, pineapples, and milk at fabulous prices, and paradoxically, fowls eggs' that were fresh and only one shilling a dozen. It was about this time that the soldier, living as frugally as any ascetic, was solemnly warned that "over-ripe fruit, such as bananas, tomatoes, oranges, and grapes should be avoided" as likely to encourage cholera! The army, weakened by dysentery, shrieked with delight!

Cheese and bacon were two popular variants in the ration. It always amused the Colonial to see the Russian Jews of the Zion Mule Corps struggling up to their cook-

[Lent by Sergt. P. Tite, N.Z.E.
MULES DUG IN UNDER THE CLIFFS IN MULE GULLY.

houses with their little bags of bacon. "It is the ration!" was the stereotyped retort to the gibes of the ribald ones. The hot sun affected the cheese somewhat. Perhaps two of the most characteristic smells of Anzac were chloride of lime and the pungent aroma of over-heated Cheddar.

This is a long story about food; but it was necessary for a soldier to eat, and most of the sickness can be attributed to the monotony of the food, the flies and the heat. Little wonder that men sickened. Trenches themselves were kept scrupulously clean, but all refuse was thrown into No Man's

Land in which were also innumerable dead bodies that it had been impossible to bury. So in the heat, the front line troops, after making the mess tin of tea, endeavoured to get a meal of meat or bread and jam. Countless hordes of flies settled on everything edible. The soldiers waved them off. The black cloud rose and descended among the filth on the other side of the parapet. Presently they were back again on the food,—and so on, from the jam to the corpse, and back again to the jam, flitted the insect swarm, ensuring that the germs of most things undesirable were conveyed to the soldier's system through his mouth.

Whatever may be the immunity of the transport and supply services in some campaigns, it is right that acknowledgment should be made of the risks run by the carriers of stores to and on the Peninsula. Whether by the trawlers or the picket boats at sea; in the ordnance and supply stores on the beaches; or on the mule tracks of the precipitous ridges and winding valleys—the men of the Navy, the Indian Supply and Transport, the Zion Mule Transport, and of our own Australian and New Zealand Army Service Corps carried their lives in their hands, for the enemy had the range to a yard of every landing stage, dump and roadway.

CHAPTER XII.

Midsummer at Anzac.

The most debated area in Anzac was that narrow strip of No Man's Land opposite Quinn's and Courtney's Posts, at the head of Monash Gully. The post on the other side of Courtney's was Steel's Post, just opposite which was the Turkish work known as German Officers' Trench. Hereabouts the front lines were a little farther apart. The Turk took advantage of this by bringing artillery fire to bear on Steel's and sometimes on Courtney's. Many were the anxious moments when the firing persisted a little longer than usual, as the garrisons could not help being a little apprehensive for the safety of their posts perched so perilously on the crest line.

THE FLY NUISANCE.
Flies, unlike men, love light rather than darkness. The wise soldier aired his blankets during the day and so kept the flies out while he snatched a little rest before going on work or watch.

The lines were so close together opposite Quinn's Post that neither side could afford to try the effect of artillery on the front-line trenches. This was fortunate, for a few well-aimed high explosive shells might have tumbled the whole structure into Monash Gully. But what Quinn's lacked in artillery duels, it more than made up for with its hand-grenade fights. Here, in common with the rest of No. 3 and No. 4 Sections, the enemy held the higher ground. Every day and every night a hail of cricket-ball bombs descended on the fire trenches, those falling in the communication trenches bounding merrily down hill until brought to rest by a traverse. Aeroplanes came over now and again, ineffectually dropping bombs and little steel darts. Whatever their lying propaganda boasted, their airmen never registered a hit on post or pier.

Mining at Quinn's Post.

Quinn's had a fatal fascination for the Turk. During May the enemy commenced mining in earnest, and this was a serious menace to the safety of the Anzac area. Successful underground operations by the enemy would mean that Quinn's might slide down into Monash Gully, so vigorous counter-mining was resorted to. Galleries were driven out under the front-line trenches; T-heads were put on to each gallery—these heads connected up made a continuous underground gallery right round the front of the post. Using this as a base, protective galleries were driven out in the direction of the advancing tunnels of the Turk. The object of this counter-mining was to get under or near the opponent's drives, and destroy them by means of small charges, calculated to break in their tunnels, but not to make a crater in No Man's Land above.

In those early days, sensitive listening appliances were not available. Underground it is very difficult to estimate the distance away of sounds recognized, for even old coal miners have little experience of parties working towards them. In constructing railway tunnels, the engineers working from both ends have the data referring to both drives. But in military mining the work of the enemy is shrouded in the "fog of war," so mining under these conditions is a most exciting process. Having driven the estimated distance to meet the enemy, the question constantly arises, "Will it pay us now to fire a camouflet?" The knowledge that the enemy is very likely considering the same

[Lent by Sergt. P. Tite, N.Z.E.

question adds a little to the tension. Then the listener reports that the enemy has ceased working. "Has he gone for his explosive, or is he only changing shift?" These and countless other speculations are constantly being made by the miner of either side. Each hesitates to fire his charge too early, as it may not achieve the maximum result. But if one waits too long the enemy will achieve that maximum! So both sides speculate until one makes a decision, which is announced to the opponents by a stunning explosion and a blinding crash if the effort is successful.

Twice Turkish tunnels had been detected nearing our lines. These were destroyed by small charges sufficient to break them down, for we could not afford to use a heavy charge, as it might threaten the stability of the hillside.

The Death of Major Quinn.

But at 3.20 on the morning of May 29, an ear-splitting explosion brought everyone in Monash Gully to his feet. A mine had wrecked No. 3 Subsection in Quinn's Post. Instantly, the musketry and bomb duel burst into life. Flashes of flame ran round the enemy's trenches and ours. The bursting of enemy shells fitfully illuminated Monash Gully. The detonations of hand-grenades, the bursts of machine-gun fire, the spluttering of musketry, the crashes of shrapnel and high explosive thundered round and round the head of Monash Gully, echoing and re-echoing in the myriad cliffs and valleys. In the confusion, a party of about twenty Turks rushed our front trenches. At last an effort was being made to break the Anzac line. As No. 3 Subsection was blown in, the men in No. 4 Subsection were cut off from Subsections 1 and 2, but all held stubbornly on. Reinforcements hurrying up to the stricken post could see, by the light of the bursting shells, the garrison clinging doggedly to the hillside. Some of the men off duty quickly clambered up the break-neck tracks. Led by the gallant Major Quinn, the defenders pushed forward in short rushes until they were once again sheltering in the broken front-line trench of Subsection 3. The party of Turks were now isolated within the post; barricading both ends of their little section of trench, they clung to the shelter of the traverse and recess. It was now breaking dawn. The machine guns on Russell's Top and Pope's Hill swept the region in the front of Quinn's with a devastating enfilade fire; but showers of bombs indicated that the Turk was still close up to the post. Major Quinn, realizing what his post meant to Anzac, warned his men for a counter-attack. Presently, the observers on Pope's and Plugge's Plateau saw the little band clamber on to the parapet, and with bayonet and bomb hurl themselves into the enemy's ranks, which momentarily wavered, then broke and fled. Back filtered the garrison, to realize that their beloved leader was mortally wounded, killed in the defence of the post that bore his immortal name.

The Turks did not attack again. Anzac was still intact. But imprisoned in our lines were sixteen brave Turks, who, in the confusion after the explosion, had stormed our front-line trench. They could not be reached by bombs, but an enterprising soldier persuaded them to surrender. Hesitatingly, out they came. They had been taught to distrust "these cannibals from the South Seas," even as we had been warned against falling into Turkish hands. With many salaams and ingratiating bows they filed down the pathway, somewhat disconcerting an R.E. officer by solemnly kissing his hand.

The Turks opposite Quinn's never neglected their opportunities. Their mine explosion made a fair-sized crater between the two front-line trenches. Next morning the periscope revealed a blockhouse built of solid timbers planted in the crater. This, being a direct threat to Quinn's, was too much for the section of New Zealand Engineers, who, with the men of the 4th Australian Brigade, had held the post from the first week. Two adventurous sappers volunteered to creep out across the debris of No Man's Land and demolish the menace by means of gun-cotton. This they accomplished with great skill, destroying the blockhouse and killing the occupants. The Turk, however, was persistent. Time and again he roofed over the crater; but with hairbrush bombs—two pounds of gun-cotton tied on to a wooden handle—with kerosene, benzine, and other gentle agents in the art of persuasion, the Turkish garrison were kept most unhappy, even though they were all promoted to the rank of corporal. About this time it was learned that the Ottoman soldiers had christened this set of trenches "the Slaughterhouse," but it must be said that the Turks operating in No. 3 Section, especially opposite Quinn's, earned the respect of all who fought against them.

Early in June the New Zealand Infantry Brigade took over this No. 3 Defence Section. The posts once held by General Monash's famous 4th Brigade were now garrisoned by men from Auckland, Wellington, Canterbury and Otago. The New Zealand Engineers still kept up their sapping and mining. The No. 1 Company had been on duty without relief from the landing, until relieved by the No. 2 Company, which arrived on June 3, and took over the sapper work within the section.

"The Agony of Anzac."

A periscopic view of No Man's Land was a terrible sight— littered with jam tins, meat tins, broken rifles and discarded equipment — every few yards a dead body and hosts of buzzing flies. Chloride of lime, with its hateful associations, was scattered thickly on all decaying matter, and the scent of Anzac drifted ten miles out to sea. In this fœtid atmosphere, with the miners on both sides burrowing under the posts like furtive rabbits, hand-grenade throwers carrying on their nerve-racking duels, stretcher bearers constantly carrying out the unfortunate ones, digging and improving the trenches under a scorching sun—is it any wonder that the men of Anzac were looked at almost pityingly by the reinforcements and the rare visitors from Helles and the warships? Let one of these visitors speak:—

> "The soul of Anzac is something apart and distinct from any feeling one gets elsewhere. It is hard to write of its most distressing feature, which is the agony it endures. But it is quite necessary, in justice to the men, that this should be said. There is an undercurrent of agony in the whole place. The trace of it is on every face—the agony of

danger, of having seen good men and great friends die or suffer, of being away from home, of seeing nothing ahead, of sweating and working under hot suns or under stars that mock. Let there be a distinct understanding that the agony is not misery. The strong man bears his agony without misery; and those at Anzac are strong. What the men endure should be known at home.''

It is true that the Australians and New Zealanders did not altogether realize how badly off they were. The Turk had said a landing was impossible—yet a landing had been forced. The Turk had boasted he would drive the infidel into the sea—the perspiring daredevils refused to be driven. Lack of water, lack of ammunition, monotony of food, rebellious stomachs, the loss of brothers and friends—all these things the men of Anzac triumphed over. The two young nations had found their manhood on these barren Turkish hillsides. Whatever our enemies and the benevolent neutrals thought, the Australian and New Zealand Army was confident in itself, confident in its leaders, confident in the wisdom of the High Command that deemed it necessary to prosecute the enterprise.

A Sortie from Quinn's Post.

Lying along the flank of the Turkish communications, the Australian and New Zealand Army Corps was a constant thorn in the side of the enemy troops journeying to reinforce the Ottoman army in the Krithia zone. The enemy kept a large general reserve with which he could reinforce his troops at either Krithia or Anzac. When the British attacked on the southern sector it was the duty of the Anzac troops to simulate an attack in force, so preventing Turkish reinforcements being sent from opposite Anzac to the south, and by making frequent sallies causing the Turkish commander to become uncertain in his mind as to the real attack. But always, in the first few months, Anzac was ''playing second fiddle to Helles.''

On June 4 the redoubtable soldiers at Helles made another great attempt on Achi Baba. The Anzac troops co-operated

A SCENE IN MONASH GULLY.

As the Turkish snipers at the head of Monash Gully could enfilade stretches of the road, sandbag traverses were built at the most dangerous points.

[Lent by Sergt. P. Tite, N.Z.E.]

by threatening the Turkish defences in the direction of Gaba Tepe, and by two raids, one on the trenches opposite Quinn's, the other on German Officers' Trench.

At first it was the custom to capture the first-line trench and to endeavour to keep it. In practice this was rarely successful. The front line of a trench system is generally lightly held; a surprise attack by determined troops can almost rely on being successful if the element of surprise is availed of. But to take a trench is one thing; to hold it another. Remember that the rest of the front line is still held by the enemy, who, working from traverse to traverse, can bomb down it. The second and third lines are also intact, with good communication trenches leading from them to the broken firing line. Bombers can also work down these communication trenches; ammunition, food and water, and (most important of all) hand-grenades, can arrive in unlimited numbers and in comparative safety. All of these things required by the attackers lodged in the enemy's trenches must come over the bullet-swept, shrapnel-torn surface of No Man's Land. By the end of a day, unless reasonable communications can be provided, the troops who so easily captured the hotly-contested position find that they must choose between annihilation or retreat. So it was raiding grew up. This appealed more to the primitive instincts of man—the sudden dash into the enemy, the attempt to achieve the maximum amount of damage in the minimum time, and to get to the home trench again before the enemy reinforcements could arrive. This method was particularly valuable when it was considered necessary to destroy the entrances to enemy galleries, to interfere with the progress of enemy saps, and to obtain prisoners for identification by the Intelligence Department.

The sortie from Quinn's Post on June 4 was a typical example of the early method. If ever an attack was organized to succeed this one was. Eager volunteers from the Auckland and Canterbury Battalions were selected to carry out the work, and at 11 p.m. a heavy artillery fire was to be directed on the surrounding communication trenches. An assaulting party of sixty men was to dash across the thirty yards of No Man's Land, take the opposing trench and transpose the

Turkish parapet. Two working parties were detailed to follow the first line. These men carried filled sandbags with which to build a loopholed traverse at each end of the captured trench; other parties were to commence two communication trenches from the new work to the old. The 4th Australian Infantry Brigade was held in reserve.

In the dark, the eager groups made ready to carry out their hazardous task. It is a strange impulse that prompts thoughtful men to face death so eagerly. But up there in the gloom of the dark Gallipoli night, at the very salient of the Anzac line, only twenty yards from a stubborn foe, these daring young infantrymen carefully examined their rifles and hand-grenades, finally adjusting their equipment, and peered at their wristlet watches slowly ticking off the leaden-footed minutes. Precisely at 11 a.m., Nos. 1 and 2 Batteries on Plugge's Plateau and Walker's Ridge joined with the 4th Australian Battery in shelling the Turkish communications. Our howitzers near the beach dropped shell after shell in the trenches leading to Quinn's. The 21st (Jacob's) Mountain Battery added its contribution to the din. Under cover of this noise and the darkness the two groups of attackers crept over the parapet of Quinn's, across the wreckage of No Man's Land, and fell on the Turkish garrison before the alarm could be sounded. A few Turks were bayonetted and twenty-eight taken prisoners. But every minute of darkness was priceless. About seventy yards of trench had been taken, the parapet shifted over, and the flanking traverses commenced. Now the Turks opposite Courtney's commenced to enfilade the captured position with machine-gun fire—the Australian party attacking German Officers' Trench had not been successful. Presently the Turkish counter-attack commenced. Bombs were showered on the working parties struggling to complete the traverses and communications. It was obvious that when daylight came the trench would be difficult to hold, especially if the machine guns opposite Steel's Post were not silenced. The work in the captured trench was now complete, and the Australians were asked to carry out another attack on German Officers' Trench. This sortie failed about 3 a.m. An hour after, a

THE BOMB-PROOF SHELTERS AT QUINN'S POST.
The hillsides were so steep that a sufficient number of men could not be accommodated near the front line.

bomb and fire counter-attack by the enemy destroyed our flanking traverses, wrecked the overhead cover, and pushed our men back, step by step, until we held barely thirty yards of captured trench. When dawn came the Turks became more insistent, the machine-gun fire increased in intensity, and the trench was filled from end to end with bursting hand-grenades. Our men were now taken in front and in flank by skilful grenade parties, until, at 6.30, we were finally driven down our new communication trenches to our old front line. Our gains were nil; our casualties numbered 137, including one officer and thirteen men killed. Lieut.-Colonel C. H. Brown, who as Brigadier-General Brown, was later killed in France—one of the most popular and capable officers of the New Zealand Staff Corps—was, as officer commanding Quinn's Post, severely wounded by a Turkish hand-grenade.

Eventually Quinn's became the stronghold of the line. This was not accomplished in a day or without enormous labour. But, inspired by their officers—particularly the new commander of the post, Lieut.-Colonel Malone, of the Wellingtons—the men of the New Zealand Infantry Brigade and the New Zealand Engineers made Quinn's Post comparatively safe. Iron loopholes were put in, bombing pits constructed, and wonderful bomb-proof shelters built in terraces on the hillside. It was a tremendous work. Because of the pitiless heat and the incessant sniping, the troops watched and waited during the day; but as soon as it was dark the working parties, on their backs, carried the sandbags, timber, iron, ammunition, hand-grenades, water and food, up that shrapnel-swept Valley of Death in order that Quinn's Post might be safe.

The Last Attack on Anzac.

Day by day the soldiers clinging to their posts at Anzac were filled with speculations as to the progress made at Helles. Great bombardments seemed to be of daily occurrence. Sometimes we could fancy that the great clouds of dust and smoke were rolling appreciably nearer. On June 27/28 the masses of smoke and flame seemed greater than ever. Then we learned that Helles was being attacked, and we were asked to take off a little of the strain. The extreme right of our line was now held by the 2nd Australian Light Horse Brigade, supported on the right by the veterans of the heroic early-morning landing—Maclagan's 3rd Australian Infantry Brigade. These units carried out dashing attacks on the extreme right. The diversion was entirely successful, and drew formidable Turkish reserves towards Anzac.

Indeed, as the hours slipped by, it seemed that the object of the Light Horse and Infantry was more than achieved, for it was reported that more and more of the finest Turkish regulars were being concentrated opposite Anzac.

On the night of June 29, about 9.10, the enemy expended thousands of rounds ineffectually against our extreme right— evidently firing at nothing in particular, as most of the bullets sailed aimlessly out to sea. This was the Turk's usual method of advertising an attack somewhere else. Sure enough, during the night that attack developed opposite Pope's and Russell's Top. The 3rd Light Horse Brigade (consisting of the 8th, 9th, and 10th Regiments) were now taking turns with the New Zealand Mounted Brigade in No. 4 Defence Section. The machine guns were never taken out of the line, Australian and New Zealand guns staying in even when their respective brigades were withdrawn to "rest."

In the moonlight, about an hour after midnight, the Turk, calling on his God, surged forward to the attack on No. 4 Section. In the half light the machine gunners found the range, and mercilessly cut up the attacking waves. But they were not to be denied. On and on they pressed, right up to the parapets. Several Turks bravely jumped into our trenches and were killed. They certainly were game. Around Pope's, too, they threw wave after wave, which faded away under the hail of lead.

On the Nek we had constructed several trenches, which were not yet joined up. Down between these new trenches came the enemy, only to be assailed with a cross-fire which almost annihilated the attack. Further to the left, General Russell had an excellent secret sap—a trench with no parapet to advertise its existence. Working round our left flank, the enemy blundered into this concealed tench, and lost over 250 men. Nowhere was the line broken, and the attack melted away.

What a sight No Man's Land presented that morning of June 30! The majority of the three fresh battalions of Turkish troops lay dead or wounded out there in the open; and of the dead men on the parapets, each had a rough haversack filled with dates and olives, the ever-present Turkish tobacco, and filled water-bottles. The prisoners taken said that their orders were to break the line at all costs. Enver Pasha himself was reported to be present, but prisoners' statements in

A CROSS-EXAMINATION.
The officer on the left of the group is Capt. the Hon. Aubrey Herbert, M.P., our divisional interpreter; the one with his back to us is Colonel G. J. Johnston, the C.R.A. of the Division, an officer loved by his subordinates for his fairness and his enthusiasm for the guns.

matters of this kind are always open to doubt, as there is a certain amount of temptation to answer in a manner calculated to please the interrogating interpreter.

This was the last attempt the enemy made to break the Anzac line.

The Soldier and His Clothes.

Two factors worked a change in the Army's clothing. The first was the Turk. His snipers picked out anyone wearing distinctions, with the result that officers cut off their conspicuous badges of rank and sewed small worsted stars or crowns on the shoulder-straps; otherwise, ranks were indicated on the shoulders of the shirts by indelible ink pencil. The N.C.O.'s and men took off their metal badges, the ink pencil being again in request to draw the badge and unit indications on the cap.

The heat was responsible for other modifications. Tunics were the first to go, and bit by bit the soldier shed his garments until he stood only in his boots, his shortened trousers, a shirt, and a cap. Riding breeches, cut well above the knee, made a most roomy pair of shorts. While no two men wore their trousers the same length, each one seemed to pride himself on having the ends as raggedly and unevenly cut as possible. The hot sun burned the exposed parts of the body a rich brown; so, when men went in bathing, it was easy to deduce by the amount of white skin exactly what garments had been preserved. On brown backs it was amusing to see a white V, testimony that the soldier still sported a pair of braces!

For some unknown reason, slouch hats, which would have been invaluable were left behind at the base. Many of the Mounted Rifles arrived with the brims of their felt hats cut off, leaving only a little peak fore and aft, like the old-time policeman's shako. New Zealanders were forbidden to wear helmets in Egypt, but the soldier of understanding smuggled his away with him, and a very proud man he was who sported one on the Peninsula. The sailor men were very keen on getting slouch hats; many a bearded face was shaded by the broad brim of a Colonial hat.

Dugouts on Wellington Terrace.

The Soldier and His Clothes.

If three was one thing the soldier had enough of, and to spare, it was socks. The good people at home put a pair into every parcel. The Ordnance issued them as well. It is hard to say what socks were not used for. The soldier who wrote, "Thanks for the socks—they will come in useful," doubtless spoke the truth.

Some things the men always craved for. Good Virginian tobacco and cigarettes were always welcome—the ration was of very inferior quality; sweets were always in great demand; owing to living under such primitive conditions, most watches went wrong, and were very difficult to replace; a "salt water soap" that would lather in salt water was looked for almost in vain; while tinned milk was worth any trouble and risk to procure. These were the days before the Y.M.C.A. made its welcome appearance.

About this time the Intelligence Department discovered that the Turk might use gas, so primitive gas helmets were procured from England. Woe betide any luckless soldier caught without his respirator. It is not suggested that the Turk was too humane to use gas, but luckily the masks were never needed, principally because the ground was so broken, and the "prevailing" winds could not be depended on. As our front line was so closely involved with that of the enemy, the enemy certainly would have received a fair share of the poisonous fumes intended for the infidels.

CHAPTER XIII.

The Preparations in July.

The decisive repulses in June made the Turk very chary of attacking. On our side it was evident that the forces at the disposal of Sir Ian Hamilton were not sufficient to win through. After months of desperate attack and dogged defence the month of July saw the enemy still holding the high ground at Helles and Anzac. At Anzac there was a cheery optimism. Everyone was satisfied that with reasonable reinforcements we would win through to the Narrows.

By now the front-line trenches were secure and the units settled down to the routine of trench warfare. Troops holding the line have a good deal of time in which to talk and think. One of the most dreadful phases of soldiering is the monotony. It is then that the soldier becomes "fed up." Men at these times will growl and argue about anything. Three debatable subjects never lost their attractiveness — oysters, medals, and the horizon. The oyster question raged furiously. Perhaps the Turkish shells suggested it; perhaps the soldier was thinking of what he would eat when he got home again; but, with an Aucklander present, it was never safe to say that Stewart Island oysters were the finest in the sea. The medal question was a perennial one. What medals would be struck for the war? Would there be a different one

THE BARRICADE IN THE BIG SAP.

SOLDIERS BATHING IN ANZAC COVE.

[Photo by F. H. Dawn

for the different campaigns—France, West Africa, Gallipoli, and all other theatres? Would the clasps be names of actions or only dates? It was persistently rumoured that the new Sultan of Egypt would give a medal to each of the troops who lined the Cairo streets on his coronation day. The Sultan supplied the answer to this by dying before his alleged promise could be fulfilled. The great line of transports and warships stretching from Cape Suvla down to Tenedos suggested the horizon. What was the horizon? There seemed to be no end of definitions, all of which could be traversed by learned persons present. Some ships would be hull down and some with only the masts and smoke showing. This raised the question as to whether one could see past the horizon, a suggestion scouted by the majority of the debating society, but warmly applauded by an enthusiastic minority.

Late in the afternoon, when the little groups assembled behind the firing line to prepare the evening meal, men would talk of their favourite foods, and speculate as to where the first big meal would be eaten when the great work was com-

SUNSET FROM ARI BURNU.

plete. Smoking the ration cigarette after tea, the New Zealander would watch the sun set behind the rose-tinted peaks of Samothrace and would picture again the sunset in his own beloved country, would hear the water tumbling and splashing in the creek, would see the sheep and horses cropping the sweet green grass of Maoriland—when "Whizz! crash!" would come the Turkish gunners' evening hate. Back with a start would the soldier come to the shells, the heat, the stench of chloride of lime, and the steadily increasing rows of little crosses on the hillside.

Units not engaged in the front line were officially "resting" in Rest Gully. Paradoxically, it was an accident if one got an hour's respite there! In civil life, where labour is expensive and difficult to obtain, all means of labour-saving devices are available to do laborious work. Near the firing line there is no room or concealment for these cumbrous instruments. On the other hand, labour is plentiful. So it happens that a multiplicity of men, with primitive picks and shovels, are available for any necessary work. On the Peninsula a spell of "rest" inevitably meant being detailed for a working party.

The Amenities of Anzac.

The noise of battle frightened away all the little song birds that had so charmed us in the spring. But there was always something of interest. The common tortoise of Europe—with a hard shell about 12 inches long—loving a quiet place shaded from the sun, crept into our dugouts during the night, so that in addition to having nocturnal visitors who caused a certain amount of irritation and annoyance, we had these larger "Pilgrims of the Night" to create a little amusement, for there is something comical about these prehistoric, rubber-necked shell-backs. The fact that a tortoise is something like a turtle also appealed not a little to the company cook, who may be a lover of the antique, but not to such a degree that the tortoise might notice it! Out on the Suvla Flats, red foxes played in the sun with their cubs. On the prickly scrub, the little praying mantis held up her supplicating green hands and prayed as if we were all far past redemption.

During July the shelling seemed to increase in intensity. Perhaps it was that the Turk had more information about our dispositions and shifted his guns a little further round on the flanks to enfilade the beach. Dugouts that had previously been considered safe now had shrapnel coming in the front doors, which is disconcerting, to say the least of it. But the

New Zealander, ever adaptable, drove his little dugout into the hillside at a safer angle and cheered the little trawlers as they slipped their anchors and zigzagged out of range. Early in the morning two big shells came over in pairs and dropped out to sea among the shipping. Rumour had it that they came from the "Goeben," anchored in the Straits. They certainly caused magnificent twin geysers as they plopped into the Ægean, but never once did any damage materialize. Because of their early morning regularity these guns were

[Photo lent by the Otago Women's Association
OFFICERS OF THE OTAGO MOUNTED RIFLES.
The officer drinking from the mess tin is Lt.-Col. Grigor, D.S.O., who commanded "C" parties of the N.Z.M.R. Brigade at the evacuation. Behind him is Colonel Bauchop, C.M.G., the commander of the outposts.

christened "Christians Awake." The shells really came from an old battleship, the "Hairredin Barbarossa," anchored in the Narrows between Maidos and Chanak. She had three pairs of 11-in. guns, with which she carried out her early morning bombardments. Built by the Germans, she was sold to the Turks in 1910, and finally was submarined by a British submarine on August 8, the day the New Zealand Infantry Brigade dashed up to the crest of Chunuk Bair. The most deadly gun was one (or a battery of them) fired from the Olive Groves away inland from Gaba Tepe. As this gun enfiladed the beach, it became widely known as "Beachy Bill." He it was who interfered mostly with the landing of stores, and worse still, the bathing. A long range gun firing from the other flank and emplaced in the "W" Hills, was known as "Anafarta Annie." Not many of our guns had names, but the mounted regiments on Walker's Ridge appropriately dubbed an Indian mountain gun "Rumbling Rufus."

During daylight the beach at Anzac Cove was practically deserted. "Beachy Bill" and his helpers attended to that. But when night came the hive buzzed and hummed. Picket boats brought in their barges, and the beach parties attacked the cargoes of stores and transferred them to the A.S.C. depots close at hand. Long convoys of pack mules and the little two-wheeled mule carts pulled in to the stores and the water-tanks, and started their adventurous journeys to the right and left flanks, and up the tortuous way to Monash Gully. The Turk had the range to a nicety, and knew quite well that if he dropped a few shells along the beach and on the communications some damage must be done. The marvel is he did not fire more. While the firing lasted the place was like Inferno, for in the darkness the shells could be seen red-hot overhead. The flash of the explosions would light up the busy scene—Indian drivers and their terrified mules inextricably mixed up with the piles of stores and water tins; mules braying and squealing, with the patient drivers striving to quieten them; the shells shrieking through the air; while the thunderous detonations punctuated the rhythmic lapping of the waves upon the beach, the moans of the wounded, and the insistent cries of "Stretcher bearer."

Reinforcements Promised.

After the unsuccessful attack on Krithia early in May, Sir Ian Hamilton cabled Home for two more Army Corps, pointing out that apparently we were to be left to our own resources in the campaign; the Greeks had decided not to move at all, and the Russians had been so punished by the Austro-Germans as to give up all hope of moving against Constantinople from the Black Sea. The General, in his Third Despatch to the Secretary of State for War, goes on to say:—
"During June your Lordship became persuaded of the bearing of these facts, and I was promised three regular divisions, plus the infantry of two territorial divisions. The advance

guard of these troops was due to reach Mudros by July 10; by August 10 their concentration was to be complete."

Now let us see what troops are available for a new trial of strength with the Turk. The following troops were already on the Peninsula:—

At Helles:

The French Army Corps	1st Division 2nd Division
The 8th Army Corps	29th Division (Regular Army) 42nd (East Lancs.) Division (Territorials) 52nd (Lowland) Division (Territorials)
General Headquarters Troops	Royal Naval Division

At Anzac:

The A. & N.Z. Army Corps	1st Australian Division N.Z. & Australian Division

New Troops Promised for an Offensive:

The 9th Army Corps	10th (Irish) Division 11th (Northern) Division 13th (Western) Division
The Infantry Brigade only of	53rd (Welsh) Division 54th (East Anglian) Division

All of the troops—owing to the demands of the French front—were woefully deficient in artillery. The 9th Army Corps were part of the New Army—generally known as Kitchener's Army—and, of course, had not seen service. The infantry of the 53rd and 54th Divisions were of the Territorial Force, and likewise were inexperienced in war. These were the troops it was determined to lead against seasoned soldiers —inured to hardship and fighting for their native soil—the veterans of the Turkish Regular Army.

But when and where should these reinforcements be used?

The time was easily settled. In war, as in many other things, there is no time like the present. The summer was well advanced; the scored hillsides gave every indication of torrential autumn and winter rains; the naval staff knew that winter storms would seriously hamper their work. But the last troops could not arrive until early in August. As darkness was essential to any surprise attack, it was necessary to carefully study the phases of the moon. It was decided that as soon as the 53rd and 54th Divisions reached the

[*Lent by Sergt. P. Tite, N.Z.E.*

HEADQUARTERS SIGNAL OFFICE.

Signallers, telephonists, and linesmen risk their lives day and night sending and carrying messages and repairing wires. Snipers watch the wire and pick off the linesmen. It is significant that the only New Zealand V.C. awarded during the campaign went to a signaller.

scene of operations they would be kept on their ships as a general reserve. The weather, the moon, and the anticipated arrival of these reinforcements determined August 6 as the latest date for the commencement of the operations, for by the end of the second week the moon would be unfavourable.

So far, we knew what troops were available, when they would arrive, and the most desirable time to use them. Next, we must examine the proposals as to where they should be used to gain the greatest advantage.

Where should the Troops be Used?

In his classical Third Despatch, General Sir Ian Hamilton has clearly shown the different suggestions for employing the new troops. They were resolved into four practicable schemes, which may be summarized as follows:—

(1) Every man to be thrown on to the Helles sector to force a way forward to the Narrows. This was rejected because it was difficult to deploy a large body of troops in such a confined area. Further, the whole of Krithia and Achi Baba had been specially prepared against such a frontal attack.

(2) Embarkation on the Asiatic side of the Straits, followed by a march on Chanak. The number of troops available was not considered sufficient to press this to a victorious conclusion.

(3) A landing at Enos or Ibriji for the purpose of seizing the Isthmus of Bulair. Against this project it was known that the Turkish lines of communication were not only by way of Bulair and down the Narrows, but also by way of the Asiatic coast across from Chanak to Kilid Bahr. The naval objections to Bulair were overwhelming: the beaches were bad, and, worse still, the strain on sea transport would be tremendous. We know how difficult it was at Anzac, but a new base at Bulair would add another fifty miles to the sea communications, already threatened by enemy submarines.

(4) Reinforcement of the Australian and New Zealand Army Corps combined with a new landing at Suvla Bay. There was a reasonable chance of success in first winning Hill 971, then across the low ground to Maidos. From thence both the Turkish land and sea communication might be cut. This plan was also acceptable to the naval authorities. The distance to Suvla Bay was approximately the same as to Anzac. There was also a tolerably good harbour that might be made submarine proof. The water supply would be difficult, but it was reasoned that efficient organization would

Where should the Troops be Used? 191

mitigate this evil; in any case, it was known that this area was not so heavily entrenched as the other three suggested landing places.

The total allied force was known to be inferior to the enemy, but it was thought that with skilful generalship this superiority might be nullified. The aim of strategy is to concentrate a superior force at the decisive point. The advantage is always with the attacker, as the side attacked must be in sufficient strength all along the line and must keep sufficient reserves in hand until the enemy's real attack definitely materializes. Wherever Turkish troops were stationed in large numbers it was necessary to arrange feint attacks—away on the flanks opposite Mitylene on the Asiatic coast, and away up at Bulair. Holding attacks to keep the enemy pinned down in their areas were to be carried out at Helles and at No. 1, No. 2, and No. 3 Defence Sections at Anzac. Having induced the enemy to become committed all along the general line, it was intended to burst out from the left flank of Anzac, at the same time land new troops at Suvla—the whole to push on towards Chunuk Bair, Hill Q, and Hill 971. These heights in our hands the fall of Maidos, Gaba Tepe, and eventually Kilid Bahr was only a matter of time.

The strategical and tactical situation may be easier grasped diagrammatically :—

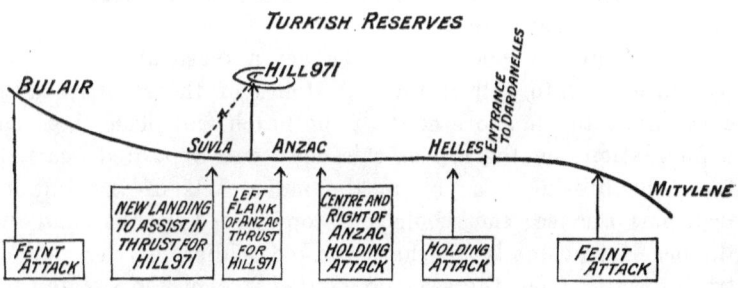

The general idea was that at Bulair and Mitylene enemy forces would be immobilized, and that the Turkish reserves on the Peninsula would flow towards Helles and the right of Anzac. As soon as these reserves were committed the troops of Anzac and Suvla would press towards Hill 971 and turn the Turkish flank.

In anticipation of this advance, a party of selected officers and scouts lived day and night out on the Suvla Flats and in the Turkish territory on the Sari Bair. These were the men who were selected to guide the troops over the new ground to be attacked.

Two other important works were put in hand at once in the Anzac area; the first, to widen the long communication trench from Anzac to the outposts; the second, to make a road available for wheeled traffic along the beach. In order not to make the enemy suspicious, this had to be done after dark, as the entire area was under the observation and rifle fire of the enemy on the heights.

Making the Beach Road.

Night after night the troops who were "resting" crept with their picks and shovels along the beach, to make the necessary road. This after-dark activity is most trying—each man working as silently as possible with his rifle at his elbow. Any noise is a magnet certain to attract machine-gun fire. Even in daylight it takes careful management to collect working parties and the necessary transport at the right spot, but in the darkness and in a region where enemy scouts and snipers roamed as soon as daylight failed, the difficulties were increased a hundredfold.

Sand makes a poor road. To get a reasonable result it was necessary to collect the big stones of the seashore and carry them to the shore edge of the beach and place them as a foundation; on the top of this, clay was deposited—carted from the hillside near by in the mule carts of the Indian transport service; the whole was top-dressed by the sand of the beach, and finally, the hard-worked soldiers carried petrol tins of water from the sea and poured it over the surface to make the material set. So, harassed by the splutter of machine guns night after night, and weakened by the heat of the day, the faithful souls of the working parties steadily carried the road from Anzac Cove along North Beach towards the Suvla Flats.

[Photo by the Author

THE "BIG SAP" NEAR FISHERMEN'S HUT.
This view is looking back towards Walker's Ridge and was taken before the sap was widened to 5 feet.

Working on the Big Sap.

To get troops quickly and secretly from Anzac to the outposts and to the foot of the deres up which the assaulting columns must approach the Turk, it was necessary to widen the communication trench known as the "Big Sap." This trench had been evolved as the outposts were established, and at many places could be enfiladed by the enemy on the heights; and nowhere was it wide enough to take troops two abreast. The pack mules used it by day, and though the soldier cared little for Turkish shells, he lived in fear of the donkey's steel-shod hoofs; it was no uncommon sight to see the soldier, disbelieving the warning "No kick! No kick!" of the Indian muleteer, climb out of the trench and risk a bullet rather than encounter a transport mule.

THE MAORI AT ANZAC.

A convential figure carved in the clay wall of the Big Sap. The telegraph linesmen of the Signal Troop have condescended to drop their wire a little to avoid the figure.

Partly the way was through the sandhills—here the necessary width of 5 feet was easy to attain; but in the harder clay, the pioneer working parties had been content to make a narrow slit, leaving the hardest work still to do. All through July the men of No. 4 Defence Section toiled at their herculean task—the Australian Infantry of the 4th Brigade, the N.Z. Mounted Rifles and Australian Light Horse from Walker's Ridge, and best workers of all, the Maori Contingent from No. 1 Post.

Man is naturally a lazy animal. When men work hard, there is always some incentive. The Maori soldier, picked man that he was, wished to justify before the world that his claim to be a front-line soldier was not an idle one. Many a proud rangitira served his country in the ranks, an example to some of his Pakeha brothers. Their discipline was superb, and when their turn came for working party, the long-handled shovels swung without ceasing until, just before the dawn, the signal came to pack up and get home.

Where the trench was liable to enfilade fire, its direction was altered, and here and there overhead protection was built with some of the precious timber and sandbags. At every few hundred yards a recess was cut to enable troops to stand aside while mule trains or passing troops moved up or down. Leaving nothing to chance, infantry parties, two abreast, marched through the trench from end to end to ensure that nowhere would there be a check.

Now these communications were complete, and July came and went, and still there was no big attack. But vast

[*Lent by Rev. Wainohu, C.F.*
WITH THE MAORIS AT No. 1 POST.

quantities of ammunition, and piles of peculiar foodstuffs that signified Indian troops to the initiated, showed that something was in the offing. With August, the transfer of the new English troops from the neighbouring islands commenced.

Before this could happen the soldiers of Anzac were called on to do one more big digging task—dugouts and shelters had to be made, and terraces formed on the already crowded hillsides, in order that the large bodies of new troops might be hidden from the enemy aeroplane observers. For the first nights of August our men worked feverishly at the terraces. Hope ran high, for here at hand was the help so long and earnestly prayed for. During the nights of August 3, 4, and 5, the beach masters and military landing officers disembarked the New Army troops intended for Anzac. After the tiresome monotony of three months' dogged holding on, months of incessant picking and shovelling, months of weakening dysentery, plagues of flies, and a burning sun, the men of the New Armies and of India were arriving, and a great blow would be struck. Sick men refused to attend sick parade in the mornings, and in the hospitals, and on the Red Cross barges, proud men wept because they were too weak to strike a blow.

CHAPTER XIV.

The Battle of Sari Bair.

Part I.

The Preliminaries.

The great battle, apart from the feint attacks away at Bulair and Mitylene, was to comprise four distinct operations, all closely dependent one on the other.

1. An attack in force at Cape Helles on the afternoon of August 6. This would tend to commit Turkish reserves to an action far away from Anzac.

2. The Australian Division, holding the line from Chatham's Post to Russell's Top, was to make several attacks on the afternoon of August 6. These would serve to immobilize or distract the enemy reserves known to be concentrated at Koja Dere, behind Mortar Ridge, and at Battleship Hill.

3. A great assault by the N.Z. and Australian Division, assisted by the newly-arrived 13th Division and a brigade of Indian troops, advancing up the three deres that lead to the peak of the Sari Bair—up the Sazli Beit and the Chailak to Chunuk Bair, and up the Aghyl towards Hill Q and Koja Chemen Tepe.

4. A new landing at Suvla Bay by the 9th Army Corps, which would pass over the Suvla Flats early on the morning of August 7, and linking up with the left flank of the army from Anzac, would press up towards the height of Koja Chemen Tepe, to prolong the line towards the Anafarta villages.

The Struggle at Helles.

After a preliminary bombardment on the afternoon of the 6th, the infantry at Cape Helles dashed to the assault of the Turkish trenches at 3.50. Thus was the greatest battle in the Gallipoli campaign commenced by the men of Helles.

ANZAC COVE EARLY IN AUGUST, 1915.

[*Lent by Col. Falia, C.M.G., D.S.O.*

The bloody and stubborn combat lasted a full week, the Turks attacking and counter-attacking with two fresh divisions. The East Lancashire Division, assisted by the war-worn 29th Division, clung tenaciously to ground they had won—in particular, a small area of vineyard about 200 yards long and 100 broad, on the west of the Krithia Road. So fierce was the fighting for this small piece of cultivated land that this week-long battle is always referred to as "The Battle of the Vineyard." The object of this attack was fully achieved. No Turkish soldier could leave for Anzac or Suvla while this blow was being threatened at Achi Baba.

The Battle of Lone Pine.

Let us pass from the tragic vineyards of the south to the hungry hills of Anzac. During the afternoon of August 6, the slow bombardment of the enemy's left and centre was increased in intensity. The 1st Battery of New Zealand Field Artillery, firing from Russell's Top, was detailed to cut the wire in front of the Turkish Lone Pine trenches. The "Bacchante" searched the valleys which were believed to contain the enemy's reserves, while the monitors engaged the batteries at the back of Gaba Tepe and at the Olive Groves. This bombardment was intended to make the Turk believe that at last a determined effort was to be made from the Anzac right in the direction of Koja Dere and Maidos. The enemy felt that this was the heart thrust, and he waited in his well-placed cover for the inevitable assault. At 4.30 p.m., the New Zealand battery concentrated again on the Lone Pine trench, and the 1st Australian Infantry Brigade mustered in Brown's Dip ready for the assault.

Those awful hours of waiting! Platoon commanders fidgeting with their wristlet watches that seem to tick off the minutes so slowly. Men smoke cigarette after cigarette, and talk in undertones. At last the word comes, "Get ready." Everywhere men crowd on to the firestep. "Over the top!" Men pull themselves up over the parapet and, regaining their feet, rush for the opposing parapet with its angry spurts of flame. Across that bullet-swept No Man's Land race the impetuous men of Australia. Line after line sweeps on, but not to fall into an open fire trench on to the foe. These trenches are roofed with timber, which has to be torn up. A merciless machine-gun fire mows down the attackers. Some run round the back, get into the communication trenches and fight their way into the underground fort. So, with hand-grenade and bayonet, the 1st Australian Infantry Brigade overpower the stubborn Turks within the fortress.

With the cry of "Allah! Allah!" reinforcements arrive for the enemy. The weary victors again repel the foe. Night brings no peace. But the captors of Lone Pine fight on, for they know full well that by their vicarious sacrifice they have pinned down all the Turkish reserves on the Ari Burnu front, and have left a minimum of the enemy to resist the Anzac and Suvla thrust for the peaks of Sari Bair.

Against German Officers' Trench.

The attack at Lone Pine drew many Turkish reserves to Anzac. Everywhere the enemy was on the alert. What wonder, then, that the occupants of German Officers' Trench were ready for the 6th Australians? At 11 o'clock on the night of the 6th, mines were exploded at the end of the trench nearest the Turk. At about midnight, the artillery momentarily ceased, and the Australian infantrymen crept from the end of their tunnelled communications which had been constructed under No Man's Land. The first and second waves of men were mown down almost to a man. The attack on trenches defended with scientifically-manned machine guns was almost a forlorn hope.

The Glory of the Australian Light Horse.

At Quinn's, Pope's, and Russell's Top the line was held by the Australian Light Horse. In common with their brothers of the infantry, attacks from these places were to be made.

Units of the 3rd Light Horse Brigade were holding Quinn's. From here, two hundred men in four lines of fifty each were to dash across No Man's Land in an endeavour to simulate a determined attack. Most of these gallant troopers died on the parapet from a hail of machine-gun fire.

From Pope's it was determined to attack Dead Man's Ridge. This effort was at first a little more successful. Three trenches were occupied, but after about two hours' desperate fighting our men ran short of bombs, and tried to withdraw, losing heavily during the operation.

The attack from "The Nek" was as glorious, as tragic, and, alas! as unsuccessful as from Quinn's. In the first line there were 150 men of the 8th Light Horse Regiment. When the artillery stopped, about 4.25 a.m., the Turk commenced a barrage of machine-gun fire. The Victorians clambered up on their firesteps, and at the word dashed into the awful storm of lead. Down went the whole line. But the second line, with a few scaling ladders, was ready to go over the top. Out they sped to certain death. The scaling ladders lay forlornly out on the fatal "Nek." The third line—150 men of the 10th Light Horse—followed and shared the fate of their comrades. The fourth line was stopped. Out of 450 men who started there were 435 casualties! Turkish prisoners stated that they never lost one man! Surely in military history there is no more splendid record of sacrifice than was enacted that fatal morning at Quinn's Post and Russell's Top.

But the Australian effort from the right and centre of the Anzac line had borne fruit, for at Rhododendron and on the Asma Dere, New Zealanders and other Australians were advancing to the stronghold of the Turk. Down at Suvla a great British landing was proceeding almost unopposed.

Part II.

The Anzac Thrust for "971."

The attack from the left of Anzac was perhaps one of the most complicated in history. The huge sprawling mass of the Sari Bair system was broken by a multiplicity of water-courses, the sides of which were often sheer cliffs, scored and fissured by torrential winter rains. The only possible means of approaching the peaks was by way of these water-courses. Now, it is a well-known military axiom

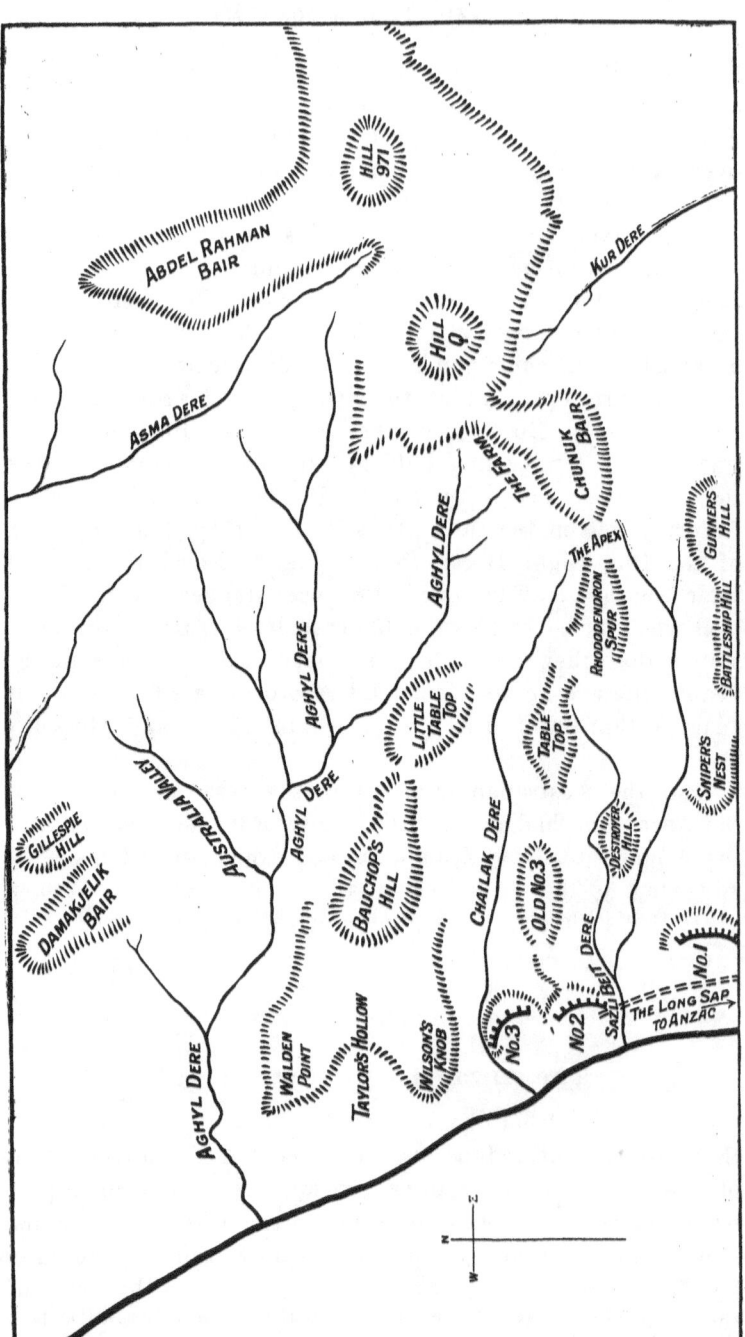

A SKETCH MAP TO ILLUSTRATE THE BATTLE OF SARI BAIR.

The area represented is about 5,400 yards by 3,000 yards. The distance from the mouth of the Sazli Beit Dere to the Apex is approximately 2,300 yards; and about 3,700 yards to the top of Hill 971.

that troops cannot pass safely through a defile until the heights are made secure; it was also known that no troops could push up through two and a half miles of these savage, scrub-covered hills and be fit to fight a battle with a fresh, determined foe at the top. So the work had to be mapped out in stages.

Soldiers know that with more than one body of troops operating there is always a risk of someone being late. In night operations this risk is intensified. Further, it is very difficult to fit in what the staff officers call their "time and space problem." The men could not all go up one gully. They would arrive at the top a few men at a time, and could not attack on a broad enough front, but only at one point. So it was arranged that the force under the command of Major-General Godley should be divided into four columns—two to break the line and open up the lower parts of the deres; the other two following shortly after, and proceeding up the three main deres, pass through the covering forces to the assault of Chunuk Bair, Hill Q, and Koja Chemen Tepe.

During the nights of August 3, 4, and 5, the New Army troops were landed at Anzac, marched along the "Big Sap" to their prepared bivouacs on the hillside, and remained under cover until the eventful night. The 29th Indian Brigade, consisting of one Sikh and three Ghurka regiments, also arrived and went to their allotted place on the left. This made available:—

- The N.Z. and Australian Division (less the Australian Light Horse, who were at Quinn's, Pope's, Russell's Top, and Walker's Ridge.
- The 13th (New Army) Division (less five battalions).
- The 29th Indian Infantry Brigade; and
- The Indian Mountain Artillery Brigade.

The Organization of General Godley's Army.

Right Covering Force—(Brigadier-General A. H. Russell):
- New Zealand Mounted Rifles Brigade;
- Otago Mounted Rifles Regiment;
- Maori Contingent;
- Field Troop, N.Z. Engineers.

The task assigned to this force was to clear the lower ridges of the Sari Bair system, seizing the Turkish posts known as Old No. 3 Post, Big Table Top, and Bauchop's Hill. The advance was to commence from No. 2 and No. 3 Posts at 9 p.m. on August 6, a movement which would enable the right assaulting column to get within striking distance of Chunuk Bair with a minimum of fatigue.

Left Covering Force—(Brigadier-General J. H. Travers):
    4th Battalion South Wales Borderers;
    5th Battalion Wiltshire Regiment;
    Half 72nd Field Company.

Composed entirely of units from the 13th (New Army) Division, this column was to march northwards along the flat ground; then strike inland and seize Damakjelik Bair. This force would be able to hold out a helping hand to the new army landing at Suvla, and would also protect the left flank of the left assaulting column moving up the Aghyl Dere.

Right Assaulting Column—(Brig.-General F. E. Johnston):
    New Zealand Infantry Brigade;
    Indian Mountain Battery (less 1 Section);
    1st Field Company, N.Z. Engineers.

This column was to move up the Sazli Beit Dere and the Chailak Dere, commencing to move up these gullies at 10.30 p.m. Having cleared Rhododendron Spur, an attack was to be made on Chunuk Bair, eventually holding a line from Chunuk Bair to the head of Kur Dere, behind Hill Q.

Left Assaulting Column—(Brigadier-General H. V. Cox):
    29th Indian Infantry Brigade;
    4th Australian Infantry Brigade;
    Indian Mountain Battery (less 1 Section); and the
    2nd Field Company, N.Z. Engineers.

The leading troops of this column were to cross the mouth of the Chailak Dere at 10.30 p.m. towards Walden's Point and up the Aghyl Dere, pass through the left covering force, assault Koja Chemen Tepe, and occupy a line from Koja Chemen Tepe to the head of Kur Dere, thus joining up with the right assaulting column.

Divisional Reserve:

6th Battalion South Lancashire Regiment }	at the
8th Battalion Welsh Regiment (Pioneers) }	Chailak Dere;
39th Infantry Brigade }	at the
Half 72nd Field Company }	Aghyl Dere.

The troops were ordered to be at the foot of the valley mentioned at 1 a.m. on the morning of August 7, to be used at the discretion of the General Officer Commanding.

For artillery support, in addition to the divisional artillery already in position, there were two squadrons of H.M. Navy:

(a) A southern squadron of five vessels, stationed off Gaba Tepe, detailed to fire at Chunuk Bair and the plateau on which Lone Pine was situated, and

(b) A northern squadron of two monitors and two destroyers, which were to engage targets on the northern and western slopes of Sari Bair.

The entire expedition was woefully deficient in heavy guns. Heavy howitzers, for searching reverse slopes, were desperately needed. A pathetic entry in General Godley's "Order of Battle" is, "Corps artillery: one 6in. howitzer!" Once again the men of Anzac were asked to do with their bayonets and rifles what should have been done with heavy guns.

The Night of August 6.

We must now look at the scene near No. 2 and 3 Posts. At Helles and Lone Pine the battles were raging. Turkish reserves were being called up in both places. So far everything was going well. With the fall of darkness the four Anzac columns began to prepare for their arduous night march and assault.

Everybody was to travel light. Kits and tunics were discarded. In short sleeves and web equipment, with a rifle and fixed bayonet, the men may not have looked uniform, but they were animated with a spirit that would dare anything. Just before dark men sewed white patches on their backs and on their sleeves, so as to indicate in the gloom who was friend and who was foe. Officers spoke to their men. The principal injunction was to press on up the hill. If any man lost touch, he was to join the nearest party and go resolutely on.

The Right Covering Force.

The four regiments of New Zealand Mounted Rifles were the first to move. It was their duty to break the Turkish line for the infantry brigades. At 9.30 p.m. they were to move out from the shelter of No. 2 and No. 3. The Wellington Mounted Rifles were to take Destroyer Hill and then Table Top. The Auckland Mounted Rifles were to take Old No. 3 Post, while the Otagos by way of Wilson's Knob, and the Canterburys by way of Taylor's Hollow and Walden's Point, were to clean up the lower ridges and capture Bauchop's Hill. This should give us the line, Destroyer Hill—Table Top—Bauchop's Hill, and open up the Sazli Beit, the Chailak and the Aghyl Deres for the infantry.

The Capture of Old No. 3.

Old No. 3 Post was that high piece of ground taken and abandoned at the end of May. Falling down towards the sea, it resolved itself into two lower spurs, on which were our No. 2 and new No. 3 Posts.

Every night, as soon as it was dark, the destroyer "Colne" stood in and went through the performance of throwing her searchlight on the heavily fortified slopes of Old No. 3, and commenced a half-hour's bombardment. The light guns of the destroyer did not cause much material damage to the carefully constructed overhead cover; but it became the custom for part of the garrison to leave their trenches and retire to their dugouts in the rear of the post on the southern banks of the Chailak Dere. Now, a searchlight beam, while it illumines everything in its path, makes the surrounding darkness appear blacker and even more intensified. As the bombardment continued, the Auckland Mounted Rifles crept up the Sazli Beit Dere. In fifteen minutes the party was lying quietly at the foot of the fortress. Squadron commanders got their final instructions, and a small party of strong men, picked for their skilled work with the bayonet, crept up through the scrub towards the crest. Led by a scout, this party dodged from bush to bush until they came to a sentry post of the enemy. Silently closing in from every side, the four New Zealanders sprang upon the sentries and overpowered them. "Crack!" went a rifle. One sentry had discharged his rifle harmlessly in the air as a New Zealand bayonet did its deadly work. So far we had no casualites.

[Lent by Lieut. Moritzson, M.C., M.M., N.Z.E.
ROUGH COUNTRY.
Calculated to throw any troops out of direction.

Up on the crest the destroyer's shells were crashing into the barbed wire and the heavy wooden beams of the overhead cover. In a few minutes the attacking party was lying all round the crest on the southern side. Presently the guns stopped, and the searchlight faded away. This was the signal! The Aucklanders rose and, spreading fanwise, went straight for the post. Into the covered trenches dived the Mounted Riflemen. The garrison fought gamely enough, but there could only be one end to it. The main body of the garrison came pouring back from their reserve trenches towards the post; but, caught in the open, they were no match for the men from Auckland. In a short time the whole work was completely in our hands. There was now time to closely examine the post. The trenches were roofed, just like those of Lone Pine, with heavy baulks of 8 x 3 sawn timber covered with sand bags. The guns on the destroyer had made no material impression on this cover, as shells striking it had glanced off and buried themselves uphill. In the front trenches was discovered a dugout with a complete equipment for electrically firing the 28 small square iron mines placed in front of the posts. Without the destroyer ruse and the quick, clean work of the attackers, the casualties would have been very heavy; as it was, we had only twenty casualties, while close on one hundred Turks lay dead within the Post and in its neighbourhood. The Auckland Mounted Rifles had signally avenged the Mounted Brigade losses at the end of May.

The Capture of Table Top.

Following on the heels of the Auckland Mounted Rifles up the Sazli Beit Dere, the Wellington Regiment silently cleaned up Destroyer Hill. As the Auckland Mounted men were stealing on Old No. 3, their comrades of the Wellington Mounteds were creeping up the Chailak Dere towards Table Top. Silently up the gully went the mounted men, the 6th Squadron leading. The 2nd Squadron was to take Table Top itself, and the 9th was to hold it afterwards. The first objective was Destroyer Hill.

It was quite dark, and difficult to see the way, but these gullies had been well reconnoitred by the scouts, and the column pressed on, dragging their telephone wire with them. After resting for a minute, the front line crept round a corner and came under heavy rifle fire. The leaders dashed straight at the flashes of rifle fire twenty yards away. Major Dick at the head of his men cried out "Come on, boys" when down he fell. But enough surged forward to overwhelm the party of Turks guarding the communication trench.

This was really a very strenuous piece of work, for from Table Top on one side, and Baby 700 on the other, communications ran down to Destroyer Hill. As fast as the enemy here was overpowered, more Turks crowded down to be dealt with.

The troopers took up a position above a well-defined track and picked off the enemy as they came along it.

[*Lent by Capt. Janson. W.M.R.*
THE PATH TO VICTORY.
The Wellington Mounteds crept up this dere and advanced up the spur from where the cross is shown.

Presently a line of men came in single file down the ridge. They were to pass just above the anxious little group of mounted riflemen who were painfully conscious of their bright white patches. Were they our men, or were they

Turks? By their chattering it was discovered they were a party of a hundred Turks on surrender bent. To the relief of the 6th Squadron, they filed past to our rear talking and laughing.

Meanwhile the squadron told off to assault Table Top stole quietly up to the head of the gully. With rifles spluttering in the scrub and bullets moaning on their flight out to sea, the Wellingtons scaled the steep clay sides of Table Top and went straight for the Turks. The fight did not last long. Up came the 9th and made the position secure. By his boldness and impetuosity the New Zealand Mounted man had again outclassed the enemy.

The path taken was the secret of success. The 6th Squadron who had taken the first trench came at Table Top from the front, and it took them over half an hour's hard climbing—cutting steps in the clay with bayonets—to reach the top. Foresight and ingenuity, boldness and determination were alike combined in these first successful captures.

A platoon of Maoris led by a Wellington officer also crept quietly up the Chailak Dere in order to get round the back of Table Top to co-operate with the Wellingtons. In the gully between Bauchop's Hill and Old No. 3 a party of Turks fired on the Maoris, who saw red and slew the Turks to a man. Chasing the enemy up the gully, the Maoris never stopped until they were round the back of Table Top, and were only with great difficulty restrained from tackling Sari Bair by themselves!

Bauchop's Hill.

The Otago and the Canterbury Mounted Regiments were to move off from No. 3 Post, traverse the flat ground to the northward, wheel to the right, and work up towards the high ground of Bauchop's Hill.

Lying in the low ground from about 9 o'clock, the South Islanders saw the white beam of the searchlight on the scrub and heard the scream of the destroyer's shells. At 9.30 the searchlight went black out. The men rose quietly— this was the signal for which they had been waiting. The

Otagos wheeled to the right toward the trenches on Wilson's Knob—trenches they had lain opposite and observed with periscopes the last two months of waiting. Spurts of rifle fire ran round the scrub above Taylor's Hollow and on Walden's Point. Pushing up the Chailak Dere, the other squadrons of the Otagos came to the heavy barbed-wire entanglements stretching right across the dere and enfiladed by fire trenches on the spur. There was nothing to be done but tear the obstruction away. A section of the Field Troop of New Zealand Engineers, gallantly led by their subaltern, attacked the wire with great determination and, after sustaining many casualties, succeeded in opening the dere to the Otagos and Maoris who pressed on up the gully towards their objective.

LITTLE TABLE TOP.
Little Table Top was of little military importance, but its water-scored cliffs are typical of the surrounding country.

The Canterburys with some Maoris in support, advanced in short rushes across the flat ground towards the trenches on the foothills. Not a shot was wasted. Bayonets alone were used. A Turkish machine gun on the spur leading to Walden's Point was responsible for many casualties, and this section of the attack was momentarily held up. "Tap, tap, tap" went the gun, exacting a heavy toll; but a subaltern, named Davidson, who gained the ridge higher up, collected a few ardent spirits, and with fixed bayonets.

charged straight down the slope. The dirt thrown up by the angry bullets flicked in their faces as they ran straight for the gun. Down tumbled the subaltern, killed leading his men, but the remnants of the party fell upon the gun crew. The keen bayonets did their silent work, and the gun ceased its death-dealing tapping.

Methodically and irresistibly the Otagos and Canterburys pushed up the spurs until the greater part of Bauchop's Hill was in our hands. Many a duel between surprised Turk and desperate New Zealander was fought that night in the tangled scrub. The ground was so broken, the twists in the gullies so confusing, that all cohesion was lost. But the troopers knew that their duty was to press on up the hill, so up the hill they went. Trench after trench was taken at the bayonet point by Pakeha and Maori. Presently three great cheers announced the final capture of the hill. But the losses were severe. Many officers were shot down, including gallant Colonel Bauchop, who fell mortally wounded, and Captain Bruce Hay who had taken charge of a hesitating line, was killed shortly after he had bravely rallied them and led them on.

By now the Sazli Beit Dere, the Chailak Dere, and part of the Aghyl Dere was opened; the N.Z.M.R. Brigade had decisively smashed the Turkish line.

The Left Covering Force.

When the attack on the lower slopes of Bauchop's Hill was well under way the Left Covering Column moved out over the flat ground towards the mouth of the Aghyl Dere. Having rounded Walden's Point they at once came under the fire of the enemy. But pressing on, the advance guard of the 4th South Wales Borderers cleared all before them. The New Army men, resolutely led, were capable of great things. An hour after midnight they saw through the gloom the dark mass of the Damakjelik Bair, and quickly put the Turks to flight.

The lower reaches of the Aghyl Dere were now held by us on both sides; our left flank was secure; the army landing at Suvla had a definite point to reach out to.

The Right Assaulting Column.

By midnight the four battalions of the New Zealand Infantry Brigade were on their way up the deres to the assault of Chunuk Bair. There had been some delay at the start, as the overs from the high ground fell among the units as they marched along to the foot of the deres. The Canterburys went by way of the Sazli Beit, and the Otagos, Aucklands and Wellingtons proceeded up the Chailak.

The night was so dark and the country so rough and unreconnoitred that the leading files often crept up little branches of the main dere, and retracing their steps, caused a certain amount of confusion among the troops behind. So

[Photo by *Guy.*
MAJOR FRANK STATHAM, OTAGO INFANTRY BATTALION.
Who with his brother, was killed in action on Chunuk Bair.

it happened on one of these occasions that part of the Canterburys struggled in the inky blackness of the night into a nullah that led them away from the objective. This caused a certain amount of delay, enemy rifle fire was very insistent, but clearing trench after trench, the men pushed slowly up the gullies. Stumbling over the boulders of the dry watercourse, charging each clump of scrub that spat out tongues of fire, the men of the infantry brigade pushed doggedly on.

Going up the Chailak, some of the Otago Infantry lost their way and "took Table Top" only to be gruffly ordered away by the Wellington Mounteds who had taken it some hours before! Part of the other two companies of the Otago Infantry—the 8th Southland and the 10th North Otago—passed Table Top at dawn and resolutely pressed up the dere, led by Major Frank Statham, a dauntless-spirited soldier and a born leader. About an hour after dawn this small band of heroes entered the Turkish communication trench running across the lower slopes of Rhododendron Spur from the Chailak Dere. They met with little resistance—indeed on reaching a point where they could overlook the Sazli Beit Dere, they were astonished to see the valley crowded with scared Turks streaming back towards Battleship Hill. Some of the bolder spirits of the Otagos went right on to the Apex and Chunuk Bair! If there had been a dozen leaders of the Statham type—men who understood country and men of resolution—the whole of Chunuk might have been ours by nine o'clock. The enemy was certainly demoralized and on the run.

A signalling officer of the Ghurkas now arrived and sent a message back to his brigade slowly proceeding up the Aghyl Dere.

The broken country delayed the rest of our brigade. The Canterburys proceeding up the Sazli Beit had some trouble at Destroyer Hill because, as we know, the Turkish communication trenches all led in that direction and fresh fugitive Turks were constantly arriving. It was well light before the Canterburys reached the lower slopes of Rhododendron. These slopes were for some time called Canterbury Ridge, but the older name of Rhododendron survived.

As it was now light, and the attack undoubtedly late, Chunuk could not be taken by surprise. But looking down towards the Suvla Flats, we were heartened by the great flotilla of ships and barges in Suvla Bay. Hope

The Right Assaulting Column.

again ran high, for help seemed close at hand. With another effort the brigade pressed forward and reached the small depression now known as the Apex, but then christened the Mustard Plaster.

Orders came that an effort must be made to take Chunuk. The machine guns of the Otago Battalion established themselves along the front, thus securing the right flank, and doing great execution to the Turks who were being driven up the gully and were seemingly not aware that we had a footing on Rhododendron. The Wellington guns were then dug in on the left of the Otagos, but lined so as to face north and thus command Chunuk Bair which our infantry must assault. The Auckland guns were just a few yards behind; those of the Canterburys had not yet arrived. The order came for the advance with only half the guns posted. There was a little hesitancy, but Major S. A. Grant gallantly rushed forward and led the Aucklands over the crest. A thousand yards of the heights, thick with Turkish rifles, carried out rapid fire on that small band of heroes. Nothing could live in it and with the exception of a few survivors who gained a deserted Turk trench 120 yards in front, the whole were either killed or wounded. The gallant Major Grant was mortally wounded, dying from his wounds that evening. At this point, if the Turks had pushed out a counter attack, they could have cleared the Apex; but the machine guns were invaluable; they cut up the crest between them and undoubtedly saved the sadly harassed line.

The troops were now very tired. An advance of a little more than a mile over most difficult country had been achieved. Taking advantage of what little cover was available, the left flank threw out little parties to get in touch with the Left Assaulting Column, which, as we know, consisted of the 4th Australian Brigade and the 29th Indian Brigade.

This column in pushing up the Aghyl Dere had met very strenuous opposition, but had surprised many Turks and driven them up the gully. The Aghyl Dere forks about 2000 yards from the sea; the Australians went up the northern one so that the Suvla army, after getting in touch with the New Army troops on Damakjelik Bair could push on and prolong General Monash's left. By dawn, this brigade had reached the ridge overlooking the head of the Asma Dere.

The Indian Brigade, guided by Major Overton, of the Cantterbury Mounted Rifles, proceeded up the southern fork of the Aghyl Dere towards The Farm, which lay beneath the crest of Chunuk Bair. Poor Overton and his companion scout were killed while leading up the dere. After receiving the message from their signalling officer the right flank

MAJOR OVERTON'S GRAVE.

of the Indians felt out towards Rhododendron, and succeeded in coming into touch with the New Zealand Infantry Brigade; the 14th Sikhs felt out towards their left and came into touch with the 4th Australians.

The exhausted line made repeated efforts to get on, but the Turks were now thoroughly alive to the threatened turning movement and hastily flung fresh troops on to Abdel Rahman spur to impede the Australians, who were standing at bay in truly awful country—standing at bay with their left flank in the air—in touch with no one. The Suvla Bay was full of ships, but there seemed no movement towards the vital hills.

All that day the troops lay out on the hot hillside exhausted with their heavy night march. True the ambitious programme of the operation order had not been achieved in its entirety, but a marked and valuable advance had been made. The Anzac troops felt that at last they had room to breathe, for Anzac had been very cramped. Here, after four months of waiting and watching, we were standing on new ground. There was a certain thrill and a little pardonable pride in the realization that these strongly entrenched and defended hill-sides had been taken by a citizen soldiery from the flower of the Turkish Army.

There was one disagreeable disadvantage in holding these steep hills—that was the supply of water, ammunition and food. But the Indian Supply and Transport Corps was equal to the emergency. As soon as it was dark the drabis of the supply columns started with their pack mules, and though they paid a heavy toll in men and animals, undeterred they gallantly soldiered on.

The Canterbury machine guns arrived at the Apex that evening. The gunners, dead beat, had carried their guns, tripods, spare parts, their own rifles and equpiment, with one hundred and twenty rounds of ammunition in their pouches, and a box of ammunition between every two men. They had marched and fought the clock round. Now they had to stand by and hold the line. There was no time for sleep. It was dig, dig, dig, and bury the dead.

The survivors of the Aucklands stayed out in their bomb-swept trench. The Otagos were withdrawn to the Rhododendron for reorganization.

So the night passed with the Auckland Battalion in front of the Apex; the Ghurkas and the Sikhs on the ridge overlooking The Farm; the 4th Australian Brigade on the Asma Dere. The New Zealand Mounted Rifles dug in and improved their line from Destroyer Hill to Table Top and Bauchop's Hill. General Travers's force was secure on Damakjelik Bair. But the Anzac Army was not yet in touch with the troops at Suvla.

Part III.

The Attack of August 8.

That night the whole of the attacking force was reorganized in three columns:—

Right Column—Brigadier-General F. E. Johnston.
    26th Indian Mountain Battery (less one section).
    N. Z. Infantry Brigade.
    Auckland Mounted Rifles.
    Maori Contingent.
    8th Welsh Pioneers } from the 13th Division
    7th Gloucesters. } in Reserve.

The Right Column was to assault Chunuk Bair at dawn on the 8th. The Auckland Mounteds and the Maoris were to be brought up from the Right Covering Column.

Centre and Left Columns—Major-General H. V. Cox.
    21st Indian Mountain Battery (less one section).
    4th Australian Infantry Brigade.
    29th Indian Infantry Brigade.
    9th Royal Warwicks.
    9th Worcesters.
    7th North Staffords.
    6th South Lancashires.

The centre of this force was to attack Hill Q; the left was to attack the Abdel Rahman spur—the two attacks converging on Koja Chemen Tepe, the highest point in the range.

We must look in turn at the left, the centre, and the right.

Away on the left the Australians of the 4th Brigade moved up the Asma Dere towards the lower slopes of Abdel Rahman Bair. The intention was to gain a footing, then wheel to the right, and work up this rugged northern spur towards Koja Chemen Tepe. By this time, however, Turkish reserves had accumulated all along the rear slopes of the whole mountain system. With machine guns and shrapnel the Ottoman soldiery assailed the Australians, who were presently almost surrounded. Hopelessly outnumbered, wearied with incessant fighting, the gallant 4th Brigade fell back to its former line.

In the centre the men of the 39th New Army Brigade and the Indians fared little better. Pushing on past both sides of The Farm the troops assailed the lower spurs leading up to Hill Q and the left of Chunuk. But the Turkish machine gunners and riflemen were fresh from reserve. They held the high ground with all its advantages, they were fighting in a country with which they were familiar, and compelled our line to come to a definite standstill on the slopes overlooking The Farm.

The Capture of Chunuk Bair.

On the right things were going better. At dawn the men of the Wellington Infantry Regiment were ready again to attack the fatal crestline. The tired troops of yesterday were once again to essay the seemingly impossible.

At 4.15 in the grey of the morning, the Wellington Infantry and the 7th Gloucesters, led by Lieut.-Colonel Malone, commenced the desperate struggle for Chunuk Bair. So far as the New Zealanders are concerned, August 8, 1915, was the blackest day on the Peninsula. But the prize was the strategical key to the Gallipoli Peninsula. Win the Ridge and we should win the Narrows. Open the Narrows to the Navy, and Constantinople was ours! Surely a prize worth fighting for. So from the scanty trenches on Rhododendron Spur leapt the Wellingtons and the 7th Gloucesters.

By their dash and audacity the crestline was soon gained. We now had a footing on the ridge, and to cling to that foothold and extend from it was now the pressing need. The Wellingtons and Gloucesters started to dig in, but the enemy evidently made up his mind to cut the New Zealanders off. A body of snipers picked off all the machine gun crews. When Malone's battalion was seen marching along the skyline four machine guns were pushed up to him. These guns never came back. When half way up the ridge a veritable hail of lead burst round them, and they were so badly damaged that only one gun could be reconstructed from the remnants of the four; but it got into position and did good service until the whole of the gun crew were killed or wounded.

Two machine guns that were to support the right flank of the attackers from the Apex were pushed forward on the slope to avoid being silhouetted against the crest line. The Turkish snipers now concentrated on these guns. Soon all the personnel were killed or wounded. A Maori machine gun close by lost their officer killed and had nine other casualties, but a few men fought their gun all day without a murmur. This was the only machine gun left in action on this flank.

The devoted party on the crest was assailed with every variety of shell, hand grenades and maxims. Time after time, Turks advanced to the attack but were driven off at the point of the bayonet. The Gloucesters who had lost all their officers now came down the ridge to the help of the New Zealanders. They seemed dazed, but instinct and the example of the New Zealanders convinced them that the bayonet was the weapon for the Turk. Time and time again they charged and cleared their front.

The Glory of New Zealand.

This forward Turkish trench became a veritable death trap. Not far behind it was another line that resolved itself into our real line of resistance. But some ardent spirits of the Aucklands, Otagos and Wellingtons decided to stick to their forward line. No one—except the dozen badly-wounded survivors—can conceive the horrors of that awful front line trench. It was practically dark when they arrived in the early hours of the morning. When daylight came it proved to be a fatal position. About ten or fifteen yards to their front the ground sloped rapidly away into a valley until again it revealed itself about six hundred yards away. When it was light this far away hill was seen to be occupied by about a battalion of Turks—a battalion advancing to attack this forward trench of Chunuk! A few long range shots were all that could be fired. Then came the long wait while the attackers crossed the gully. To the waiting New Zealanders—the New Zealand infantrymen who had penetrated farthest into Turkey—the minutes seemed hours. But a shower of hand grenades announced the beginning of the end. From the dead ground in the

The Glory of New Zealand.

front came bombs and more bombs. Away from the left came the Turkish shrapnel. To fire at all, our men had to stand up in the trench and expose themselves almost bodily to view. One by one they died on Chunuk, until after a few hours desperate struggle against overwhelming forces the only New Zealanders left alive were a dozen severely wounded. But not for a long time did the first Turk dare show his head. Then into the trench several crept with their bayonets to kill the wounded. Fortunately a Turkish sergeant arrived and saved the lives of the wounded who were carried off to the German dressing stations behind Hill Q. In all the history of the Gallipoli Campaign there is no finer story of fortitude, no finer exhibition of heroism and self-sacrifice, than was shown in this forward trench of Chunuk on that desperate August morning. Here died some of the noblest characters in the New Zealand Army. August 8 was a day of tragedy for New Zealand, but no day in our calendar shines with greater glory.

All that day midst the shriek of the Turkish shrapnel, the dull booming of the British naval guns, the incessant rattle of musketry and machine gun fire, that heroic band held on. With their faces blackened with dust and sweat, with the smell of the picric acid assailing their nostrils, with their tongues parched for the lack of water, up there in the blazing heat of the August sun those gallant souls held on.

The Auckland Mounted Rifles and the Maoris arrived at Rhododendron about 3 a.m. and were ordered to the firing line about 11 o'clock. The Aucklanders went out to help Colonel Malone on the ridge. On came the Turks again. The line of infantry and mounteds drove them back at the point of the bayonet. A portion of Chunuk Bair was undoubtedly ours, but at what a cost! Many of the finest young men of the Dominion lay dead upon the crest. Colonel Malone himself, one of the striking characters in the New Zealanl army, was killed as he was marking out the trench line.

It was during this struggle for Chunuk Bair that Corporal Bassett of the Divisional Signallers undertook to carry the telephone line up on to the ridge and gained the first V.C.

THE APEX AND CHUNUK BAIR.

These photographs were taken after the Armistice in 1918, and clearly show the distinction between Chunuk Bair and Hill 971, which was 1,400 yards away. No British Troops ever got on to Koja Chemen Tepe (or Hill 971). When New Zealanders say they were on "the top of 971," they mean "the ridge of Chunuk Bair." Hill Q is about 600 yards from the highest point of Chunuk Bair. Koja Chemen Tepe is 800 yards further on than the crest of Q.

LOOKING TOWARDS KOJA CHEMEN TEPE (HILL 971) FROM CHUNUK BAIR.
Hill Q is the high ground to the right.

for New Zealand. In full daylight, with the approach swept by rifle and machine gun fire, with the Turkish field artillery from Abdel Rahman mercilessly searching the slopes, Bassett dashed and then crept, then dashed and crept again, up to the forward line on Chunuk. These lines were cut again and again, but Bassett and his fellow linesmen of the Signals went out day and night to mend the broken wires. No V.C. on the Peninsula was more consistently earned. This was not for one brilliant act of bravery, but for a full week of ceaseless devotion.

The Maoris were sent over more to the left and most gallantly hung on to an almost untenable position in the neighbourhood of The Farm. They suffered grievous losses uncomplainingly. At dusk the Otago Infantry went out to reinforce what was left of the Wellington and Auckland Infantry, the 7th Gloucesters, and the Auckland Mounteds. Already the Otagos had suffered terribly, but throughout that awful night of August 8 all previous experiences were as nothing. It was a night of agony by thirst, of nerve-wracking bomb explosions, and of bayonet jabs in the dark.

In the darkness a little much-needed water was carried out to the thirsty men. Hand grenades, food and reinforcements went out to the battered trenches; more machine guns were sent—three from the Cheshire Regiment, three from the Wiltshires, and one from the Wellington Mounted Rifles. The Cheshire guns came back as there was ample without them. This second lot of four guns was never seen again.

Still another effort had to be made, for the hold we had on Chunuk had to be increased. It was the most important capture, so far, in the whole campaign; but the Suvla army still clung to the low ground at Suvla, leaving the Australians with their left flank out in the air waiting for the necessary support to carry them on to victory up the Abdel Rahman.

There was no time to lose. The partial success on Chunuk must be exploited. We could not afford to wait on Suvla.

The Ghurkas Attack Hill Q.

Once again on the night of August 8 the columns were reorganized for the attack:

No. 1 Column—Brigadier-General F. E. Johnston.
  26th Indian Mountain Battery (less one Section).
  Auckland Mounted Rifles.
  Wellington Mounted Rifles.
  N.Z. Infantry Brigade.
  7th Gloucesters.
  8th Welsh Pioneers.

The Wellington Mounted Rifles came up from Table Top during the night, but the other troops were already on Chunuk Bair. Their duty on the morrow was to consolidate their position, and if possible extend it.

No. 2 Column—Major-General H. V. Cox.
  21st Indian Mountain Battery (less one section).
  4th Australian Infantry Brigade.
  29th Indian Infantry Brigade.
  39th Brigade (less the 7th Gloucesters).
  6th Battalion South Lancashire Regiment.

This column was to attack the heights of Hill Q.

No. 3 Column—Brigadier-General A. H. Baldwin.

6th East Lancashires.	From the
6th Loyal North Lancashires.	38th Brigade.
10th Hampshires.	From the
6th Royal Irish Rifles.	29th Brigade.
5th Wiltshires.	40th Brigade.

These troops were from the Army Corps Reserve. They were to assemble in the Chailak Dere on the night of the 8th, move up to Rhododendron Spur in the dark, and getting in touch with the No. 1 Column on Chunuk Bair, move up the slopes towards Hill Q.

Troops moving up defiles in the dark are always late, for so many factors seem to work adversely. Wounded men and transport mules will persist in coming down and blocking the road. Wounded men are generally past caring about the fortunes of the fight. Indian mule drivers know they have to get back to their depot and are perhaps not told the proper track to take. This, of course, is soon

The Ghurkas' Attack Hill Q.

regulated when things are normal; but while a fight is on there is a good deal of confusion.

No. 1 Column carried out its task and held on to Chunuk Bair; the Ghurkas struggled up the steeps of Hill Q, their ranks becoming visibly thinner and thinner until the watchers from the posts below wondered if there would be enough momentum to carry them to the top. But they undoubtedly did get there. The Navy now commenced firing over the crest in order to debar the Turk from pressing a counter-attack. Some of the shells fell short among the Ghurkas. Instead of getting help from Baldwin, who was only at The Farm, a few heavy shells crashed on to the summit. This was one of the tragedies of Anzac. Instead of help came our own shells. It is the price that must be paid for artillery support in broken country. These things are unavoidable—they are the misfortune of war.

A Sikh and a Ghurka.

But the enemy saw his chance. Launching a counter-attack, the gallant handful of survivors was swept off the crest and into the valley below. Simultaneously a flood was loosed on the 4th Australians; wave after wave was hurled against the New Zealanders up on the shoulder of Chunuk Bair; flushed with success and confident in the overwhelming superiority of numbers, wave after wave of skirmishers was thrown around Baldwin's forces at The Farm until the column was well-nigh annihilated. General Baldwin himself was killed with many of his commanding officers. The survivors retired to their original position on the ridge overlooking The Farm.

The only force to hold its ground was General Johnston's on Chunuk Bair, where a poor trenchline of 200 yards was occupied. Our fellows were too exhausted to dig in the hard ground and rock of the crest-line. It was impossible to put out wire.

This brings us to the end of Sunday, August 9. The battle at Lone Pine was still raging. Down at Suvla, high officers were trying to infuse a little energy into an army that had become moribund.

Worn out with three days and three nights of fighting under a merciless sun, with a short ration of water, suffering tremendous losses, the New Zealanders and other troops on Chunuk Bair were withdrawn for a little rest on the evening of August 9. Their place was taken by the 6th Loyal North Lancashires and the 5th Wiltshires. It was estimated that more than two battalions could not be usefully employed on the ridge.

We Lose the Crest of Chunuk.

At dawn on the 10th, these two battalions had disappeared! Some of the North Lancashires who escaped explained that the Wiltshires arrived tired and did not dig in; they were attacked by the Turks with knives and bombs; the Wiltshires ran in towards the Lancashires and the machine guns, and so masked their fire. So were these two battalions wiped out!

About 6 a.m. the Turks delivered their famous counter-attack down the slopes of Chunuk Bair, and endeavoured to get at the New Army regiments on the left of the Apex. But the four machine guns of the Canterbury Battalion were on the left front of the Apex, and the two remaining guns of the Auckland Battalion were on the Apex itself; two guns of the Wellington Battalion were back on the Rhododendron with the Maori gun and the flank gun of the Otago Infantry —these four could fire over the heads of the guns on the Apex, and commanded the whole of the approaches from Chunuk Bair. The small details of training, generally found so irksome, now proved of value. The gunners had already attended to their guns at the first streak of day.

A Canterbury gunner, finding his gun difficult to adjust reported to the N.Z. Brigade Machine Gun Officer, who was sighting the gun on to the ridge when the first line of the Turkish attack came over at that very point. This gun had the range at once, and followed by keeping the sights a little in advance of the enemy. The other guns quickly took up the rat-a-tat; the range was sent to the other five guns. The N.Z. Mounted Brigade machine guns on Table Top and Bauchop's Hill also found a good target at extreme range. The New Zealand field guns, especially the howitzers, also opened up at once.

[Photo by Col. Falla, C.M.G., D.S.O.
A NEW ZEALAND 4.5 HOWITZER.

The Turkish line consisted of from 250 to 300 men at about one pace interval. By the time they reached a point immediately in front of the guns, the whole of the N.Z. machine guns were concentrated at that point in accordance with the orders hurriedly issued. Thus was created a death zone through which the enemy could not pass. They fell over literally like oats before a reaper. Twenty two lines came down each as true and steady as the first. They moved at a jog trot with their rifles at the port. The machine gunners with the assistance of the Navy and the Field Artillery mowed down line after line until the Turkish effort was spent. A number of Turks crawled back during the forenoon. They were not molested by the machine gunners, who admired their bravery so much as to leave them alone.

The New Zealand Infantry Brigade was relieved at 2 p.m. that day, but the machine guns were left in to stiffen up the New Army regiments.

At about 2.30 a.m. there was an attack and much confusion. The Turks showed on the top of the Apex, but the two flank guns of the Canterbury Battalion quickly dispersed them. Order was only restored at daylight. The presence of the N.Z. machine guns had saved the situation. The N.Z. Infantry Brigade again came in with the Aucklanders on the Apex. The next morning the Turks occupied the point of the Apex, and it was decided to take a Vickers Maxim out to the front and open up on them from an unexpected quarter. The gun was just in position when a peculiar incident occurred. An Otago man of the 5th Reinforcements was working in front of where the gun took up position. He was told to stop work when the gun was ready and to crouch down so that the gun could fire over him. Against all the rules of war he immediately lighted his pipe. The Turks, only 80 yards away, opened fire with about twenty rifles on to the light. Their rifle flashes disclosed their position and the machine gun drove them out.

The New Zealand Infantry were relieved again in a short time and the machine gunners moved back to Rhododendron. On the first morning after their move back, a blockhouse was found to have been built in No Man's Land during the night. It now became plain what the Turks had been trying to do, but this had been prevented as long as the N.Z. Infantry were in possession. This blockhouse was a great nuisance to our men at the Apex, until it was summarily dealt with by the Canterburys later in the month.

Part IV.

The Battle of Sari Bair.

The Suvla Landing.

We know that the thrust towards Koja Chemen Tepe from Suvla Bay failed. Let us examine the causes of the failure. For of what use is history if we do not seek to understand its lessons?

The story of the failure at Suvla Bay is not only the story of the misfortune of war. It ranks with the tragedy of Kut-el-Amara as an illustration of what must happen to a nation which accepts world-wide responsibilities and does not keep itself in a state of preparedness for possibilities.

The people of the British Empire did not realize that an efficient army was the complement to a powerful navy. For battleships cannot cross deserts or climb mountains. Indeed, battleships, as every soldier who was on Gallipoli Peninsula knows, are of incalculable value for moral effect, but for supporting troops ashore in mountainous country they are almost useless. Their guns cannot get at the enemy behind the crest. Only on rare occasions can ships' guns search reverse slopes. Ships are built to fight ships—not to act as army corps artillery.

No regular soldiers were available for these subsidiary operations in the East, but the next best—an army corps of the New Army—was available for this advance over broken, unreconnoitred country.

The 9th Army Corps, under Lieut.-General Sir F. Stopford, was organized as follows:—

The 10th (Irish) Division (Lieut.-General Sir B. Mahon) was composed of the 29th Brigade (detached for service at Anzac), the 30th Brigade, and the 31st Brigade.

The 11th (Northern) Division (Major-General F. Hammersley), consisted of the 32nd, the 33rd, and the 34th Brigades.

The 13th (Western) Division (Major-General F. C. Shaw), was also taken from the Suvla Army to act at Anzac. The three brigades were the 38th, 39th, and the 40th.

In that four of his brigades were landed at Anzac, General Stopford did not have anything like an army corps. His divisional artillery was lamentably weak, and his corps artillery almost non-existent. True, he had the support of some warships, but as we know, this support is not so much material as moral.

It was estimated that a force of 20,000 rifles would overpower a thin screen of Turks, which was reckoned at about 4000.

The 53rd and 54th Territorial Division (of infantry only) were to arrive later and be used as a general reserve.

The Hill Features of the Suvla Plain.

The country was not so hilly as at Anzac. From Lala Baba, looking due east, one saw the high ground running from the Gulf of Saros round towards the two Anafartas and so to the underfeatures of Sari Bair near Abdel Rahman Bair.

The plan of campaign was to land during the night of August 6/7 at three beaches to the north and south of Nibrunesi Point, push back the screen of enemy scouts holding the sparsely-wooded plain and rolling country, and occupy the hills about Anafarta, and so take a measure of the strain off the direct push for Koja Chemen Tepe. Having got astride the high ground near Anafarta the Turkish communications from Bulair to their Ari Burnu front would be imperilled.

A reference to the map will show that the conception was a reasonable one if the country was not strongly held. Resolute troops, vigorously led, might have reasonably achieved a success. But Chance did not smile upon our efforts, and instead of closely examining the structure of this high ground inland, we must look at the tactical features much nearer the coast line.

On the extreme left flank, and overlooking the Gulf of Saros, was the long ridge known as Kiretch Tepe Sirt. The southern foothills of this range merged into an expanse of

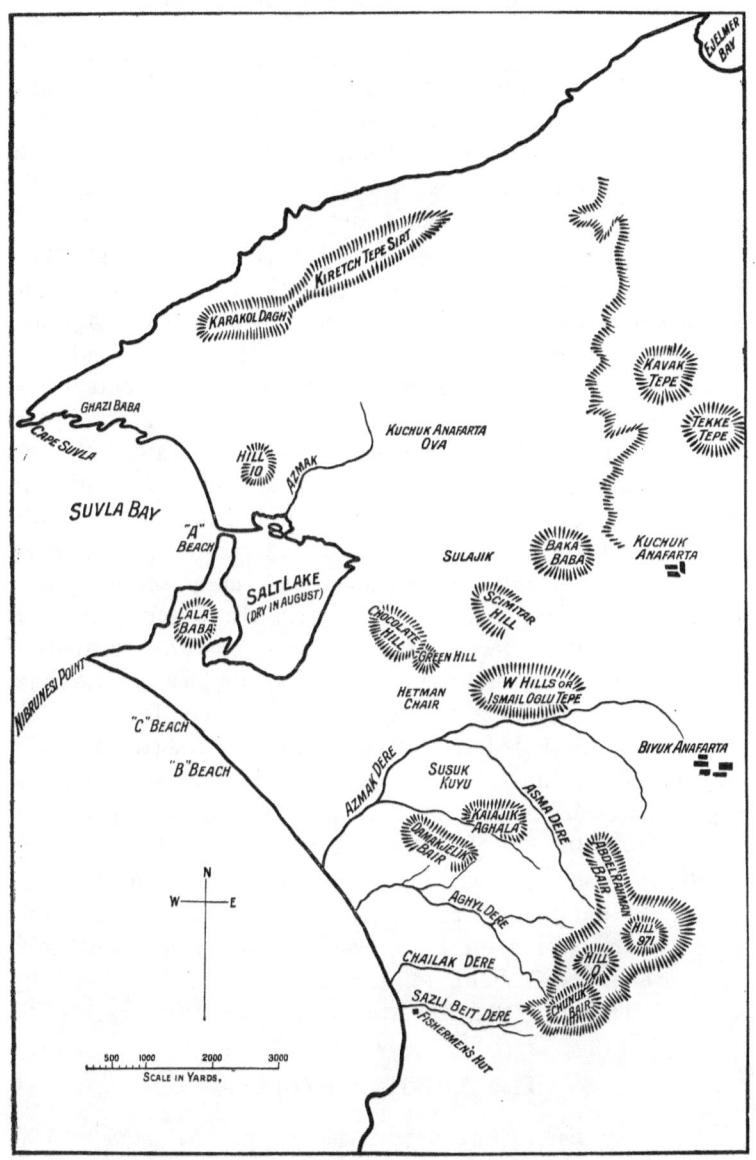

SKETCH MAP OF THE SUVLA AREA SHOWING THE LANDING BEACHES.
The landing place most used in the later stages was near Cape Suvla, just inside Suvla Bay.

cultivated land, bounded on the east by the Anafarta Hills, and on the west by the Salt Lake. During the winter months the Salt Lake takes all the flood waters from the surrounding hills, and the rough weather brings in the salt water. But in August the water had disappeared and there was a circular expanse of grey, sticky sand, measuring a mile across.

About a mile in a south-easterly direction from Lala Baba was the tactical feature christened "Chocolate Hill." The gorse and grass on this hill caught fire during the fighting, and one part of it became a more pronounced reddish-brown than ever. The southern portion was not burnt, and is distinguished on the map as Green Hill. Standing on Chocolate Hill and looking towards the west, one saw, half left, the high ground called Scimitar Hill, and half right, the ill-starred Ismail Oglu Tepe, known to our men as "W" Hills. The "W" Hills looked down on to the valley of the Asmak Dere, which ran into the sea about two miles south of Lala Baba, and running generally in a westerly direction towards Biyuk Anafarta, threw out two forks, one to the foot of Abdel Rahman Bair, the other towards Kaiajik Aghala (Hill 60). The latter fork was the Asma Dere, which running up past Hill 60, drained the watershed of Abdel Rahman Bair. Just to the south of the Azmak Dere, and between Kaiajik Aghala and the sea, was the high ground of Damakjelik Bair.

So it was intended that the Suvla Army, pushing on across the flat plains of Suvla in the early morning, should get in touch with their New Army comrades on Damakjelik and prolong the right of the new Anzac line held by General Travers's and the 4th Australian Brigades.

The Landing Beaches.

The day before the battle the component parts of the Army Corps were widely scattered. Part was at Mitylene, 120 miles away; part was at Mudros, 50 miles away; the remainder at Kephalos, on Imbros, about 16 miles away. As soon as it was fully dark, these three bodies of troops were speeding on their way to Suvla. Three beaches were

TROUBLE AT THE BEACHES. 233

to be used. Beach A was in the centre of Suvla Bay. Beaches B and C were to the south of Nibrunesi—B for infantry and C for the disembarkation of artillery.

At 8 o'clock on the night of the 6th, the force sailed from Kephalos with its collection of water boats, barges and lighters. At 9.30 p.m., the flotilla silently crept towards Nibrunesi, and the disembarkation commenced. The 32nd and 33rd Brigades got ashore expeditiously at Beach B and rushed Lala Baba.

Then occurred the first disaster. Beach A was not reconnoitred, and the barges containing the 34th Brigade ran aground. Men jumped into the water and waded ashore. A few Turkish snipers on Hill 10 and Lala Baba crept among the troops, who were new to war. In the dark, confusion reigned. When daylight came the troops were ashore, but that was about all. There was no pressing on. The men were shaken by their experience of the night. The line ran round from Lala Baba across the flat ground to Hill 10.

Trouble at the Beaches.

Just as it was getting light, six battalions of the 10th Division arrived from far-distant Mitylene. These troops were to go out to the extreme left flank. They should have landed at Beach A, but owing to the shallows and the difficulties already experienced there, the Navy took them to Beach B, south of Nibrunesi! This again upset the prearranged plan. These battalions fell in and marched along the mile and a half of open beach towards the left flank, passing behind and through the men who had earlier experienced the mess caused by inefficient reconnaissance.

By the time the remaining battalions of the 10th Division arrived, the Navy had found a small landing place in one of the little bays on the southern side of Suvla Point, just inside Suvla Bay. These men of the Irish Division scrambled ashore and pushed on to the high ground of Karakol Dagh.

When noon came the sun beat down on those poor citizen soldiers, worn out and tired by their long sea journeys, harassed by daring snipers in the dark, not very resolutely led, not at home in this hot and dusty country, tortured by thirst, the improvized and intricate machine went to pieces at the first rough jolt. Most of that day the Suvla Army sat down and waited for something to turn up. But during the afternoon some bold spirits led two battalions of the 11th Division across the flat ground and secured a foothold on the Chocolate Hills. So, from a point above Karakol Dagh, the line ran through Hill 10 and past the Salt Lake to the Chocolate Hills, about two miles from the outpost of their New Army comrades on Damakjelik Bair.

That night the Anzac troops, as we know, were holding the line Damakjelik-Asma Dere-Rhododendron Spur.

The Morning of August 8.

This morning—the morning when Malone stood triumphant on the crest of Chunuk Bair; when the Australians were pluckily attempting to carry Abdel Rahman—passed strangely inactive at Suvla. Following on their exhaustion and the heat of the midday sun, the men undoubtedly suffered agonies from thirst. There was water in the Suvla Plain, but no proper provision was made to take advantage of it. Instead, much effort was directed towards getting the supplies known to be somewhere at hand in ships and lighters. So one thing reacted on another—the bad landing beach at A caused exhaustion in the troops disembarked there, and was the cause of greater confusion when the troops for the left flank were landed on the right. This caused delay, which meant that more of the precious water was consumed than was allowed for. As a matter of fact, such was the lack of ordinary supervision, numbers of men landed without any water in their water-bottles at all! Those who had water consumed it during the waiting of the day. So General Stopford brought off mules to carry water in preference to artillery horses, and created a further excuse for delay—not enough supporting artillery! At the Anzac landing horses could not be landed, but willing men manhandled the guns up precipitous cliffs to their positions. No one seemed to think of this at Suvla. But the Generals in command seemed fairly satisfied with the progress of things. General Hamilton, over at Imbros, from where he could best keep touch of his widely-scattered army, got so uneasy that he could not resist hurrying to Suvla to see why the advance had been hung up. Nothing was done, but one battalion, the 6th East York Pioneers, occupied Scimitar Hill and dug in for the night. It was decided to make an advance early in the morning. Then an extraordinary incident occurred. The higher command evidently did not know where the battalions were. The 6th East Yorks were considered to be the freshest, and were ordered to the attack on another hill in the morning. This battalion had taken Scimitar Hill, but those in command did not seem to know it. Accordingly, the 6th East Yorks abandoned their position on this valuable hill without an effort and marched back to Sulajik!

[*Lent by Rev. Wainohu, C.F.*]
THE ROLL CALL OF THE MAORIS AFTER THE AUGUST FIGHTING.

The Next Day—August 9.

Early in the morning the 32nd Brigade attacked the hills towards Anafarta, but were repulsed and continued to occupy a line running north and south through Sulajik.

This day the New Zealanders clung to the ridge of Chunuk Bair, the Ghurkas and 6th South Lancashires struggled on to Hill Q, but the Suvla Army, worn out with fatigue and thirst, lay along the low ground stretching from the Chocolate Hills towards Kiretch Tepe Sirt.

In this day's attack on Scimitar Hill, serious scrub fires broke out and held the attention of the troops for the rest of the day. At noon the units fell back to a line between Sulajik and Green Hill.

A New Move that Failed.

General Hamilton concluded that on this right flank success would be delayed, and decided to land part of his reserve—the infantry brigades of the 54th Division—up at the new landing place near Cape Suvla, so that they might advance, with the 10th Irish Division, along Kiretch Tepe Sirt, then thrust towards Kavak Tepe and capture the line Ejelmer Bay to Anafarta, thus turning the Turkish flank.

The infantry of the 53rd (Territorial) Division landed during the night of the 8/9th, and were to assist the units on the right flank. The advance of these newly-arrived territorials was a pitiable thing. Crossing the open country from Lala Baba towards the Anafarta Hills, the enemy artillery, now considerably increased, took heavy toll. The enemy again fought his sniping screen with conspicuous ability. The attack could not get on. Realizing that the troops were unequal to the situation, it was decided to dig in on a line from near the Azmak Dere, through the knoll east of the Chocolate Hill, to the ground held by the 10th Division on Kiretch Tepe Sirt.

On August 11, the infantry brigades of the 54th Division were disembarked and placed in reserve. An attack on Kavak Tepe-Tekke Tepe was planned by Sir Ian Hamilton, but after a series of minor disasters the projected night march and attack was abandoned. General Stopford was now thoroughly convinced that his troops could not be expected to do more. Even if they gained the high ground, he considered that the supply of water and food would be too difficult and well-nigh impossible to arrange. There seemed nothing to do but to dig in everywhere and strengthen the line.

* * * *

So ended the great battle for the heights of Sari Bair. The Turk still held the higher ground at Helles, Anzac, and Suvla.

Part V.

After the Battle.

The Trenches on the Crest of Chunuk.

There has been placed on record a statement that the trenches on the crest of Chunuk were badly sited. No soldier of experience would have made such a criticism if he understood the facts. Bare justice is due to Colonel Malone and those New Zealanders who took Chunuk and held it. It has been said that the trench line was the wrong side of the crest, and that there was not a good field of fire.

What would anyone else have done?

We all know that a trench should have the best field of fire. But one can easily get in a training manual what one seeks for in vain during a pitched battle! In the carefully prepared treatise, principles are laid down and their application is expounded. But the enemy is not firing bullets and hand grenades in the book. The ground in the book, too, is easy to dig.

Look for a moment at this sketch of a typical crest.

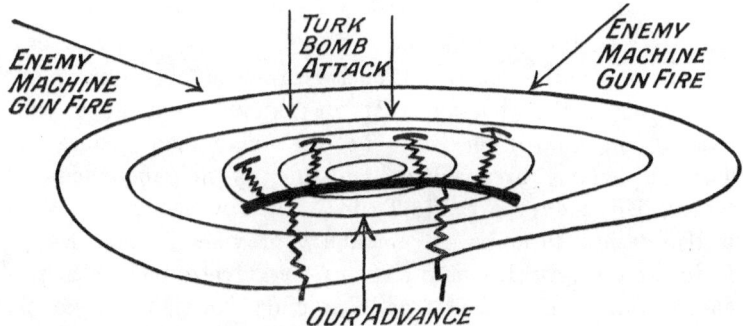

It is obvious that the trenchline we have gained is the best possible one under the circumstances. No one contends that it is the best one theoretically, but at least one has a certain amount of protection. Anyone who goes forward on to the crest itself is killed by bomb or rifle fire; anyone who goes over the enemy's side of the crest to dig posts that have a good field of fire is also sure to be killed. This, however, does not deter determined soldiers from trying. The men who did try on Chunuk were buried long after by the Turks, and cannot reply to criticism—criticism which is cheap, and, in this case, futile.

The only thing to do is to dig deep zig-zag saps through the crest line, put T heads on each sap, and so get posts with a field of fire—posts that can be connected by sapping. A determined enemy—and the Turk was very determined—will not let attacking troops do exactly what they wish, otherwise war might be made safe, and the front line become more popular than it is!

The fact remains that the trenches on Chunuk Bair were the only possible ones for such a situation. Those of us who have found it necessary to entrench on a crest line in close proximity to a determined foe, know that what was done on Chunuk could not have been done any better by anybody else; and there, for the present, the matter must stand.

The Water Problem.

The question of water was perhaps our most terrible problem during the week-end battle. It had always been one of the problems of Anzac, but that awful week in August was the culmination.

In anticipation of the offensive, great efforts were made to overcome the shortage. It was known that good wells existed on the other side of the watershed where the Turkish armies bivouacked, and in the neighbourhood of Kabak Kuyu on the Suvla Plain. Until we could get these wells, we had to make extraordinary provision. From Egypt, India and England, every class of water receptacle was procured. Milk cans came from England; fantassahs from the caravans of Egypt; pakhals from India; sealed petrol tins by the thousand, filled with water from the Nile, arrived and were stacked ready for the advance. Water from a petrol tin looks rusty and tastes abominably, but it is water, and men count themselves fortunate to get it.

The value of water in the campaign can be realized from one illustration. Success seemed within our grasp when we got a foothold on the crest of Chunuk. Tacticians of the Army consider that from there success should have been exploited—that all available reserves should have been thrown in there and so distributed along Hill Q to Koja Chemen Tepe. General Sir Ian Hamilton has put it on record that he was tempted to throw his reserves into the balance at Chunuk Bair, but each time the problem of the water supply dissuaded him from putting any more thirsty men at Anzac. That they were ultimately more thirsty at Suvla is

[*Lent by Capt. Boxer, N.Z.M.C.*
A DRESSING STATION IN THE CHAILAK DERE.

part of the tragedy, which is easy to point out now, but difficult then to foresee.

All through the fight on Chunuk Bair men's throats were parched for the want of water. Intense thirst is one of the cruellest torments man can suffer. Hot weather, hill climbing, and the excitement of fighting combine to accentuate the desire to drink. On occasions like this, the contents of two water bottles do not last long. When the New Zealand infantry went out on to Chunuk Bair, they had marched all the night before and lain out on the hillside during the torrid day. Their water was soon consumed. Water bottles were carefully collected from the dead, more carefully even than ammunition. The short supply gallantly carried up by the

Indian transport service did not go far, but it saved the situation.

Perhaps the success of the Australian and New Zealand divisions in this war was due to having in their ranks skilled and resourceful men who had spent most of their lives solving problems for themselves. In any case the New Zealand Engineers took advantage of the well near No. 2 and developed it to the full. Not that there were no difficulties. On one occasion the bearings got heated, metal ran out of the couplings, and the engine broke down. Spare parts could be made on the warships, but that meant delay. We were getting 1,000 gallons per hour, and pumping 20 hours a day. This meant keeping 2 divisions supplied; so one old sapper filed up a new bearing out of the gun-metal coupling off a service pump! Again, owing to the lubricating oil being so poor, the cylinder rings used to burn on to the piston, and had to be forced off. First one was broken, and then another. New rings were made by cutting up a Turkish 4.5 shell with a hack-saw! The job was a lengthy one, but as the shell was the right thickness, they proved to be A1. After that a few were always kept on hand. Not without ingenuity and knowledge born of experience did the troops at Anzac get the water denied their unfortunate comrades at Suvla.

The Fifth Reinforcements.

If ever mortals were projected into a hell of torture and suffering it was the men of the 5th Reinforcements. Coming straight from the transports, they arrived at No. 2 Post on August 8, and were summarily introduced to modern war. Hundreds of wounded had been carried down from the bloody slopes of Chunuk and were laid in rows in the neighbourhood of No. 2 Post, in readiness to be carried along the Big Sap, and so to the piers as soon as it was dark. These men of the 5th Reinforcements had served little apprenticeship to active service; but they had heard of the casualties of the landing at Anzac and Helles, and some have written that at first they were of the impression that these rows of wounded men were an everyday occurrence! In a sort of nightmare, not knowing whither they were going, or even the name of the dere they traversed, these men dived into the trenches on Chunuk Bair and found themselves among Wellington and Otago Infantry, Auckland and Wellington Mounteds—the heroic band of brothers clinging to Chunuk and prepared to die there. A great proportion did die there; but they held Chunuk! Into this company of heroes stumbled the men of the Fifths.

They were greeted with "dig for your lives for dawn is not far away, and if you haven't got cover by then, you're dead men!" All through the night the digging, the bombing, and the shooting continued. Rifle barrels got so hot they had to be discarded, and a rifle from a dead man used. Ammunition and water were collected. Some men used three rifles, turn and turn about.

CARRYING WOUNDED TO THE PICKET BOATS.

With dawn came the lyddite shells from the Navy. Dense rolls of yellow smoke curled round the hills. Small coloured flags were waved to indicate our position to the Navy.

The suffering from thirst was terrible. When relief did come, men crowded round the wells at No. 2 and drank tin after tin of the precious water.

The Valleys of Torment.

During the nights of August 7, 8, 9, and 10, the wounded men of Anzac seemed to encompass the sum total of human suffering. Travelling light to avoid the heat of the day, a badly wounded man who could not walk had to lie out all through the long cold night. To men without blankets and tunics, and often without a shirt because of the noonday heat, those nights were excruciating cold. Those who could walk were in fairly good stead. They could reach

[*Photo by Capt. Boxer, N.Z.M.C.*

A TRAWLER ALONGSIDE A HOSPITAL SHIP.

Under the big Union Jack are six bodies; and one under the small flag. The trawler made a trip every morning out to the three mile limit, where a solemn burial service was held—the only mourners being the padre and the seven men of the trawler.

the dressing stations near the beach, and get near the piers when the Red Cross barge came alongside. So it happened that the least wounded were always ready to be evacuated; the others had to lie in those stricken gullies until the few overworked stretcher-bearers could carry them down. The lack of facilities for evacuating wounded was as pronounced as at the landing. Of course, in war it must always happen that during big battles things will go wrong. That seems unavoidable, and conditions generally adjust themselves after a few days. But to get a parallel to the sufferings at Anzac one must go back to the days of the Crimea.

The Sazli Beit Dere and the Chailak Dere were crowded with walking cases; those who could not walk, waited in vain for stretcher-bearers, then born of desperation, crawled, crept,

IN EGYPT: THE RED CROSS CARS AND THE RED CRESCENT TRAIN.
The Christian Cross and the Mahommedan Crescent—for perhaps the first time in history—working together in the interests of humanity.

and rolled down the slopes into the gullies. Here there was a certain amount of protection against Turkish fire. Ghurkas, New Army men, and New Zealanders painfully crept towards the low ground. Perhaps the gully would lead too far away from the direction of No. 2 Post; men at the last stages of exhaustion would give up here and wait for the stretcher-bearers who could not come, for they were overwhelmed with cases nearer home. Medical officers, padres, dentists and stretcher-bearers toiled against one of the most heartbreaking experiences of the war. Up in these gullies of torment men died by the hundred—died of thirst, of awful bomb wounds and of exposure.

Down near No. 2 Post was an awful sight—a thousand wounded men lying in rows and in heaps. Crash would come a Turkish shell and the already wounded would be wounded once again. Mule trains moving up and down to the Big Sap raised great clouds of fine dust that settled on everything, increasing the discomfort already caused by wounds, fever, flies and the alternating heat and cold.

Barges full of mules would pull in to be disembarked. The stretcher bearers would help with the unloading, and without any cleaning, for there was no time to worry about the niceties, the serious cases would be placed on the bottom of the barge and towed out to the hospital ship or carrier.

When a string of Red Cross barges would come in, the walking cases would naturally crowd up to the pier in anticipation of getting off; there was a tendency to leave the helpless man on the beach, but the medical officers and orderlies watched as well as they were able, and sent the serious cases to the hospital ships as soon as possible, the less serious ones going to Lemnos by the hospital carrier.

It is difficult to conceive what clean sheets, soft food, the sight of the army nurses, and the sound of their English voices, meant to the tired men of Anzac. Worn to shadows by hardships and suffering, these men could not understand the present situation. For if their experiences had been awful, they expected little else. As pioneers in a desperate enterprise they knew the path would not be strewn with ease and comfort, but rather with danger and pain—and their expectations were realized at Anzac; but here on the hospital ships where there were warm baths, clean underclothing, and the tender ministrations of the army nurses, the suffering New Zealander was literally overwhelmed with his good fortune.

CHAPTER XV.

The Battle of Kaiajik Aghala.

When Sir Ian Hamilton realized that he could not win through to the Narrows with the force at his disposal, he cabled to England for reinforcements. The answer came that no reinforcements could be sent. Men and all the munitions of war were wanted for the Western Front. The dominant school of thought was now in favour of a winter base at Salonika. There was a keen disappointment over the Suvla failure. The people had been told that we were

[*Lent by Captain Janson, W.M.R.*
AT THE FOOT OF THE CHAILAK DERE.
Officers and men of the Wellington Mounted Rifles going out to Hill 60.

only two miles from the greatest victory of the war. And that was true! But what miles? And we were now not much nearer victory than we had been before the push, for our every post was dominated by a higher Turkish one.

Sir Ian Hamilton decided to make another effort with a regrouping of the troops at his disposal.

The only new troops he could call on were the 2nd Mounted Division, a body of British Yeomanry who had been doing garrison duty in Egypt. They were composed of young men who had served in the volunteer mounted service before the war and correspond to our New Zealand regiments of Mounted Rifles. They totalled about 5000 men, and were organized in four brigades (the 1st South Midland, the 2nd South Midland, the North Midland, and the London.)

The 29th Division, who since their desperate landing, had borne the brunt of the fighting at Cape Helles, were moved from there to stiffen the New Army division, which were dug in along the Suvla Flats.

By the night of August 20/21, all was ready for the projected attack. This was to consist of two preliminary movements.

> (1) The 29th Division was to move from Chocolate Hills against Scimitar Hill. Everywhere along the line the other units were to take the offensive to hold the enemy's reserves in check. The 13th Division was to attack at 3.15 p.m. The 34th Brigade was to attack on the plain near Hetman Chair. Next to it the 32nd Brigade was to get possession of a trench running from Hetman Chair towards "W" Hills.

> (2) The Anzac troops from Damakjelik Bair were to attack Kaiajik Aghala (Hill 60) and swing their left round to junction with the Suvla forces.

A reference to the map will show that when these two points—Scimitar Hill and Kaiajik Aghala—were taken the way would be clear for a converging combined assault on Ismail Oglu Tepe, the well known "W" Hills of Anzac. From it in a north-westerly direction ran the long spur on which—some 2700 yards away—was situated the village of Biyuk Anafarta. A similar distance away, but to the south-west, lay Kuchuk Anafarta. The occupation of Ismail Oglu Tepe would not only give us possession of the valleys running up to both these villages, but would also give us uninterrupted intercourse between Anzac and Suvla, now continually under the fire of the guns on "W" Hills. The wells in the neighbourhood were also valuable to whichever side held them.

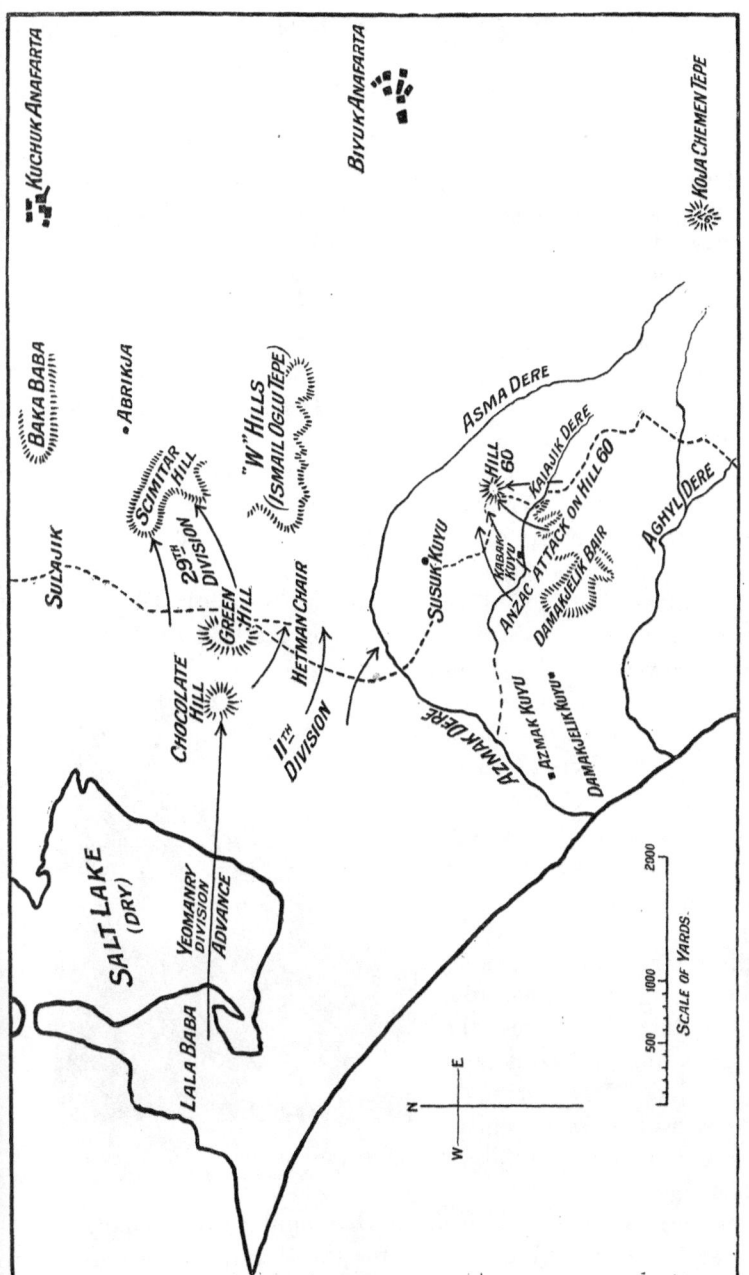

Sketch Map to Illustrate the Battles for Scimitar Hill and Hill 60.
"Kuyu" is the Turkish name for well. There were many valuable wells between Kaiajik Aghala and the sea.

The Attack on Scimitar Hill.

On the night of August 20/21, the 29th Division assembled at Chocolate Hills and prepared for the advance on the morrow. All that day they kept under observation their objective for the morrow—the ill-starred Scimitar.

The preliminary bombardment was very heavy for Gallipoli, but a mist on the Suvla plain favoured the enemy, interfering with the aim of our gunners. At 3.15 in the afternoon the 34th Brigade reached their objective—the trenches on the plain near Hetman Chair; but the 32nd Brigade lost direction, and instead of taking the communication trench leading to the "W" Hills, went far north of it and suffered heavy casualties. The 33rd Brigade went out to retrieve the situation, but made the same mistake and failed entirely in its object.

Just after 3.30, the 87th Brigade of the 29th Division, taking advantage of every bush and every fold in the ground, moved steadily from Chocolate Hill towards the Scimitar. The 1st Royal Inniskilling Fusiliers stormed the crest and chased the Turks back towards the high ground leading to Kuchuk Anafarta. But just higher than the first crest of the Scimitar were other rows of Turkish trenches. From the machine guns there, from the field guns of "W" Hills, and from Tekke Tepe, came a storm of lead. The Scimitar was swept with a devastating converging fire.

OFFICERS OF THE 29TH DIVISION IN THE TRENCHES AT SUVLA.

The 86th Brigade was to attack the right of the Scimitar, and merge with the 87th Brigade for the attack on the crest; but the badly-directed 32nd and 33rd Brigades of the 13th Division were now scattered over the ground between Green

Hill and the Scimitar. These troops got mixed with the regulars and threw them into confusion; but born of long training, led by experienced officers, companies emerged from the chaos, and pressed on to the Scimitar. Then a great fire broke out in the undergrowth and little headway could be made.

At five o'clock the Yeomanry were called from the reserve at Lala Baba. With their hearts in their mouths, the watchers from the Anzac hills saw the long lines extend in open order and move across the wide expanse of plain. Right across the dry Salt lake the troopers quickly marched. The wonder is that so few casualties occurred. They had some difficulty in pressing through the scattered men of the 13th Division round the Chocolate Hills; but by 7 o'clock at least one brigade was at the foot of the Scimitar. Darkness fell as they commenced to work their way to the crest. The converging fire again swept the crest and they too suffered the fate of the Inniskillings and had to withdraw after suffering fearful loss.

Scimitar Hill, which was taken so easily by the 6th East Yorks and so tragically abandoned on August 8th, cost over 5000 casualities. There was not an atom of gain, for everywhere the troops fell back to the original line.

The First Attack on Kaiajik Aghala.

The attack from Anzac met with better fortune. It will be remembered that the Left Covering Force occupied Damajelik Bair on the morning of August 7. The 4th Australian Brigade which fell back from Abdel Rahman had dug in along the southern bank of the headwaters of the Kaiajik Dere.

The line to be attacked was shaped like a boomerang. The operation was divided into two parts.

(1) The 29th Indian Brigade of Ghurkas and Sikhs was to seize the important wells, principally Kabak Kuyu —the Suvla end of the boomerang.

(2) The other force under Brig.-General Russell was to storm Kaiajik Aghala, which we knew as Hill 60—this was the elbow and the Anzac end of the boomerang.

OCEAN BEACH AFTER THE AUGUST OFFENSIVE. The road along the beach, the new wharfs from
[Lent by N.Z. Y.M.C.A.

The First Attack on Kaiajik Aghala.

The troops for (2) were disposed from right to left as follows:—

(a) The 4th Australian Infantry Brigade, now reduced to about 1,400 men, had available for the attack about 400 men from the 13th and 14th Battalions.

(b) The Canterbury Mounted Rifles were already on the ground, and the Otago Mounted Rifles were brought over to reinforce them. To each of these regiments a platoon of Maoris was attached.

(c) Detachments of the 5th Connaught Rangers (10th Div.), the 4th South Wales Borderers (13th Div.) and the 10th Hampshires (10th Div.) were on the extreme left, where the South Wales Borderers had been since August 7 waiting for the joining up of the Suvla forces. The Indians, it must be remembered, were also part of the Anzac Army.

The ravine of the Kaiajik Aghala separated the Australians and New Zealanders from their objective. This ravine gradually broadened out in front of the New Army troops, and debouched on the wide open plain around the wells of Kabak Kuyu and Susuk Kuyu.

The line was to be attacked as follows:—

Kabak Kuyu.
29th Indian Inf. Brigade.

The Hill of Kaiajik Aghala (Hill 60)

Connaughts	Canterbury M.R.	Otago M.R.	13th & 14th
S.W. Borderers	Maoris	Maoris	Batt. A.I.F.
Hampshires			(about 500 men)

By some strange mischance, the artillery bombardment which was so liberal at Suvla, overlooked Hill 60 altogether. But at 3.30 the troops made ready for the advance.

The 13th and 14th Australian Battalions—those veterans of Pope's and Quinn's, the men who early in August struggled on to the Abdel Rahman—dashed down the slope. Losing heavily, they raced into the gully and up the other side. Beaten by Turkish machine gun fire, they held their ground, but could not get on.

The New Zealand attack had about 800 yards to go. Squadron and troop leaders spent the day observing the objective and the best lines of advance. They went back to their men, explained the position and made clear to everyone that the attack was to be by bayonet only, then bombs. The formation was to be in lines of successive troops; each ridge to be taken advantage of as a reforming point for a fresh advance.

There was some wonderment at the lack of artillery fire, but punctually at 3.30, over the top went the troopers. Down the slope went the Canterburys and Otagos. Troop after troop dived into the hail of death and pushed on to the first ridge to collect their scattered fragments. Each troop made its fifty yard rushes and fell down exhausted. These men had lived for months on hard rations and were weakened by dysentery and fatigue. But on they swept again. It was a triumph of resolute minds over wasted bodies. Reaching the shelter of the gully, they reformed and commenced the steep ascent. Between the large ridge and the Turkish trench there was about 100 yards of bullet-swept scrub. Dozens of the troopers fell never to rise again; the wounded crept into positions of comparative safety. The Turkish shells set the scrub and grass on fire, but luckily there was little wind, and the little there was blew the flames away from our wounded.

By now the Canterburys and Otagos had reached the first enemy trench, and a bomb fight ensued. Down the communication trench the Turk was driven. Our men came across an enemy machine gun, which was promptly turned on to the fugitives. Back came the Turk with a counter attack, but the troopers stuck like limpets to their hardly-won position.

The position now was: The Indians had seized the well, and were well round the Suvla flank of Hill 60. The N.Z.M.R. had 150 yards of the Turkish trenches; but on the right, the 13th and 14th Australians could not get on. We had a precarious hold that night, as the Connaughts sent round between us and the Indians were mercilessly bombed back again.

A most dramatic incident occurred when there was a sudden cry of "cease fire," and from the Turkish trenches on Kaiajik Aghala over 150 Turks issued with their hands held high in the air. They had rifles with them, but their movements and demeanour strongly suggested that they were willing to be taken prisoners. There was no one who could talk Turkish, so an interpreter was sent for. But before he arrived our men were out of the trenches trying to carry on a conversation with the Turks, who seemed perfectly friendly, but could not understand our words or signs that they must put down their arms and come quietly away. Suddenly shooting rang out on the right and left. But the O.C. Otago Mounteds went right out into No Man's Land towards the Turkish trenches, surrounded by a mob of Turks. He was convinced that we were about to make one of the biggest hauls of prisoners in the campaign. The few New Zealanders were hopelessly outnumbered, but still they tried to indicate by signs and pantomimic gestures that the Turks must first lay down their arms. By this time firing was brisk in other parts of the line. Some Turks who came to our trenches reached down to assist our fellows out, but our men pulled them in and made them prisoners, very much to their annoyance. The Otago colonel got right to the enemy's trench, and a Turkish officer tried to pull him in. This did not seem good enough, so in the grey of the morning the colonel, a lonely figure, retraced his steps across No Man's Land. Then firing became general, but not before we had captured a dozen of the enemy.

To this day the senior officers who were on the spot are not certain of the Turk's intention, but as it was discovered that all the prisoners and the dead carried many bombs, it is almost certain that they did not wish to surrender. The most likely story is that a few New Army men were captured out on the Suvla Flats, and told the enemy intelligence officers that we were badly shaken and perhaps would surrender. So this party came down to conduct us into their lines. But instead of finding a place in the line —if there was one—where men were willing to give themselves up, they came upon a nest of hornets that stung them very severely.

During the rest of the night, communications were dug from the old Australian trenches to their new front line on the other side of the Kaiajik Dere. The New Zealanders in the Kaiajik trenches were not in touch with the Australians on the right.

The newly arrived battalion of Australian Infantry—the 18th—now came out from Anzac as reinforcements. This was at 4.30 a.m. Two companies were taken round by the Kabak well, along an old Turkish road, and sent to attack the northern flank of the hill. At first they were very successful, but the bombing tactics of the enemy were too much for the newly arrived soldiers, who had to evacuate —about 9 a.m. on the 22nd. At 11 a.m. the N.Z.M.R. again took part of those trenches on the extreme left, and built a sandbag barricade.

The position now was that the front line trench on Hill 60 was held for about 200 yards by the New Zealand Mounted Rifles. This trench ran approximately round the 60 metre contour line. We built traverses to separate us from the enemy, who held the rest of the trench.

This attack had fallen very heavily on the troops engaged. The Canterburys, Otagos and Maoris had severe losses—the Canterburys losing 58 per cent. of their effictives, the Otagos 65 per cent. But we had taken part of the enemy's trench, and that was something—in fact, the only thing gained in the whole line from the Asma Dere to the Chocolate Hills.

We set to work on our communication trenches, and the Turks dug and dug until they made the rest of Kaiajik Aghala into a veritable redoubt.

Second Assault on Kaiajik Aghala.

For the next few days the units in the line carried on an incessant bomb and rifle duel, but it was decided to make one more effort to win the coveted hill.

In the reorganization which took place for the second attack, the disposition was as follows:—

On the right a detachment of the 4th Australian Infantry Brigade (250 men), with 100 men of the 17th Battalion,

Second Assault on Kaiajik Aghala.

A.I.F. In the centre, the four regiments of the N.Z. Mounted Rifles Brigade (300 men), with 100 men of the 18th Battalion, A.I.F. On the left were the 5th Connaught Rangers, totalling 250 men.

This attack on Contour 60 of Kaiajik Aghala was timed for 5 p.m., with an artillery bombardment for an hour prior to that. The gunners promised 500 H.E. shells over the space of 500 yards square. In our section of the attack 5 officers and 100 men of the Canterbury Mounteds were to form the first line, with special bombing parties of 20 men of the Aucklands supporting the right and left flanks; Wellington and Otago Mounted Rifles made the second line; the 18th Battalion, A.I.F. the third line. Bayonets and bombs only were to be used. The Canterbury men took up their places in the trench at 4.30 p.m. with the other regiments in the communication trench.

After a bombardment by our artillery, at 5 p.m. our men jumped out to advance and were immediately under a terribly hot fire from machine guns and rifles. But they never wavered, and with men falling everywhere they continued in one long straight line, magnificent in their courage, on into the first trench where they disappeared for 10 or 15 minutes, amongst a nest of live Turks. Finishing these off, without more hesitation, they rose again and advanced under the same withering fire, fewer in numbers, but dauntless in determination, only to meet a new foe in the enemy's shrapnel.

The casualties were fearful. But still they pressed on to the second trench, then the third. Men were falling more quickly now. Yet it was a charge to stir the heart and quicken the blood of a stoic, and so forlorn it looked against such dreadful odds. The little pink flanking flags were gradually moving forward as the artillery exploded their shells just in front of them. It was noticeable that the 4th Australian Infantry Brigade had not been able to make an advance on the right, and the troops on our left were making little headway. Our machine guns now hurried forward to take up a forward position and all hung on to the ground gained as darkness set in. Wounded, slightly and severely, now began to pour into the dressing stations.

It then became a bomb duel for the remainder of the night. The trenches were choked with dead and wounded Turks and our own people, and were so narrow that no stretchers could be used to send them out.

During the early hours of the morning the 18th Australians continued to improve and deepen their trenches. Up and down the trenches roamed the padres of the Mounted Rifles so that they might be near the men. Chaplain Grant, the beloved padre of the Wellington Mounted Rifles

[Photo by Rev. E. O. Blamires, C.F.
PADRE GRANT OUT AT HILL 60.
This picture was taken about an hour before his death.

laboured with a comrade attending to the wounded. He heard a man crying out in the scrub, so he took the risk and went beyond the barricade erected to divide our line from the Turks. Bandaging friend and foe, the two chaplains pushed on, but on rounding a traverse, they came suddenly on a party of Turks, and Padre Grant was killed instantly.

The enemy now began to enfilade with 75m. guns from the east. Their gunners knew the range to a yard, for these were his own captured trenches he was shelling. There seemed to be no escaping these terrible guns; man after man, group after group, was destroyed, but the survivors held stubbornly on. Up in the salient held by our fellows, the Turk attacked again and again, but the Mounted Rifles stood to it. New Zealanders have a tradition that they cannot be shifted out of reasonable trenches.

The 9th Light Horse, about 200 strong, were placed at General Russell's disposal and were ordered to come over from Walker's Ridge. They arrived at 10 o'clock, and an hour later two parties of 50 each, were taken over to the trenches to help hold our left. They encountered very strong opposition, and had to fall back again to a barricade, which was held by them for the rest of the night.

The position was greatly improved during the day, large working parties being kept going deepening the trenches. The work was much interrupted by shell fire from Abdel Rahman Bair.

[*Photo by Rev. E. O. Blamires, C.F.*
AFTER HILL 60: THE REMNANTS OF THE AUCKLAND MOUNTED RIFLES.

At 2 p.m. the officers of the 10th Light Horse came over from Walker's Ridge and were shown the position. A plan was unfolded whereby these Light Horsemen might attack an essential piece of trench away on the left. That night the old 10th, our comrades of Walker's Ridge, came over to Kaiajik, and at 11 o'clock, in the darkness of the night, fell upon the Turks in the remainder of the trench. This was the climax. Bomb as the Turk might, he could not shift the Light Horse and Mounted Rifles. It was here that Thossell of the Light Horse got his V.C. for holding the barricade against persistent bombing attacks. The top of Kaiajik Aghala was now partly in our hands. We never gained the whole of the crest; but what we took on August 21/28 we held till the evacuation.

Three machine guns and 46 prisoners were taken, as well as three trench mortars, 300 Turkish rifles, 60,000 rounds of small arm ammunition, and 500 bombs. The estimate of the Turkish losses was given at 5,000, but this is likely an exaggeration.

ALONGSIDE THE HOSPITAL SHIP "MAHENO."

Many of the wounded in these two battles for Kaiajik Aghala were fortunate enough to be taken aboard our own Hospital Ship—the "Maheno"—which arrived off Anzac on August 26. With what joy did the soldiers welcome the clean sheets, the hot baths, the thousand and one comforts and the sight of real New Zealand girls. After the hand-to-hand struggle at Hill 60, to lie at rest on the "Maheno" and watch the nurses was like creeping quietly into heaven.

CHAPTER XVI.

Preparing for the End.

The struggle near Kaiajik Aghala was the last pitched battle on the Peninsula. After the desperate landings in April; the trench warfare of May, June and July; the titanic efforts of August—four strenuous and bloody months—we were forced to admit that at Helles, Anzac and Suvla, we were still holding only the lower fringes of the Turkish position. The troops, weakened by continual hardships and malnutrition, were an easy prey to dysentery and

[*Lent by Lieut Carr, A.M.R.*

AN OFFICERS DUGOUT.
On the left is the soldiers pack and an empty rum jar; on the right of the "door" a petrol tin for water.

similar ailments. The dressing stations were also kept busy by men troubled with septic sores. Scratched by the prickly scrub, or with a meat or jam tin, the wounds were healed with great difficulty, which was not surprising, as the men were not strong enough to throw off or resist even the most trifling ailment.

Resting at Sarpi.

About the middle of September, taking advantage of the arrival of the 2nd Australian Division, it became possible to relieve the troops of the two veteran Colonial divisions,

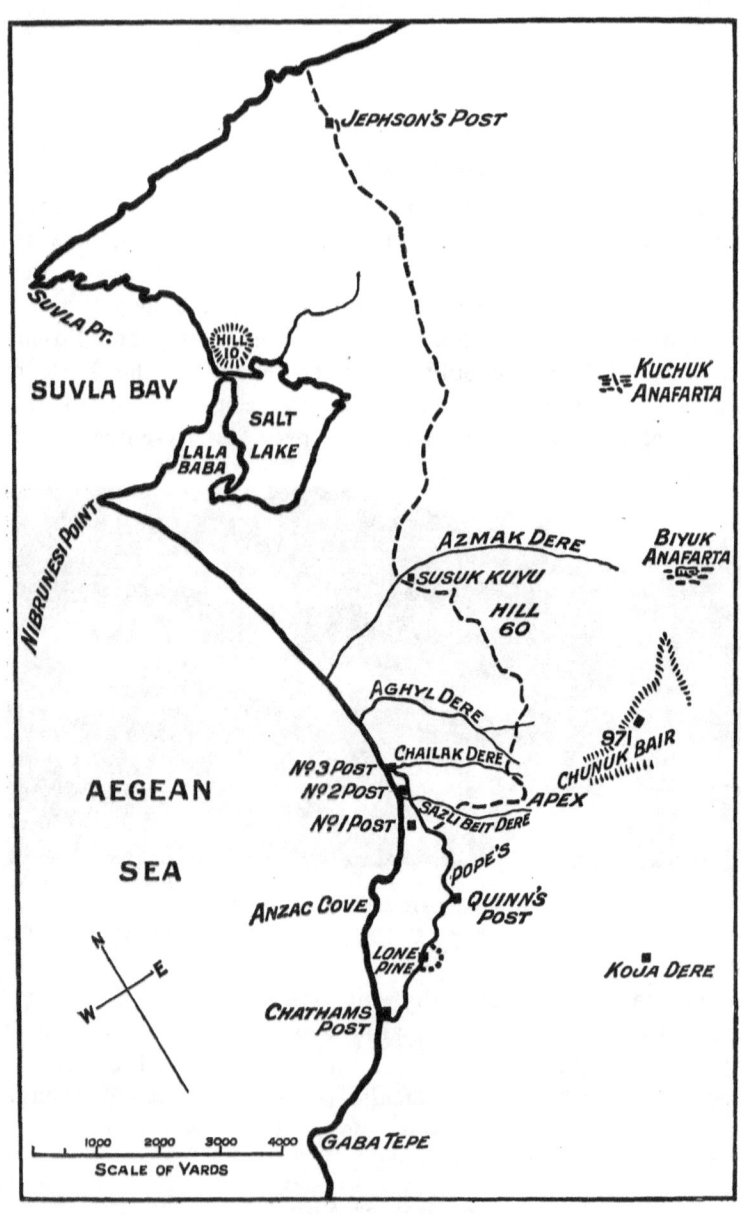

A Sketch Map of the New Anzac Line.

Chatham's Post to No. 3 Post were the original Anzac boundaries. The dotted line at Lone Pine, and from the Apex to Jephson's Post indicates the territory gained in August. The Anzac area went as far as Hill 60.

excepting the New Zealand and Australian divisional troops (artillery, engineers, A.S.C. and ambulance) who went through unrelieved right up to the evacuation.

The N.Z.M.R. Brigade at Cheshire Ridge handed over to some recently arrived Australians, leaving only a few officers and men as machine gun crews. The remainder of the brigade —20 officers and 229 other ranks—were accommodated in one small barge! It was only on occasions such as this that we could comprehend our losses. The old "Osmanieh" sailed for Lemnos, and the brigade disembarked at Mudros early on September 14, and marched by road to Sarpi Camp, about three miles from the pier. This road connected Mudros with the chief town of the island, Castro. Tents were scarce, and during the night a torrential rain made everybody most unhappy. The ground was very soft, but a hot sun made things more bearable during the day. A few tents were erected for the Infantry Brigade which was expected during the day.

The infantry battalions were in the same plight as the mounted regiments. Although having absorbed the 3rd, 4th, and 5th Reinforcements, these one-thousand-strong battalions of the landing were now pathetically weak—the strongest not totally more than 300 men. Four months of living on monotonous food, of constant hammering at the Turk, of thirst and danger and fatigue, had left its mark on the hollow-cheeked, sunken-eyed, but dauntless-spirited soldiers of Anzac. Arriving at night, the men of the N.Z. Infantry Brigade stumbled along the dark and dirty highway. Many of the troops slept by the wayside rather than struggle on and further weaken themselves. As there were few tents at the camping place, it turned out that the ones who did struggle on were in no sense rewarded, and to make matters worse, a real Mediterranean downpour set in. Daily more "Indian pattern" tents arrived, into which as many as forty men crept at night. Gradually the number of tents increased, the weather cleared, and the men made an effort to extract a little pleasure out of life.

Here at least there was no shelling, and the food, in quality and quantity, surpassed our most sanguine expectations. For the first time on active service we tasted the luxury of canteens. Even recreational institutes sprang up. Day by day the men gained strength until they were colourable imitations of the original arrivals at Anzac. How genuinely pleased we were to get the many gifts of eatables from New Zealand, and from good friends in England and Scotland—these good people can never realize what pickles, strawberry jam, condensed milk, crisp Edinburgh shortbread, illustrated periodicals, and letters meant to those war-worn, homesick men.

A gift particularly touching was a large consignment of sweets packed in tins by the school children of the Dominion. Some of the cases had evidently been stowed too near the ship's boilers, as, on being opened, there was discovered a conglomerate mass of molten sugar, tin, and little notes

A FRENCH SENEGALESE.
Dressed in white with a red sash, these troops were very vain and like all negroes could not keep their hands off the henroost.

from the various packers. Weird mixture though it was, the sweets were most acceptable, and appreciated not only for their value, but for the kindly solicitude that prompted the service.

Nurses!

The camp was thrilled when Canadian nurses were discovered on the island. With their wonderful ways, their delightful accents, and their cute little naval capes, the memory of those nurses working away in that hell-hole of Mudros should never be forgotten. On the road from Anzac, Suvla and Helles; on this dusty, rocky island; surrounded by that atmosphere of desolation and suffering caused by an aggregation of wounded and broken men—these girls, with no halfpenny illustrated paper to print their pictures and sing their praises, slaved away in the Mudros hospitals and saved the lives of many New Zealanders who must have perished had it not been for the devotion of the nurses. The soldiers of New Zealand can never adequately express their thanks for the magnificent work of those Canadian and Australian women at Lemnos, and the British, Australian and New Zealand nurses who toiled so heroically on those awful journeys in the hospital ships from Anzac to Mudros, Alexandria and Malta.

War has some compensations, after all. One begins to realize that we are so dependent on our fellows for most of the happiness and joys of life. Between the sailormen and the Colonials, too, there was a strong bond of friendship. This became very manifest after the landings, and further intimate acquaintance strengthened those early ties. The latest expression of these feelings came from the cruisers and destroyers in the bay. The crews had a "tarpaulin muster," the result of which was a present for every man in the division of half a pound of tobacco, at a time when it was specially acceptable.

Hot Baths at Thermos.

Most welcome news was that, at Thermos, about three miles away, hot baths could be had. From the day when the baths were built, they could not have been more crowded. Since leaving Egypt, five months before, hot baths were unknown, unless one was lucky and sufficiently hurt to be put aboard a hospital ship. So out to Thermos hurried the men, to whom a hot bath was a boon beyond price. The little stone building was below ground level, the inside lined with marble, and with marble basins full and overflowing in each corner so that the marble floor was also awash. The procedure was to strip off and with a little dipper pour the water over oneself. Thermos became the most popular resort on the island.

In the little villages, too, very good meals could be obtained—especially those delicious Continental omelettes made only in countries where eggs, tomatoes and fine herbs are estimated at their full value. The mild Greek beer was also most palatable. Mixed with the wine of the country, it made even the listless Anzacs quite hilarious. The quaint old windmills on the hill, and the church in the village square, where the gossips gathered together, were reminiscent of the Old World life made familiar to us in our youth by means of books and pictures. Indeed, some of these old villages seemed just like an ancient painting come to life. Flocks of sheep with little bells on their necks made sweet tinkling music as they wandered to and from their pasture lands; by the roadside the comely (if rather fat) Greek women worked in the fields, and winnowed in olden style their crops of grain and seeds; on the hillside the ancient windmills ground corn which made a most palatable brown bread; under the spreading tree in the village square, picturesque old patriarchs, apparently telling the tales of ancient Greece, were really discussing how much money they could extract in the shortest time from these open-handed, spendthrift warriors!

THE MAIN STREET IN MUDROS.

The Problem of a Mixed Coinage.

The troops certainly had plenty of money to spend, and indulged in orgies of tinned fish, tinned fruit, and tinned sausages from the naval canteens, supplemented by melons, grapes, figs and eggs bought from the villagers. The Mudros shopkeeper made a small fortune out of the exchange of English money. Generally we had English treasury notes for one pound and ten shillings. These were over-printed in Turkish, so that their value might be comprehended in captured villages, but so far Kuchuk Anafarta and Krithia had resisted our efforts to make them legal tender!

Perhaps the strangest thing of all was the readiness with which Australian silver was accepted. A few years ago it was not legal tender in New Zealand, but away up here in the Levant, and all over Egypt, it was not questioned. The emu and kangaroo signified nothing to these simple folk, but did not the other side picture King George of England?

[Photo by the Author.
THE VILLAGE PUMP.
A sentry on guard at Mudros. Greeks drawing water with the ubiquitous kerosene tin.

The change given for an English pound was enough to make the soldier join the scientists in praying for the early adoption of a universal coinage. French Colonials from Senegal and Tunis brought their own money with them; French territorials contributed francs and centimes to the medley; Egyptian labourers tendered their piastres and millemes; Greek, Turkish and Italian money circulated freely; English and Australian was as good as the best—so, when a man got his change, the silver would be Australian, the nickels would be endorsed with an inscription which was Greek in more ways than one, while the coppers bore on one side a meaningless Arabic scrawl and "Tunis" on the other!

Welcome Reinforcements.

The arrival of the 6th Reinforcements gave a tremendous fillip to the sadly depleted brigades. To the 20 officers and

200 other ranks of the N.Z.M.R. Brigade were added a draft of 30 officers and 1060 men of eager volunteers. The Infantry Brigade was reinforced in a like manner. The new men were so fresh and fit, rosy-cheeked and cheery. "Just like a lot of young schoolboys," said an officer. "I never realized before how different the newcomer was to the sun-dried, war-stained, weather-beaten Anzac."

[Lent by Lieut Carr, A.M.R.
AUCKLAND MOUNTED RIFLES AT LEMNOS.

With mixed feelings the units learned that they were to return to Anzac. This rest at Sarpi had been a great relief. Strengthened by the fresh blood of the reinforcements, strong in the veteran's knowledge of warfare, the troops once again embarked. "I'm glad we're going home," said one boy. Strange what we can get accustomed to call "Home"! Farewells were exchanged with the nurses, the sailormen and the Greek ladies gathered round the village pump. Lemnos was once again lost to view and the pleasant sojourn at Sarpi became only a memory.

The Seething Pot of Balkan Politics.

During the months of midsummer the political situation in Europe gave the staffs and soldiers of the Mediterranean Expeditionary Force something to think about. We studied the Balkan situation and knew of the different candidates and parties struggling for dominance in Greece. The boy

The Seething Pot of Balkan Politics.

from Awarua waited anxiously for the latest election return from the islands of the Cyclades!

And now the Russian armies on which we had so much depended were being hurled from line to line by the Austro-Germans. Warsaw and Brest-Litovsk fell in August; Grodno and Vilna in September. It was reluctantly admitted that no help could be expected from Russia.

Meanwhile the Green Premier, Venizelos, who had been returned to office with an overwhelming majority in June, experienced opposition from King Constantine. It was understood that the Greeks would always help the Serbians if attacked by an outside power, but to the disgust of all true lovers of freedom, the Greeks refused to move. Serbia's cup of bitterness was filled to overflowing on September 19. when a powerful Austro-German force struck again at that gallant army which but a few months before so decisively punished the Austrians. The next day Bulgaria made public a treaty (secretly signed two months before) throwing in her lot with Germany, Austria and Turkey!

King Constantine, convinced that Germany must win the war on land, prevented the Greeks coming to the assistance of their traditional friends. So it was that Serbia found herself assailed on one side by the Austro-Germans, and threatened by the Bulgarians on the other.

The French and British wished to help their ally, Serbia, but once again the old complaint was evident—a shortage of trained available men. See how this re-acted on the Gallipoli compaign: Sir Ian Hamilton was asked if he could now spare three Divisions! With the consent of the French, the 53rd (Welsh) Division, the 10th (Irish) Division from Suvla, and the 2nd (French) Division from Helles were sent to Salonika. Thus was the Gallipoli army despoiled to provide troops for the new venture at Salonika, whence with other allied troops, it was thought an effort could be made to save Serbia. But once again the allied help arrived in time only to fight a rearguard action, and Serbia shared the fate of Belgium.

Salonika absorbed more and more British troops—troops which might have made all the difference if they had been ready and released a little earlier for the attacks on Sari Bair. On the Western Front a great effort was being made to concentrate men, ammunition, and guns, for the coming great offensive, which culminated in Neuve Chapelle, Loos, and the French attacks in Champagne.

The British authorities—almost beside themselves with the demands from the Western Front; troubled by the hesitancy of the Greeks; dumbfounded by the deceitfulness of the Bulgarians; appalled by the evident collapse of the

[Photo by Col. Falla, C.M.G., D.S.O.
WATER CARRIERS OF THE 4TH HOWITZER BATTERY.
These small donkeys were purchasable in the Ægean Islands at about two pounds each.

Russians; and now faced with the necessity of providing a force at Salonika, had, in taking three divisions from the Peninsula, again demonstrated that the Gallipoli campaign did not have the whole-hearted support of those responsible for its vigorous prosecution. They had not realized that, perhaps more in war than in other matters, things done by halves are never done right.

So it was that while the troops were resting at Sarpi, the fate of the Gallipoli adventure was being decided elsewhere. All the gallantry, heroism, and sacrifice of the British, Indian, French and Colonial troops were to be sacrificed because the Allies, caught unprepared by the Central Powers, had no well-defined plan of action. Nations unprepared must always pay the price in flesh and blood.

The Responsibility of Australia and New Zealand.

In this matter the people of New Zealand are not one whit better than their kinsfolk of the Old Land, of Canada, of South Africa, of Australia. The people of New Zealand cannot preen themselves in the knowledge that they were prepared for war. The advocates of preparedness had been for years voices crying in the wilderness. A little reasoning here may be of value. For of what use is experience and history if we do not measure our shortcomings?

Ultimately New Zealand maintained a Division in the Field. At the end of the war—in that we had twelve, instead of nine battalions of infantry—we had the strongest division in all the Allied Armies.

Australia maintained five, and always four, divisions in France. Now the August offensive in Gallipoli took place just one year after war had been declared between Great Britain and Germany. Yet New Zealand—because, before the war, the people refused to comprehend the German challenge for world dominion—could not put into the field more than two brigades. It was not that the public was not warned, but the English-speaking peoples will not see that if we must do the world's work we must use worldly tools. We are men in a world of men, and despite the visionaries and the dreamers, the last appeal is to force. This may be regrettable, but unfortunately it is true!

If the Australians could have placed their four magnificent divisions at Anzac and Suvla; if New Zealand could have loosed a full division at Chunuk Bair, while the Australians went for Hill 971 and Suvla—there perhaps would be no talk of "the Gallipoli failure." Admitting that the New Army divisions were not of a calibre required for desperate fighting in rough country, they were certainly better from a soldier's point of view than the excellent material not yet available from Australia and New Zealand.

General Hamilton is Recalled.

The story of Sir Ian Hamilton's recall is best told in his own words. After describing the battle for Kaiajik Aghala, he says: "From this date onwards up to the date of my departure on 17th October, the flow of munitions and drafts fell away. Sickness, the legacy of a desperate trying summer, took heavy toll of the survivors of so many arduous conflicts. No longer was there any question of operations on the grand scale, but with such troops it was difficult to be downhearted. All ranks were cheerful; all remained confident that so long as they stuck to their guns, their country would stick to them, and see them through the last and greatest of the crusades."

"On the 11th October, Your Lordship cabled asking me for an estimate of the losses which would be involved in an evacuation of the Peninsula. On the 12th October I replied in terms showing that such a step was to me unthinkable.

[*Photo by Captain Wilding, N.Z.F.A.*
A GUN PIT OF THE 6TH HOWITZER BATTERY, N.Z.F.A.

On the 16th October I received a cable recalling me to London for the reason, as I was informed by Your Lordship on my arrival, that His Majesty's Government desired a fresh unbiased opinion, from a responsible commander, upon the question of early evacuation."

The reasons for Sir Ian Hamilton's recall were not promulgated to the men on the Peninsula, but his departure was made known to the troops through a manly farewell order. The Colonial divisions were very sorry to see him go. His commanding figure, his charming personality, his warm and expressed admiration for the "ever-victorious Australians and New Zealanders" endeared him to the soldiers, who like himself, were high-spirited, brave, optimistic, and warm-hearted. "Our progress was constant, and if it was painfully slow—they know the truth." And knowing the truth we grieved to see him go. We knew that the age of miracles had passed, and that improvized machines could not stand the rough tests of war.

General Munro Assumes Control.

The new "responsible Commander" proved to be General Sir Charles Munro, K.C.B., a soldier of much experience in former wars, and a fine record of service on the Western Front. Until General Munro's arrival on the Peninsula at the end of October, General Birdwood acted as Commander-in-Chief of the Mediterranean Expeditionary Force. No movement was attempted during this period. There seemed nothing to do but strengthen the line and prepare for the bad weather everyone anticipated.

General Munro arrived on the Peninsula at the end of October. His duty was:

(a) To report on the military situation on the Gallipoli Peninsula.

(b) To express an opinion whether, on purely military grounds, the Peninsula should be evacuated, or whether another attempt should be made to carry it.

(c) The number of troops that would be required—
   (1) To carry the Peninsula.
   (2) To keep the Straits open.
   (3) To take Constantinople.

It was not long before the General was able to report that "the positions occupied by our troops presented a military situation unique in history. The mere fringe of the coast line had been secured. The beaches and piers . . were exposed to registered and observed military fire; our entrenchments were dominated almost throughout by the Turks. The possible artillery positions were insufficient and defective. The force, in short, held a line possessing every possible military defect. The position was without depth, the communications were insecure and dependent on the weather.'' After reviewing the conditions of the troops—they could not get the necessary rest from shellfire as in France; they were much enervated from the diseases in that part of Europe in the summer; through their tremendous losses there was a great dearth of officers competent to lead—these and other considerations forced the General to the conclusion that the troops available on the spot could not achieve or attempt anything decisive.

A UNIQUE PIER AT IMBOS.

Ships sunk to make a pier at Kephalos. A close examination of this large vessel will reveal the deception—she is a merchant steamer with enough fake super-structure to make her look like a British dreadnought. Observe her own funnel with the outer imitation funnel removed. A fleet of these dummy warships often masqueraded in the North Sea as the British Fleet.

On considering the possibilities of an early success by the provision of reinforcements, he came to the conclusion that ''an advance from the positions we held could not be regarded as a reasonable military operation to expect;'' and ''even had we been able to make an advance on the Peninsula, our position would not have been ameliorated to any marked degree, and an advance to Constantinople was quite out of the question.'' Which brought the General to the point: ''Since we could not hope to achieve any purpose by remaining on the Peninsula, the appalling cost to the nation involved in consequence of embarking on an Overseas

Expedition with no base available for the rapid transit of stores, supplies, and personnel, made it [an evacuation] urgent.''

It must be remembered that the soldiers were not informed of these important decisions. It was essential to the plan that absolute secrecy should be observed, and that the enemy should be led to believe that an attack might take place at any time. It was now announced that the Mediterranean Expeditionary Force would consist of two distinct and separate parts—the ''Salonika Army'' under Lieut.-General Sir B. Mahon; and the ''Dardanelles Army'' under Lieut.-General Sir W. Birdwood.

The Great Blizzard.

With the advent of cooler weather the daily sick parades became appreciably smaller, but the men of Anzac were to have still another trial of their endurance and cheerfulness, for on November 27, the weather turned extremely cold. Next morning the troops awoke to find everything white with snow. A snowstorm is not a very disagreeable thing

[*Lent by Lieut Carr, A.M.R.*
New Zealand Troopers in the Snow.

provided one has a comfortable home and clean streets. But at Anzac everyone lived in a dugout—clay walls, clay floor, and a clay track up to the door. The mud and slush made all the tracks as sticky as glue. Locomotion became difficult. Supplies ran short.

The blizzard was almost the fiercest enemy encountered on the Peninsula. We could fight with, and often outwit, the Turk, but against snow and slush we had very little defence.

The troops were greatly indebted to some enterprising men who anticipated cold weather, and issued a small supply of whale oil with instructions how to apply it to the extremities in case of heavy frosts. This simple precaution prevented a very large number of frost-bite cases, as far as the New Zealand brigades were concerned. In comparison with the other troops we were more or less fortunate, as we occupied the higher ground on the Peninsula, and our trenches drained themselves down the slopes. But to those who had to go uphill to the trenches, the task was almost impossible. The deres which were always used as tracks became miniature rivers of mud, eventually becoming frozen and covered with snow. The troops will long remember the small hours of November 28 as they were rudely awakened by the tarpaulin roofs of their never-too-elaborate dug-outs collapsing on top of them with the weight of snow.

[*Photo by Col. Falla, C.M.G., D.S.O.*
ROUGH WEATHER AT ANZAC: A STORM IN ANZAC COVE.

The gale made playthings of the light craft in the Cove. Barges and launches broke from their moorings and completed their sphere of usefulness on the beach. The snow-covered hills presented a wonderful sight. Long icicles hung down from the parapets in the trenches. Comparatively few of our men suffered from frost bite, but it was really a very sad and pitiful sight to see long queues of stretcher bearers carrying the suffering men from the lower slopes.

The poor fellows caught it very badly, especially towards Suvla Bay, as the trenches became inundated

IN THE SNOW; ENGINEERS' DUGOUTS AT THE APEX.

[Photo by Capt. Fairchild, N.Z.D.G.]

with the rushing waters. Many of the occupants were drowned. The brigades of the 29th Division held the trenches into which drained the flood waters from the Kiretch Tepe Sirt. They suffered severely. The Newfoundland contingent, now attached as a battalion to one of these famous brigades, almost revelled in the frost and snow, as might have been expected! The casualties among the Turks, according to those who surrendered at this period (and there were quite a few) must have been enormous.

The most popular place after the blizzard broke out was the ordnance stores, as everyone was in want of extra clothing—and, thank goodness, it was available. It was amusing to see sentries on duty after their experience of the first night. It would have needed a very energetic bullet to penetrate the amount of clothing worn! This is a fair sample:—Hat, balaclava cap, (two if procurable) waterproof cape, greatcoat, tunic, cardigan jacket, shirt, two singlets, two pair of underpants, trousers, puttees, two pair of sox, straw or paper round the feet, and a pair of trench boots! After each tour of duty a compulsory tot of rum was issued. Fortunately for all concerned perfect weather set in about December 4.

This blizzard set all thinking. The chief topic of conversation was "How will we fare, supposing the bitter weather holds out for a couple of months?" as nothing in the way of stores or provisions could be landed other than in perfectly fine weather. Units who had sited their homes near the deres carved out neat villas on higher ground. Hospitals evacuated their sick as quickly as possible, and men not employed making high level roads, were busily engaged in making winter dugouts, well beneath Mother Earth—well beneath advisedly, as about this time we were almost daily informed that our airmen were locating concrete emplacements for heavy howitzers. The Turkish prisoners were also kind enough to say that a large number of heavy guns were being placed in position to blow us into the Mediterranean, which was understood to be very cold in winter.

The Visit of Lord Kitchener.

We did not get many callers, so the visit of Lord Kitchener of Khartoum to the Anzac battlefields started us speculating afresh and making wild conjectures. His visit, needless to say, was very secret. On landing he went straight to Russell's Top and right through the trenches on the Nek. Indians passed by the way were overawed and simply went down on their knees. Needless to say there were wonderful rumours as to what he did and said, but it was generally understood that the decision to evacuate the Peninsula was confirmed there and then. Viewing the country from the observing station of the 2nd Battery, N.Z.F.A., he was much impressed by the rough country. His time at Anzac was chiefly spent at that portion of the line held by the Australians, and it was impossible to suppress the outburst of enthusiam when they recognized Lord Kitchener. The men cheered and he made short speeches, but did not tarry. Soon he stepped aboard the waiting motor launch and sped away north to Suvla.

The Hours of Silence.

A mysterious order for forty-eight hours' silence was hailed with delight by the men. No work was to be attempted, not a shot was to be fired. It was well to let the Turk believe that we could stay silent if we wanted to. If he had come on to investigate, our machine guns would have punished him severely. But he was too wary, and not prepared to put his head into our noose. He made no move. Perhaps he had a hearty laugh at our tempting him, so the ruse certainly prepared him for an occasional silence that might be priceless later on. Presently he became bolder and put out a good deal of wire. The silent period was lengthened and eventually ended at midnight of November 27/28, having lasted seventy-two hours.

CHAPTER XVII.

The Evacuation.

Even as the military feat of the landing was unparalleled, so the situation now presenting itself to the staff was unique. Nowhere in history could be found any precedent. This was not an ordinary strategical or tactical retreat. With our farthest post about 3,000 yards from the sea; with a No Man's Land in many places only 20 yards wide; with the opposing trenches held by an unbeaten enemy—we had to disengage ourselves, march down narrow defiles, and embark from flimsy piers, each one of which was liable to be heavily shelled during the operation. This was no time for muddling through. Cool and ingenious brains propounded plan after plan. The orthodox thing would have been to attack everywhere but at Anzac and Suvla, and under cover of these diversions, seek to beat a retreat. But for many reasons this method did not commend itself. Already indiscreet people in high places had openly talked of evacuating the Peninsula. The Press of England had discussed the matter, and the Turk was bound to be suspicious. So it was decided that the enemy must be deceived as much as possbile. A rumour became persistent that Lord Kitchener, with a great new army, would land and make one last grand effort on Christmas Day.

Secret instructions were issued to officers that the evacuation would be accomplished in three distinct phases. First: all surplus men, supplies, and animals were to be sent away. Secondly: during December 13 and 14, a whole battalion and regiment should go out of each brigade—this alone would reduce the force by over a fourth. Thirdly: on the nights of December 19 and 20 there should embark the last rearguard, specially selected men, in numbers just strong enough to hold the line.

With the memory of the blizzard and its accompanying wind—the wrecked piers at Imbros and Anzac were mute evidence of its fury—General Munro decided to accelerate the evacuation of Anzac and Suvla. On December 8, General Birdwood was ordered to prepare a detailed plan for the daring and perilous enterprise. Almost everything depended on the weather. Unless anything unforseen happened, Rear-Admiral Wemyss undertook to remove all the troops by the night of Sunday, December 19.

Men who had battled on with complaints, only parading sick for treatment, now found that if they complained of the most trivial ailment they were sent away to the hospital ship. It was announced that only the fittest men were to be kept on the Peninsula during the winter. Every night saw the outgoing barges crowded to their fullest capacity; but as it grew light a great show of landing troops would be made—an effort that was not lost upon the Turks, who erected barbed wire more vigorously than ever.

[Lent by Lieut. Moritzson, M.C., M.M., N.Z.E.
PREPARING FOR THE EVACUATION.
The small trestles prepared by the engineers, ready for the decking. They were only to be used in case of emergency.

The evidence gradually became too strong for most men. Parties visiting the beach found ordnance and supply officers astonishingly openhanded. Tinned fish, condensed milk, different varieties of jam and other rarities could be had for the carrying away. Officers' coats, leather leggings, puttees, and many pairs of boots were appropriated. Men going back to the front line looked like itinerant hawkers. Toiling up one of the deres a trooper called to a friend "How's this for evacuation?" A brigadier overheard the remark and bounced out of his dugout. "Who's that talking about evacuation? Don't you know there's an order against using the word? Anyway, there is no evacuation!" The trooper, while lugubriously examining his assortment of ordnance stores, preserved a silence so eloquent that even the attendant staff officer had to turn his face away. "What have you got to say for yourself?" said the brigadier, who felt that he was losing ground. "Nothing," said the quiet trooper, "but I never signed for these," and he held up a pair of gum boots. The brigadier retired before the evidence of such unparalleled generosity.

The Order to Evacuate.

On December 8 it was decided to withdraw those guns that were not required for a passive defence. On December 12, 19 guns of varying calibre, belonging to the N.Z. and A. Division, were embarked. On the same day it was announced that a Rest Camp had been formed at Imbros to which units would go in turn during the winter. Some men still thought it was all a big bluff, but were inclined to be convinced upon the departure of the 3rd and 10th Australian Light Horse Regiments, the Auckland Mounted Rifles, the Otago Infantry Battalion, the Maori Contingent, the 15th Australian Infantry Battalion and other details from the New Zealand and Australian Division.

But the decision could not be concealed indefinitely, and the following order was issued on December 16:

"The Army Corps Commander wishes all ranks of your Division to be now informed of the operations that are about to take place, and a message conveyed to them from him, to say that he deliberately takes them into his confidence, trusting to their discretion and high soldiery qualities to carry out a task, the success of which will largely depend on their individual efforts.

If every man makes up his mind that he will leave the trenches quietly when his turn comes, and sees that everybody else does the same, and that up to that time he will carry on as usual, there will be no difficulty of any kind, and the Army Corps Commander relies on the good sense and proved trustworthiness of every man of the Corps to ensure that this is done.

In case by any chance we are attacked on either days, the Army Corps Commander is confident that the men who have to their credit such deeds as the original landing at Anzac, the repulse of the big Turkish attack on May 18, the capture of Lone Pine, the Apex and Hill 60, will hold their ground with the same valour and steadfastness as heretofore, however small in numbers they may be; and he wishes all men to understand that it is impossible for the Turk to know or tell what our numbers are, even up to the last portion of "C" party on the last night, as long as we stand our ground."

Officers who knew the state of affairs were greatly relieved at the decision, but sick at heart now that the blow had fallen. To give up Anzac and all that it meant! To leave the place where our brothers and friends were lying! Out there in No Man's Land graves were marked where men had fallen, but no cross had been erected, and now the chance was slipping away. Men crept out at night to pay their last visits to those lonely graves. One soldier writing home voiced the undisguised emotion of many:

"My goodness, Mother, how it did go to our hearts—after all we had gone through—how we had slaved and fought—fought and slaved again—and then to think that we had been sizzled in the heat, tortured by flies and thirst, and later nearly frozen to death. It was hard to be told we must give it up. But it was not our wasted energy and sweat that really grieved us. In our hearts it was to know we were leaving our dead comrades behind. That was what every man had in his mind. We thought, too, of you people in New Zealand and what you might think of us. Believe me, it is far harder to screw one's courage up for running away than it is to screw it up for an attack!"

But now that the decision had been made, everyone worked with a will. The horses and mules, valuable vehicles and guns were mostly embarked before the last two nights. The Division withdrew 53 guns in all, only 12 being left for the last night. The batteries were ordered to continue firing in "an extraordinary erratic manner" in order to mystify the enemy. The gunners were busy burying and otherwise destroying surplus stores. The enemy gunners were very energetic during the last three days. Round Russell's Top their shells arrived in myriads, and quite noticeably of better quality. Each battery was reduced until only one gun remained. The New Zealand gunners were determined that they would get all their horses away, and every gun. In order to facilitate an uninterrupted passage for the last night, resourceful and hard-working artillerymen prepared bridges and cuttings to get their beloved pieces away. The last gun from Russell's Top had to cross a perfect maze of communication trenches, but the men refused to rest until the ten improvized bridges were ready for the eventful night.

Preparing for the Big Bluff.

Thursday and Friday nights came, and in the darkness, crowded barges were towed out to the transports lying out to sea. On Friday night an accident occurred that certainly invited disaster. Great piles of stores in all the depots were soaked in kerosene and petrol and made ready for firing just before leaving. By some mischance the heaps at Anzac Cove burst into flame, lighting up the scene like day— with the troops waiting on the beach; the picket boats with their loads puffing in and out; and away out to sea, the waiting transports and the destroyers, ever vigilant. So light it became that the embarkation of troops had to be discontinued. Still the Turk made no sign beyond directing a few shells towards the long tongue of flame. It transpired afterwards that he was under the impression that the valuable stores had been set ablaze by his shell-fire!

By day there was little rest. There seemed to be a thousand things to be done in the short time available. Much material had to be destroyed, rather than let it fall into the hands of the Turk. Ammunition was buried or dropped into the sea. Condensed milk that would have been invaluable earlier in the campaign was destroyed by punching holes in the tins with bayonets. Jar after jar of rum was smashed. Blankets by the thousand and piles of clothing were saturated with petrol ready to be burned. Everything of value to the Turk was made valueless.

"Safe Road to Beach."

At Suvla where there was more room than at Anzac, an inner position was prepared by the erection of a strong barbed wire fence eight feet high, with great gates across the roads. At Anzac, barricades were made in all the principal deres and communication trenches. A final covering position, manned by machine gunners, was prepared. Its left flank was on No. 1 Post, and ran by way of Walker's Ridge, across to Plugge's Plateau and so down Maclagan's Ridge to the sea, very much the line decided on when the re-embarkation after the April landing was momentarily considered. Oh! the what-might-have-beens of those eight tragic months!

There were now only two nights to go, Saturday night and Sunday night. The 20,000 troops remaining at Anzac and Suvla were to be evacuated at the rate of 10,000 per night. The numbers from our division were 3491 on the second last night, and the final 3000 on the last night.

The line from Suvla to Chatham's Post was held as follows:

> 9th Army Corps—The Suvla front up to and including, Hill 60;
>
> N.Z. & A. Division—from the right of Hill 60 to the Apex;
>
> 1st and 2nd Australian Divisions—from Walker's Ridge to Chatham's Post.

The Suvla Army embarked from the piers in Suvla Bay and on the Ocean Beach. The New Zealanders and Australians on the left of Anzac had to come down the three principal deres to the piers on Ocean Beach. The Australians from the centre and right of Anzac naturally moved down Shrapnel Gully and along the beach from the extreme right towards the piers at Anzac Cove.

The New Zealand Brigades were now disposed as follows:

RHODODENDRON SPUR

HILL 60	HILL 100	CHESHIRE RIDGE	THE APEX
Wellington, Otago and Auckland Mounted Rifles		4th Aust. Inf. Brigade	Canterbury, Wellington and Auckland Infantry Battalions

The Mounted Rifles would come down the Aghyl Dere, and the N.Z. Infantry down the Chailak Dere to the Williams Pier on North Beach.

A divisional rendezvous was formed at No. 2 Post. Here the troops paraded according to a timetable, and were drafted into groups of 400—the capacity of those big motor lighters that the men had christened "beetles."

All through the night of that last Saturday at Anzac the little groups assembled, and were packed into the lighters. By 4.30 a.m. on December 19, the last beetle cleared from the shore leaving the "Diehards" of the Division, only 3,000 strong, to hold the line against a mighty army.

It was an anxious day, but there was much to do. Men devised all sorts of mechanism to keep rifles going mechanically after the last party had left. The favourite method was as follows: It takes a certain amount of pressure to pull the trigger of a rifle. After many experiments a device was perfected whereby an empty tin was suspended by a piece of string to the trigger of a loaded rifle. Another tin full of water, but with a small hole in it, was placed above the empty one, so that the water leaked into the bottom one, thus gradually increasing the weight until it was sufficient to pull the trigger!

Actors at Anzac.

In an endeavour to mystify the Turk observers, the few men left at Anzac became very energetic. With packs up they marched uphill wherever the Turk might see them. Like actors impersonating a crowd in a moving picture studio, these small bodies of men passed ostentatiously backwards and forwards until they were tired.

Reinforcement drafts always went in reserve for a time after their arrival, so down in Reserve Gully and Waterfall Gully enthusiastic parties entertained themselves and mystified the enemy by spreading out blankets to dry even as the new arrivals did! The innumerable small fires that smoked incessantly were made to smoke more copiously than ever, for the Turks must fully understand that the great new army was now arriving in strength.

Every man ate as much as he could of the tinned goods now so plentiful. Pennies were tossed freely in the air— "Heads for Constantinople; tails for Cairo!" Everybody was in great spirits and betrayed no anxiety. There was little departure from the normal, except that at the Apex there was heavier shelling than usual.

A, B, and C Parties.

The 3,000 men of the Division still to be withdrawn were divided into three: A, parties totalling 1,300; B, parties totalling 1,100; and C, parties totalling 600. All of A and B were to withdraw and embark as the parties of the preceding night—they came to the divisional rendezvous and embarked in their groups of 400. It was quickly decided that if A parties were for Alexandria, B parties must be for the Beach, and C for Constantinople.

Up the deres, great wire gates had been erected so that if the force was attacked the gates would be shut down and the garrison left to its own resource—to fight where it stood and cover the retirement until 2 a.m., and then retire down the ridges to the beach. It would not be possible to come down the ordinary communication trenches in the deres, for on the sign of an attack, the great barbed gates were to be dropped into place in the entanglements and the deres themselves heavily shelled by the warships. The "last ditchers" were to be sacrificed for the army. There was no lack of volunteers. Australians and New Zealanders; New Army men and Yeomanry; men who had been there since the landing, and men who had recently arrived as reinforcements; men of Anzac and Suvla alike—vied with each other in the endeavour to become included in the "Diehards." These men—whether they came from Midlothian or Yorkshire, Queensland or far Taranaki—were all volunteers, proud of their race and the Empire, and convinced of their personal superiority over the seemingly victorious foe. Messages were left warning the Turk he was on the wrong side, exhorting him to look after our scattered graves and the unburied dead of No Man's Land, and promising to return again and punish all the allies of the Germans.

A rear party of the No. 1 Field Ambulance was detailed to look after the wounded should disaster overtake the rearguard. They were each equipped with a surgical haversack containing field dressing and morphia. The dressing stations were left equipped with the necessary instruments, so that if the Turk did appreciate the situation and come over in force, the wounded might be tended by our own men. It was thought that life-boats from the Hospital Ships might be allowed to approach the shore and take away the serious cases. Luckily there were no casualties in the division, nor, in fact, in the Army Corps.

WATCHING FOR THE TURK.

The day was fairly quiet, but at about 11 o'clock in the morning the kinema actors had so impressed the Turks that much heavy shell was dropped into the communication trenches leading from the beach, and into the gullies where the reserves usually bivouacked. Thanks to the great dug-outs constructed for the winter, there were no casualties.

At 4 o'clock that afternoon, the Turkish shelling increased very much in intensity. Was this a preliminary bombardment before the attack? But the shelling ceased with the sunset, and everything became normal once more.

The Last Night.

The sun went down that evening on a wondrously peaceful scene. The peaks of Samothrace and Imbros were bathed in the glow of a glorious golden sunset. The sea was unruffled by the faintest breeze. Faint wisps of clouds floated lazily across the sky, fitfully obscuring the moon. As soon as it was dark men became very busy.

At ten minutes past six the last gun fired its last shot from Russell's Top, and its removal to the beach commenced over the temporary bridges, down through the wider trenches, past much barbed wire entanglement—over cliff-sides and down Walker's Ridge the proud gunners triumphantly brought their charge, and before eight o'clock were safely embarked on their waiting transports.

Two much-worn guns—not New Zealand ones, but attached to our division—were rendered useless and abandoned. One was a 5-inch howitzer in Australian Valley, the other a 3-pounder Hotchkiss in the Aghyl Dere.

All the men were travelling very light. Previous parties had taken the "Diehards" kits and impedimenta. With a rifle and bayonet and a stock of hand grenades the men of the rearguards took up their positions in the front line. Machine guns were carefully looked to. Ammunition was plentiful. If the Turk did come over he would pay a big price. As one of the normal smells of Anzac was that of tobacco smoke, men smoked packet after packet, and pipe upon pipe. Out to sea, the traffic was quite noticeable to the anxious watchers on the hillside.

A and B Parties Leave.

Soon after dusk the men of the A parties at Anzac and Suvla said goodbye to their comrades of B and C, marched to their respective divisional rendezvous, and passed down the sandbag-muffled piers to the waiting "beetles."

Early on that last night many were confident that the Turk was completely fooled. If he had wanted to attack he would have attacked before dark; if he attacked at dawn he would be too late. If he had known, as some clever people say, that we were leaving, would it not have been a "tremendous victory" if he had come boldly on and overwhelmed the "Diehards?" He certainly would have taken no prisoners—the men of Anzac would have attended to that. But the fact is: the Turk helped us at the evacuation in the same degree as he helped us at the landing!

B party commenced to leave at nine o'clock. It was very hard to go. What might happen to the waiting men of C? However, the barges were waiting and the timing could not be arranged otherwise. So, with a "Goodbye, boys! see you in Cairo!" on their lips, but with misgivings in their hearts, the second last parties left their posts and made for the rendezvous. By 11.25 all of A and B parties were safely embarked without a casualty.

Those left moved quickly from place to place, firing their rifles in order to preserve the "normality" of things. The old trench mortars coughed spasmodically, and the Turks returned the compliment. Away on Walker's Ridge several very heavy bursts of firing broke out. Men could not help questioning themselves. Was Quinn's Post holding out with so numerically weak a garrison? Quinn's that had cost so much to hold all those weary months. It was hard to give up Quinn's!

And Lone Pine! Where the glorious men of those veteran battalions made such a sacrifice for the sake of Anzac—and for the sake of Suvla. These last men, with their boots muffled in sandbags, crept back and meditated at Brown's Dip with its rows of silent eloquent graves. The dead men took Lone Pine from the Turks, the survivors held it against angry hordes, to-night the rearguard was to hand it quietly back!

The men of the New Zealand Infantry Brigade looked out towards The Farm and the fatal crest above it, and thought of those boys who in August went straight for the ridge of Chunuk and doggedly waited for the help from the left, the help that never came. Here the last New Zealanders stood fingering their trigger guards—holding the line at the Apex, only 2,000 yards from the sea. Eight months of incessant striving, a gain of 2,000 yards of bare clay hillside, a loss of so many valuable lives!

And Hill 60! Where the New Zealand Mounted Rifles had refused to be worsted when others fell back! Hill 60! Now honeycombed with galleries hewn out with such an expenditure of blood and sweat. These men of the C parties could not help feeling that the dead deserved a better fate than this. Yet what could be done? No men could have achieved more. If the men of Anzac had failed, they certainly had been faithful failures.

No pains were spared to make everything appear normal. Some men went round lighting candles in the empty dugouts, others concocted placards to welcome the Turks. The soldiers bore no malice. "Goodbye Johnnie, see you soon in the Suez Canal;" and "Remember you didn't push us off, we simply went," are typical. Others were more amusing if not quite so polite! Men wandered up and down firing occasional shots, and at 11.30 the message came round to the men in the line that everywhere the plans were working without a hitch and well up to time. In front of the Apex and near Hill 60 the Turks were putting out more wire in anticipation of the big attack on Christmas Day. They evidently interpreted the shipping off the coast as the prelude to a big attack.

The Last Anxious Moments.

Midnight came and the firing died down as was the normal custom. Slowly the minutes crept by. One o'clock! Still there was no alarm. Some men began to feel the tension very keenly. Everybody else was safe. Would C party get away? At 1.30 the first of the C parties commenced to come in. At 1.45 the duty machine gun at the Apex fired three shots three times in rapid succession. This was the signal for all the machine guns of our infantry brigade to withdraw. With a quarter of the remaining infantry, the gunners marched down the gullies and joined up with the other detachments. The organization worked like clockwork. One party was two minutes early in the Chailak Dere and was halted by its captain until, to the second, the little party resumed its march and dovetailed into the long column now winding down the gully towards the muffled piers.

At two o'clock another party left. The men of the last group were now looking anxiously at their wristlet watches,

[*Photo by Capt. Wilding, N.Z.F.A.*
OFF ANZAC: A GUN OF THE 6TH HOWITZER BATTERY.

which had been carefully synchronized. At about 2.15 each man in the trenches quietly walked out into the nearest communication trench. There was little time to lose. The gate in the Chailak Dere was to be closed at 2.25. Here a staff officer carefully checked the numbers and made sure that all were accounted for.

The New Zealand Mounted Rifles.

Between the 4th Australian Brigade on Cheshire Ridge and the Welsh Horse at Hill 60, were the New Zealand Mounted Rifles. They had the farthest to march from the left flank. But officers had stepped it out and carefully timed the journey from their front line trench to the pier. With careful timing of watches, they got away their A and B parties to the minute.

Last of all came the Canterbury Mounted Rifles, who were steadily sticking to their schedule time of 2 miles per hour. Hand-grenades were tossed into the sea. The motor barges were quickly crowded. As the loaded "beetles" moved slowly out from Anzac a deafening roar and a blinding explosion occurred. Our great mine on the Nek had been detonated. The Turk trenches instantly burst into flame.

[*Lent by Lieut. Lockyer, W.M.R.*
The Wastage of War.
Boots dumped on the wharf at Alexandria after the evacuation.

Fires broke out among the piles of stores. The bay seemed crowded with motor barges and flotillas of trawlers.

Once on the warships the men were hurried below to a meal of hot cocoa, steaming pea soup, and every delicacy the ships' stores could offer.

By 3.40 a.m. the embarkation was complete. Men could hardly realize that the work was accomplished without a terrible disaster. Restraint was thrown aside. New

Zealanders from the Apex and the Lone Pine rearguard of Australians danced wild measures with the sailors on the iron decks.

As the ships moved over towards Imbros, Suvla and Anzac burst into flame. All the stores were afire now and the great tongues of flame seemed to reach to the very heavens. Right along the line Turkish rifles and machine guns opened, but caused no casualties, as most of the bullets plopped harmlessly in the water.

So we said good-bye to Anzac. Next morning the Turk rubbed his eyes and proclaimed a great victory.

The Evacuation of Helles

It was thought that we might hold Helles as we hold Gibraltar, but Mudros was considered an easier base for a naval power. The poor souls of the 29th Division, after being withdrawn from Suvla, hardly had time to rest a day at Mudros before they were ordered to return and hold the line at Helles. They were bitterly disappointed, but were they not tried and trusted Regulars? The Territorials they relieved went back to Egypt for a New Year's dinner in peace; the brigades of the 29th went back to the firing line. This perhaps was the greatest test of the 29th, for the men were sure that the bluff of Anzac and Suvla could not be repeated. They made ready for a heavy rearguard action to cover their retirement. During the days of waiting, it rained and blew until they were perhaps the most miserable men on earth. At least they should have been—but they were British regular soldiers, and there was nothing to do but stick it. So the troops who bore the brunt of the bloodiest landing were to bear the brunt of the evacuation. But a miracle again happened! The Turk could not make up his mind when we were going, and he could not make up his mind to attack. On the night of January 9, the coup came off. There was much heavy shelling of piers and landing places, but the casualties were infinitesimal, though much equipment was lost. The enemy was again baulked of his prey!

CHAPTER XVIII.

The Return to Anzac.

Three years in succession the valleys of Anzac were flooded with the crimson poppies of the Aegean Spring. During these three years the New Zealanders in France and Palestine shared in the vicissitudes and the dearly-bought victories of the Allied Armies.

THE GREAT TURKISH VICTORY MONUMENT ON THE NEK.

While the soldiers were fighting, some of the politicians of England—a few of whom had been prominent in reducing Army and Navy expenditure before the war—enquired with great deliberation into the rights and wrongs of the

---

The illustrations in this Chapter are by Col. Findlay, C.B. and Capt. Douglas Deans of the C.M.R.

Gallipoli campaign. Money that would have been better spent in hand grenades in 1915 was lavishly poured out in trying to discover who was to blame for this and who should be censored for that. It may be said with pride that the people of New Zealand—and the people of Australia, too—did not indulge in recrimination. They knew that the armies were not to blame, and were content to leave it at that.

While commissions investigated ancient history the triumphant Turks erected great monuments on the Peninsula—monuments to commemorate the defeat of the infidels.

* * * *

But the months slipped by, and nearer and nearer crept the forces enveloping the Central Powers. The Bulgars felt the pressure first. When they finally broke and fled up the Seres Road, our airmen bombed them unmercifully. Caught in their mountain passes, they were killed in thousands by our low-flying planes. So was Bulgaria finally bombed out of the war by British airmen.

On October 26, 1918, British cavalry and armoured cars entered Aleppo and cut the Constantinople—Baghdad railway. On October 29, General Marshall's forces on the Tigris severed the Turkish communications at Mosul. The Turkish armies were everywhere helpless.

One day at the end of October a little launch with General Townshend on board slipped out from Chios down near Smyrna, carrying a white flag. A representative of Vice-Admiral Calthorpe, the British naval commander in the Aegean, conducted the liberated hero of Kut-el-Amara and the fully-accredited representatives of the Turkish Government to Mudros—the Mudros of our rendezvous and of our Rest Camp—where the Turkish representatives signed the Armistice terms, preparatory to an unconditional surrender. This was on the evening of October 30. The Armistice came into effect at noon on the following day.

The end of 1918 saw British and French warships lying off the Golden Horn and British soldiers on guard at the forts of Chanak and Kilid Bahr.

Was it not prophesied that one day a New Zealander would sit on London Bridge and survey the ruins of the metropolis? In the year of grace, 1918, the real modern New Zealanders—with the dust of the desert still on their faded tunics, complete with their wristlet watches and folding kodaks—stand on the famous Galata Bridge and snapshot the imperturable Turkish boatmen who seem but faintly interested in the doom of the Ottoman Empire. There in their old slouch hats stand the war-worn troopers—young crusaders who have contributed their full share to the humbling of those despots who for centuries have been the curse of Western Europe.

GOING ASHORE AT MAIDOS.

Among the troops to re-occupy Gallipoli were the Canterbury Mounted Rifles, who, in December, disembarked at Maidos, and with their comrades of the 7th Australian Light Horse, did not hesitate to sit as conquerors on the giant guns of Kilid Bahr.

Up the valley towards Lone Pine they rode, until they came to the Turkish victory monument erected on the site of the famous Australian salient. Then over to Koja Chemen Tepe, to stand in silence where British soldiers had never stood before. This was the moment of triumph: this was the prize for which we had striven in 1915, and now, after all these years, the prize was ours—on the one hand the great forts and Point Nagara running out into the rushing waters of the Narrows; on the other side the great

THE TRIUMPH OF ANZAC.
Men of the Canterbury Mounted Rifles sitting on a 14-inch gun at Kilid Bahr.

RHODODENDRON SPUR FROM THE APEX.
Notice the luxuriant growth of thistle in the old trench lines.

THE PROMISED LAND: THE COUNTRY BEHIND KOJA CHEMEN TEPE.

panorama of the Aegean Sea—Samothrace and Imbros in the distance; the Salt Lake and the fatal plains of Suvla; away South, the forbidding hump of Achi Baba; and closer in, the Anzac beaches, Russell's Top, the tangled steeps of Walker's Ridge, The Farm, and the ridge of Chunuk. These men of the Canterbury Mounted Rifles were the triumphant victors, but slowly they rode down the winding ways of dry watercourses looking for the last resting places of brothers and comrades-in-arms. Never a yard but somebody stopped and silently searched for an indentification disc.

And here on the Nek was the great monument erected by the Turks in honour of their victory in December, 1915!

Down the Aghyl Dere where the gallant Overton rests under the shade of the Turkish trees; out to Hill 60 where the white bones lie in heaps; along to Ari Burnu where the graves are thickly crowded; and so to Anzac Cove itself. Here, pathetic beyond words, were the skeletons of old barges and boats—rotting in the smooth white sand once pockmarked by thousands of hurrying feet; here on the sandy beaches the Turk paid the men of Anzac the greatest compliment, for they had wired the beach against another landing! Did not the daredevils say they would come back? Was it not wise to prepare for possibilities? But the soldiers who went so quietly away in December, 1915, chose to come another way as victors.

This is the end of the Gallipoli campaign. The men of New Zealand were there at the start—here they are as the victors at the end.

* * * *

And now that the struggle is over, now that the great guns of Chanak are silent, and the hillsides once peopled with busy men are again given over to the song birds and the wandering Turkish shepherds—what is the gain to the world? What is the gain to New Zealand?

For assuredly there is some gain? Our eight months struggle—even if it grievously tried us—undoubtedly weakened the military power of the Turks. But it did more. It taught the New Zealander many things. It taught him lessons that stood him in excellent stead on the battlefields of the world. It taught him to respect his own strength and capabilities. For before the war we were an untried and insular people; after Anzac, we were tried and trusted. Before Anzac we had few standards; after Anzac, we knew that, come what may, if it were humanly possible—and often when it seemed almost impossible—New Zealanders would not be found wanting, but would prove irresistible in attack, steadfast and stubborn in defence—and what more can anyone ask of soldiers?

Even as in the war we lost our insularity and found our national spirit, so at Anzac we found our brothers-in-arms, the gallant sons of Australia; and we did our work together —for if the initial "A" stands for Australia, New Zealand furnished the very necessary pivotal consonants. So in the future we must stand together and carry the white man's burden in these Southern Seas.

A Turkish Victory Monument behind No. 1 Post.
The design is carried out with shell-cases. The monument itself was knocked down by our troops.

And if Anzac means suffering, a hopeless longing, aching hearts and a keen sense of loss to many in this land of ours, the gain cannot be measured—for the miner at Quinn's Post did not sweat at the tunnel face in the interests of self; the middies of the picket boats and the men of the trawlers were not working for dividends; the nurses on those hospital ships did not toil the long nights through for praise or notoriety; the women who waited so bravely and patiently at home in hourly dread of the telegraph boy, thought nothing of themselves. One and all made their willing sacrifices for the common good. And that is the message of Anzac to the people of New Zealand: Place the interests of the community before the interests of self, follow in the footsteps of the early pioneers, and make New Zealand a sweeter place for the little children.

ANZAC COVE TO-DAY.

Anzac Cove.
(*From Leon Gellert's "Songs of a Campaign"*)

There's a lonely stretch of hillocks:
   There's a beach asleep and drear,
There's a battered broken fort beside the sea.
   There are sunken trampled graves;
And a little rotting pier:
   And winding paths that wind unceasingly.

There's a torn and silent valley:
   There's a tiny rivulet
With some blood upon the stones beside its mouth.
There are lines of buried bones:
   There's an unpaid waiting debt:
There's a sound of gentle sobbing in the South.

January, 1916.

New Zealand Transports of the Main Body.

		Tons	Knots	Port of Departure	Units on Board	Numbers Carried
N.Z.T. No. 3	"Maunganui"	7,527	16	Wellington	Headquarters Staff, N.Z.E.F. Headquarters N.Z. Infantry Brigade Field Troop N.Z.E. Wellington Infantry Battalion (West Coast Coy.) N.Z. Mounted Field Ambulance	38 Officers 528 Men 204 Horses
N.Z.T. No. 4	"Tahiti"	7,585	17	Lyttelton	Canterbury Mounted Rifles Regt. Wellington Mounted Rifles Regt. (1 Squadron) Canterbury Infantry Battalion (1 Company)	30 Officers 611 Men 282 Horses
N.Z.T. No. 5	"Ruapehu"	7,885	13	Port Chalmers	Otago Mounted Rifles Regt. (1 Squadron) Otago Infantry Battalion (less 2 Companies and Machine Gun Section)	31 Officers 785 Men 244 Horses
N.Z.T. No. 6	"Orari"	6,800	12	Wellington	Wellington Mounted Rifles Regt. (East Coast Squadron and 2 Troops) Surplus horses from other transports	16 Officers 269 Men 728 Horses
N.Z.T. No. 7	"Limerick"	6,827	13	Wellington	N.Z. Field Artillery Brigade (in part) Wellington Infantry Battalion (No. 7 and 8 Platoons)	21 Officers 495 Men 348 Horses
N.Z.T. No. 8	"Star of India"	6,800	11	Auckland	Auckland Mounted Rifles Regt. New Zealand Field Ambulance	30 Officers 652 Men 395 Horses
N.Z.T. No. 9	"Hawkes Bay"	7,207	13	Port Chalmers	Otago Mounted Rifles Regt. (less 1 Squadron) Otago Infantry Battalion (2 Companies and Machine Gun Section)	40 Officers 930 Men 569 Horses
N.Z.T. No. 10	"Arawa"	9,372	12	Wellington	Wellington Infantry Battalion (less West Coast Coy. and 7 and 8 Platoons) Wellington Mounted Rifles Regt. (less 2 troops) Field Artillery Brigade (in part) Signal Troop N.Z.E.	59 Officers 1,259 Men 215 Horses
N.Z.T. No. 11	"Athenic"	12,234	12	Lyttelton	Headquarters Mounted Rifles Brigade Canterbury Mounted Rifles Regt. (2 Squadrons) Canterbury Infantry Battalion (less 1 Company)	54 Officers 1,259 Men 339 Horses
N.Z.T. No. 12	"Waimana"	10,389	14	Auckland	Auckland Mounted Rifles Regiment Auckland Infantry Battalion N.Z. Signal Company N.Z. Divisional Train	61 Officers 1,400 Men 496 Horses

In addition to the units mentioned each transport carried the usual details—Naval Transport Officer, Medical Officers, Chaplains, etc. N.Z.T. No. 1 (s.s. "Moeraki") and N.Z.T. No. 2 (s.s. "Monowai") took the Samoan Force in August, 1914.

Transports Carrying the New Zealand and Australian Division from Alexandria to Gallipoli, April 1915.

Name of Transport.	O.C. Troops.	Adjutant	Units on Board
"ACHAIA"	Major H. Hart Wellington Battalion	Lieut. A. J. Cross Wellington Battalion	Wellington Infantry Battalion (2 Companies)
"ITONUS"	Lt.-Col. W. G. Malone Wellington Battalion	Capt. M. McDonnell Wellington Battalion	Wellington Infantry Battalion (less 2 Companies) Canterbury Infantry Battalion (2 Companies)
"KATUNA"	Major F. Symon R.N.Z.A.	Capt. Clyde McGilp N.Z.F.A.	Headquarters Field Artillery Brigade 1st Battery N.Z.F.A.
"LUTZOW"	Lt.-Col. A. Plugge Auckland Battalion	Capt. A. G. B. Price Auckland Battalion	Divisional Headquarters Auckland Infantry Battalion Divisional Signal Company (Headquarters and No. 1 Section) Canterbury Battalion (less 2 Companies)
"GOSLAR"	Major F. Fergusson Royal Engineers	Capt. F. Waite N.Z.E.	Headquarters Divisional Engineers, N.Z. Engineers No. 1 Field Company New Zealand Engineers Headquarters New Zealand Infantry Brigade No. 1 Field Ambulance, New Zealand Medical Corps Headquarters No. 2 Company Divisional Train and Details, N.Z.A.S.C. Divisional Signal Company (Brigade Section)
"ANNABERG"	Lt.-Col. A. Moore Otago Battalion	Lieut. J. S. Reid Otago Battalion	Otago Infantry Battalion
"HAIDAR PASHA"	Lt.-Col. Pope 16th Battalion	Capt. R. T. McDonald 16th Battalion	16th Battalion Australian Infantry (Headquarters and 3 Companies)
"SEEANGBEE"	Major H. R. Carter 15th Battalion	Capt. C. P. Corsor 15th Battalion	13th Battalion Australian Infantry (1 Company) 15th Battalion Australian Infantry (2 Companies) 16th Battalion Australian Infantry (1 Company)
"AUSTRALIND"	Lt.-Col. Cannan 15th Battalion	Capt. W. C. Willis 15th Battalion	4th New Zealand Howitzer Battery and Ammunition Column 15th Battalion Australian Infantry (less 2 Companies)
"SEEANGCHUN"	Lt.-Col. R. E. Courtney 14th Battalion	Capt. O. M. H. Dare 14th Battalion	Headquarters 4th Australian Infantry Brigade 14th Battalion Australian Infantry
"CALIFORNIAN"	Major I. T. Standish R.N.Z.A.	Lieut. C. Carrington N.Z.F.A.	3rd Battery New Zealand Field Artillery Ammunition Column, New Zealand Field Artillery Brigade 4th Australian Field Ambulance
"ASCOT"	Lt.-Col. G. J. Burnage 13th Battalion	Capt. J H. A. Durrant 13th Battalion	13th Battalion Australian Infantry (Headquarters and 3 Companies) 4th Australian Company Divisional Train (Headquarters and Supply Section)
"SURADA"	Major F. B. Sykes Royal Artillery	Lieut. V. Rogers R.N.Z.A.	2nd Battery New Zealand Field Artillery No. 2 Brigade Ammunition Column

Establishment of Main Body, N.Z.E.F.

Units.	Officers.	Other Ranks.	Total.
HEADQUARTERS STAFF	16	68	84
NEW ZEALAND MOUNTED RIFLES BRIGADE—			
Headquarters	6	28	34
The Auckland Mounted Rifles Regiment	26	523	549
The Canterbury Mounted Rifles Regiment	26	523	549
The Wellington Mounted Rifles Regiment	26	523	549
Field Troop, N.Z.E.	3	74	77
New Zealand Signal Troop, N.Z.E.	1	32	33
New Zealand Mounted Field Ambulance	8	70	78
NEW ZEALAND INFANTRY BRIGADE—			
Headquarters	4	18	22
The Auckland Battalion	33	977	1,010
The Canterbury Battalion	33	977	1,010
The Otago Battalion	33	977	1,010
The Wellington Battalion	33	977	1,010
DIVISIONAL TROOPS—			
The Otago Mounted Rifles Regiment	26	523	549
Divisional Artillery—			
1st Field Artillery Brigade—			
Headquarters	5	38	43
No. 1 Field Battery	5	141	146
No. 2 Field Battery	5	141	146
No. 3 Field Battery	5	141	146
No. 1 Brigade Ammunition Column	3	131	134
Divisional Signal Service—			
New Zealand Signal Company (3 Sections)	4	109	113
Divisional Transport and Supply Units—			
Divisional Train—			
No. 1 (Divisional Headquarters) Company	5	90	95
Army Service Corps (attached to units)	4	125	129
Divisional Medical Units—			
New Zealand Field Ambulance No. 1	13	182	195
Dental Surgeons (unattached)	10	...	10
SERVICES AND DEPARTMENTS—			
Veterinary Surgeons (unattached)	3	...	3
General Base Depot	1	4	5
Army Pay Department	1	5	6
Chaplains	13	13	26
Total	351	7,410	7,761

New Units Raised during Gallipoli Campaign.

Additional Units Formed in New Zealand.

Unit.	Date of Despatch.	Officers.	Other Ranks.	Total.
DIVISIONAL TROOPS—				
Divisional Artillery—				
2nd Field Artillery Brigade—				
Headquarters	12 June, 1915	1	38	39
No. 4 (Howitzer) Battery	14 Dec., 1914	5	141	146
No. 5 Field Battery	17 April, 1915	5	141	146
No. 6 (Howitzer) Battery	12 June, 1915	5	141	146
(B) Howitzer Battery Ammunition Column (for No. 6 (Howitzer) Battery)	12 June, 1915	1	40	41
Divisional Engineers—				
No. 2 Field Company, N.Z.E.	17 April, 1915	6	211	217
Divisional Transport & Supply Units—				
Divisional Train—No. 4 Company	17 April, 1915	5	80	85
Divisional Medical Units—				
New Zealand Field Ambulance No. 2	...	10	182	192
SERVICES AND DEPARTMENTS—				
No. 1 Stationary Hospital	21 May, 1915	8	86	94
No. 2 Stationary Hospital	12 June, 1915	8	86	94
2 Mobile Veterinary Sections	14 Dec., 1914	2	26	28
2 Veterinary Sections	14 Dec., 1914	4	226	230
Total Additional Units formed in New Zealand		60	1398	1458

Additional Units Formed by N.Z.E.F. (Egypt).

Unit.	Date of Formation.	Officers.	Other Ranks.	Total.
DIVISIONAL TROOPS—				
Divisional Artillery—				
2nd Field Artillery Brigade—				
Divisional Ammunition Column		5	233	238
(A) Howitzer Battery Ammunition Column		1	40	41
No. 2 Brigade Ammunition Column		1	46	47
No. 3 Brigade Ammunition Column		3	66	69
Divisional Engineers—	Feb., 1915			
Headquarters		2	11	13
No. 1 Field Company, N.Z.E.		6	211	217
Divisional Train—				
No. 2 (New Zealand Infantry Brigade) Company		5	80	85
No. 3 (New Zealand Mounted Rifles Brigade) Company		5	80	85
Total	...			
TOTAL		28	767	795
Main Body	...	351	7410	7761
Units raised during Gallipoli Campagn	...	88	2165	2253
TOTAL (This does not include reinforcements.)	...	439	9575	10014

The Staff and Senior Officers of the New Zealand and Australian Division.
This picture was taken in Egypt, 1914. Those marked with a Star are now deceased.

Top Row from Left.— *Capt. C. H. J. Brown; Hon. Capt. W. T. Beck; Capt. J. W. Hutchen; Major J. A. Luxford; Lieut. Kettle; Lieut. J. Anderson; *Lieut. J. M. Richmond; Capt. H. M. Edwards; Capt. N. W. B. Thoms; *Lieut. C. M. Cazelet; Capt. C. H. Jess, A.I.F ; Capt. R. E. Coningham; Capt. W. P. Farr, A.I.F.; Lieut. Tahu Rhodes; Major J. G. Hughes, D.S.O.

Second Row.— *Lt.-Col. C. E. Thomas, V.D.; Lt.-Col. N. C. Hamilton; *Lt.-Col. R. E. Courtney, V.D., A.I.F.; Lt.-Col. Hon. J. L. Beeston, V.D., A.I.F.; Major H. G. Reid, A.S.C.; Capt. W. S. Berry, A.I.F.; *Capt. G. A. King; Major C. G. Powles; Major A. C. Temperley; Major C. Shawe; Major G. R. Pridham, R.E.; Major E. M. Williams, A.I.F.; Capt. J. E. Hindhaugh, A.I.F.

Third Row.—Lt.-Col. P. C. Fenwick; Lt.-Col. H. Pope, A.I.F.; Lt.-Col. J. H. Cannan, A.I.F.; Lt.-Col. H. J. Burnage, A.I.F.; Lt.-Col. J. Findlay; Lt.-Col. W. Meldrum; Lt.-Col. C. E. R. Mackesy; Lt.-Col. J. B. Meredith, A.I.F.; *Lt.-Col. F. M. Rowell, A.I.F.; Lt.-Col. R. T. Sutherland, A.I.F.; Lt.-Col. R. M. Stodart, A.I.F.; Lt.-Col. G. N. Johnston, R.A.; *Lt.-Col. A. Moore, D.S.O.; *Lt.-Col. A. Bauchop, C.M.G.; *Lt.-Col. C. M. Begg; *Lt.-Col. W. G. Malone; *Lt.-Col. D. McB. Stewart.

Sitting.—Lt.-Col. J. P. McGlinn, V.D., A.I.F.; *Col. N. Manders, R.A.M.C.; Lt.-Col. W. G. Braithwaite, D.S.O.; Brig.-General A. H. Russell, A.D.C.; Col. E. W. C. Chaytor, T.D.; Major-General Sir Alex. Godley, K.C.M.G.,C.B.; Col. H. G. Chauvel, C.M.G., A.I.F.; Col. J. Monash, V.D., A.I.F.; *Lt.-Col. F. E. Johnston; Lt.-Col. J. J. Esson; Lt.-Col. A. R. Young.

The Men of Anzac.

Although this volume deals specifically with the doings of the New Zealanders at Anzac, the Colonials who were there quite recognize that they played only a part in the Great Game. They fully appreciate the magnificent work of the Navy and of their French and British comrades who braved the same dangers, and worked together against the common foe.

The Men of Anzac know that a war correspondent cannot be in three places at once. What he sees he describes, and what he does not see he obviously must collect information about, and cannot do justice to. So perhaps the glory of the Anzac landing was magnified at the expense of the men who landed at Helles. Australians and New Zealanders alike agree that the Helles landing called for a greater show of discipline and self-sacrifice than was needed at Anzac—for Anzac was a surprise landing, Helles was not. But considerations of space, and the fact that volumes have already appeared dealing with the work of our British, French and Indian comrades, precludes full justice being done to their work in these pages.

In our own army there are two groups of soldiers that have to a certain extent been overlooked.

Even in the Colonial Armies we depended for light and a certain amount of leading on British Regular Officers—officers loaned before the war to the Colonial Forces,—and it is right that mention should be made of them here. For what in the days of its infancy would the N.Z. Expeditionary Force have been without the services of Colonel Braithwaite—"Dear Old Bill"—Colonel Johnston of the Gunners; Colonel Pridham of the R.E's; Major Temperley of the Infantry Brigade Staff, and a dozen others? They contributed much more than has been acknowledged to the initial successes of our New Zealand Army.

Of the second group it is difficult to write. It may have been noticed that most of the soldiers mentioned in this volume are men who were killed in action. There is perhaps more in this than meets the eye. For the men killed in action and the mortally wounded are those who put the fear of death into the Turk—men who by their impetuosity and their eagerness to close really established the Anzac front line. This meant personal leadership and absolute contempt for death. These men were often not officers—often they were privates, but natural leaders nevertheless. They were not necessarily university men or large employers of labour—sometimes they were miners and taxi-drivers—they were of the glorious democracy of the Front Line. Anyone, whatever his rank or social standing, could have demonstrated his claim to be a leader of men at Anzac.

We know that the list of decorations does not recognize all the gallant deeds performed on the field of action; and those left alive in the following list of soldiers decorated would be the first to admit that they knew of men long since killed who deserved greater reward. Think of a few of them: Lieut.-Colonel Stewart, of the Canterburys, who died on the day of the landing fighting for Walker's Ridge; Lieut.-Colonel Malone who died on the crest of Chunuk; Lieut.-Colonel Bauchop, mortally wounded in the advance that smashed the Turkish line; Major Statham, impetuous leader of men, who died in the forefront of the battle—each of these admittedly heroic souls passed away without receiving a decoration.

And these officers were only worthy of the men in the ranks—men who if they had lived, might have become great and famous soldiers, but who sacrificed themselves thus early in the struggle so that we who survived might carry on: Sergt. Wallace, one of our most promising Rhodes Scholars, who came straight from Oxford to a soldier's death while sapping out in front of Pope's; and the well-beloved Arthur Carbines, who, disregarding the terrors and the dangers on the crest of Chunuk, died so tragically endeavouring to rescue the body of his Colonel, the gallant Malone—these men are typical of the scores who received the small wooden cross which is the only distinction that the gallant thruster is likely to receive; and some do not have even a wooden cross, but die so far forward that they are buried by the Turks in name'ess graves and to these is the greatest honour!

New Zealanders decorated and mentioned in despatches.

VICTORIA CROSS.

Corporal Cyril Royston Guyton Bassett, N.Z. Divisional Signal Company: "For most conspicuous gallantry and devotion to duty on the Chunuk Bair ridge in the Gallipoli Peninsula on the 7th August, 1915.

After the New Zealand Infantry Brigade had attacked and established itself on the ridge, Corporal Bassett, in full daylight and under a continuous and heavy fire succeeded in lying a telephone-line from the old position to the new one on Chunuk Bair. He had subsequently been brought to notice for further excellent and most gallant work connected with the repair of telephone-lines by day and night under heavy fire."

London Gazette, 15th October, 1915.

CORPORAL C. R. G. BASSETT, V.C.
(Now Lieutenant Bassett, V.C., D.S.O.)

KNIGHT COMMANDER OF THE MOST HONOURABLE ORDER OF THE BATH. (K.C.B.)

Major-General (temp. Lieutenant-General) Sir A. J. Godley, K.C.M.G., General Officer Commanding, N.Z. Expeditionary Force.

KNIGHT COMMANDER OF THE MOST DISTINGUISHED ORDER OF SAINT MICHAEL AND SAINT GEORGE. (K.C.M.G.)

Colonel (temp. Brigadier-General) Sir A. H. Russell, General Officer Commanding, N.Z. Division.

COMPANIONS OF THE MOST HONOURABLE ORDER OF THE BATH. (C.B.)

Colonel E. W. Chaytor, N.Z. Staff Corps, New Zealand Expeditionary Force (Staff).
Lieutenant-Colonel J. Findlay, Canterbury Mounted Rifles Regiment.
Major (temp. Brigadier-General) F. E. Johnston, N.Z. Infantry Brigade (The Prince of Wales's Own, North Staffordshire Regiment).

NEW ZEALANDERS DECORATED.

COMPANIONS OF THE MOST DISTINGUISHED ORDER OF SAINT MICHAEL AND SAINT GEORGE. (C.M.G.)

Lieutenant-Colonel W. M. Alderman, Auckland Infantry Battalion (Commonwealth Military Forces).
Lieutenant-Colonel C. M. Begg, N.Z. Medical Corps.
Lieutenant-Colonel (temp. Brigadier-General) W. G. Braithwaite, D.S.O., Headquarters, N.Z. Expeditionary Force (Royal Welsh Fusiliers).
Lieutenant-Colonel A. B. Charters, Otago Infantry Battalion.

[Photo by Bartlett & Andrew.
LIEUT.-COLONEL W. G. BRAITHWAITE, C.M.G., D.S.O.
(Royal Welsh Fusiliers)

Major (temp. Lieutenant-Colonel) J. J. Esson, Staff Headquarters N.Z. Expeditionary Force.
Lieutenant-Colonel P. C. Fenwick, N.Z. Medical Corps.
Lieutenant-Colonel J. G. Hughes, D.S.O., Canterbury Battalion (N.Z. Staff Corps).
Reverend J. A. Luxford, Chaplain, 3rd Class, N.Z. Chaplains Department.
Lieutenant-Colonel W. Meldrum, D.S.O., Wellington Mounted Rifles.
Lieutenant-Colonel W. H. Parkes, M.D., N.Z. Medical Corps.
Lieutenant-Colonel A. Plugge, Auckland Battalion.
Major (temp. Lieutenant-Colonel) G. S. Richardson, N.Z. Mediterranean Expeditionary Force, (N.Z. Staff Corps).
Lieutenant-Colonel F. Symon, N.Z. Field Artillery (Royal N.Z. Artillery).
Lieutenant-Colonel R. Young, Auckland Battalion.

COMPANIONS OF THE DISTINGUISHED SERVICE ORDER. (D.S.O.)

Major H. E. Avery, No. 1 Company Divisional Train (N.Z. Staff Corps).

Honorary Captain W. T. Beck, N.Z. Ordnance Corps (attached N.Z. Staff Corps).
Major C. H. J. Brown, Canterbury Battalion (N.Z. Staff Corps).
Captain A. C. B. Critchey-Salmonson, Canterbury Battalion (Royal Munster Fusiliers).
Major N. S. Falla, N.Z. Field Artillery.
Captain B. S. Finn, N.Z. Medical Corps.
Lieutenant-Colonel R. R. Grigor, Otago Mounted Rifles.
Major N. C. Hamilton, N.Z. Army Service Corps (Army Service Corps).
Major Herbert Hart, Wellington Battalion.
Major N. F. Hastings, Wellington Mounted Rifles.
Major H. C. Hurst, Canterbury Mounted Rifles.
Major G. A. King, Headquarters N.Z.M.R. Brigade (N.Z. Staff Corps).
Major Eugene Joseph O'Neill, F.R.C.S., N.Z. Medical Corps.
Captain (temp. Lieutenant-Colonel) C. G. Powles, Headquarters, N.Z.M.R. Brigade (N.Z. Staff Corps).
Major G. S. Smith, Otago Battalion.
Major I. T. Standish, N.Z. Field Artillery (Royal N.Z. Artillery).
Major (temp. Lieutenant-Colonel) F. B. Sykes, N.Z. Field Artillery (Royal Artillery)
Major W. McG. Turnbull, Otago Battalion (N.Z. Staff Corps).
Major Fred Waite, N.Z. Engineers.
Major R. Wyman, Auckland Mounted Rifles Regiment.
Major R. Young, Wellington Battalion.

MILITARY CROSS. (M.C.)

Captain L. G. D. Acland, N.Z. Army Service Corps.
Lieutenant W. G. A. Bishop, Otago Infantry Battalion.
Captain D. B. Blair, Canterbury Mounted Rifles, (N.Z. Staff Corps).
Lieutenant G. R. Blackett, Canterbury Mounted Rifle Regiment.
2nd Lieutenant R. T. R. P. Butler, N.Z. Engineers (Royal Engineers).
Captain G. E. Daniell, N.Z. Field Artillery (Royal N.Z. Artillery)
Reverend P. Dore, Chaplain, 4th Class, N.Z. Chaplains Department.
Captain T. R. Eastwood, Headquarters Staff, N.Z. Expeditionary Force (The Rifle Brigade, Prince Consort's Own).
Captain T. Farr, N.Z. Field Artillery.
A. Greene, Chaplain, 4th Class (Salvation Army), N.Z. Chaplains Department.
Captain R. N. Guthrie, N.Z. Medical Corps.
Captain P. B. Henderson, Canterbury Infantry Regiment (N.Z. Staff Corps).
Captain G. H. Holland, Auckland Infantry Battalion.
2nd Lieutenant R. McPherson, N.Z. Field Artillery.
Lieutenant A. N. Oakey, N.Z. Engineers.
8/1048 Sergt.-Major A. W. Porteous, Otago Infantry Battalion.
Captain J. M. Richmond, N.Z. Field Artillery (N.Z. Staff Corps).
Captain J. M. Rose, Wellington Infantry Battalion (N.Z. Staff Corps).
Captain L. M. Shera, N.Z. Engineers.
2nd Lieutenant W. H. Stainton, N.Z. Maori Contingent.
Captain H. Stewart, Canterbury Infantry Battalion.
Captain N. W. B. B. Thoms, Headquarters N.Z. and A. Division (N.Z. Staff Corps).
Lieutenant F. K. Turnbull, Wellington Infantry Battalion.
Lieutenant F. M. Twistleton, Otago Mounted Rifles.
Captain J. A. Wallingford, Auckland Infantry Battalion (N.Z. Staff Corps).
Captain F. A. Wood, Auckland Mounted Rifles (N.Z. Staff Corps).

DISTINGUISHED CONDUCT MEDAL. (D.C.M.)

4/85a Sergeant A. W. Abbey, N.Z. Engineers.
13/5 Trooper L. J. Armstrong, Auckland Mounted Rifles.
6/884 Sergeant A. A. Atkins, Canterbury Infantry Battalion.
10/1731 Private C. R. Barker, Wellington Infantry Battalion.
6/194 Private H. Barlow, Canterbury Infantry Battalion.
10/274 Corporal P. H. G. Bennett, Wellington Infantry Battalion.
8/1370 Acting Sergeant-Major P. C. Boate, Otago Infantry Battalion.
9/129 Sergeant J. Campbell, Otago Mounted Rifles.
3/317 Private J. F. Cardno, N.Z. Medical Corps.
4/363 Sapper A. L. Caselberg, Signal Troop, N.Z. Engineers.
2/83 Driver N. Clark, N.Z. Field Artillery.
3/158 Private J. Comrie, N.Z. Field Ambulance.
13/606 Private L. Crawford-Watson, N.Z. Medical Corps.
4/506 Sapper B. L. Dignan, Divisional Signal Company, N.Z. Engineers.
2/444 Acting Sergeant C. J. K. Edwards, N.Z. Field Artillery.
4/188a Lance-Corporal F. J. H. Fear, N.Z. Engineers.
6/227 Private A. J. Findlay, Canterbury Infantry Battalion.
12/1627 Sergeant J. H. Francis, Auckland Infantry Battalion.
8/465 Quartermaster-Sergeant L. S. L. L. Graham, Otago Mounted Rifles.
7/516 Corporal G. G. Harper, Canterbury Mounted Rifles.
7/517 Sergeant R. P. Harper, Canterbury Mounted Rifles.
8/872 Sergeant A. G. Henderson, Otago Infantry Battalion.
3/168 Private W. J. Henry, N.Z. Field Ambulance.
2/147 Acting Sergeant J. F. Hill, N.Z. Field Artillery.
4/203a Sapper E. A. Hodges, N.Z. Engineers.
2/115 Bombardier D. C. Inglis, N.Z. Field Artillery.
14/43 Sergeant F. Jenkins, N.Z. Divisional Train.
9/1316 Sergeant J. Little, Otago Mounted Rifles.
10/2228 Private F. Mahoney, Wellington Infantry Battalion.
8/33 Sergeant F. Mitchell, Otago Infantry Battalion.
3/269 Sergeant-Major F. W. Moor, N.Z. Medical Corps.
8/1302 Private R. C. McLeod, Otago Infantry Battalion.
7/764 Trooper D. J. O'Connor, Canterbury Mounted Rifles.
10/1307 Private F. O. O'Connor, Wellington Infantry Battalion.
16/407 Private Tau Paranihi, Maori Contingent.
7/583 Trooper H. Pidgeon, Canterbury Mounted Rifles.
2/1252 Gunner J. Rankin, N.Z. Field Artillery.
12/1015 Corporal W. J. Reid, Auckland Infantry Battalion.
6/1129 Corporal H. Rhind, Canterbury Infantry Battalion.
11/442 Sergeant-Major W. Ricketts, Wellington Mounted Rifles.
6/978 Sergeant W. J. Rodger, Canterbury Infantry Battalion.
4/208a Corporal C. W. Salmon, N.Z. Engineers.
4/60a Corporal C. W. Saunders, N.Z. Engineers.
6/1399 Sapper E. G. Scrimshaw, N.Z. Engineers.
3/95 Lance-Corporal W. Singleton, N.Z. Field Ambulance.
8/1837 Lance-Corporal H. D. Skinner, Otago Infantry Battalion.
12/1799 Corporal H. Spencer, Auckland Infantry Battalion.
3/447 Lance-Corporal G. Steedman, N.Z. Field Ambulance.
6/1156 Private T. Stockdill, Canterbury Infantry Battalion.
10/1674 Private J. W. Swan, Wellington Infantry Battalion.
6/157 Sergeant B. N. Tavender, Canterbury Infantry Battalion.
12/1062 Private G. A. Tempany, Auckland Infantry Battalion.
2/146 Bombardier J. P. Thomson, N.Z. Field Artillery.
12/472 Sergeant R. Tilsley, Auckland Infantry Battalion.
12/1020 Corporal F. W. Watson, Auckland Infantry Battalion.

4/450 Sapper K. T. Watson, N.Z. Engineers.
6/741 Private C. M. Wilson, Canterbury Infantry Battalion.
14/76 Lance-Corporal J. Wimms, N.Z. Divisional Train.
11/941 Trooper J. H. Winter, Wellington Mounted Rifles.

MENTIONED IN DESPATCHES.

* Mentioned twice.   † Mentioned three times.

4/85a 2nd Corporal A. W. Abbey, D.C.M., N.Z. Engineers.
*Captain L. G. D. Acland, M.C., Divisional Train, N.Z. Army Service Corps.
4/513 Sergeant G. D. Alexander, N.Z. Engineers.
13/64 Sergeant F. Allsopp, Auckland Mounted Rifles.
13/5 Trooper L. J. Armstrong, D.C.M., Auckland Mounted Rifles.
10/1731 Private C. R. Barker, D.C.M., Wellington Infantry Battalion.
Lance-Corporal P. G. Barratt, Wellington Infantry Battalion.
Lieut.-Colonel A. Bauchop, C.M.G., Otago Mounted Rifles.
Captain W. T. Beck, D.S.O., N.Z. Army Ordnance Corps (attached N.Z. Staff Corps).
Lieut.-Colonel C. M. Begg, C.M.G., N.Z. Medical Corps.
3/233 Lance-Corporal T. Biggar, N.Z. Medical Corps.
Lieut. W. G. A. Bishop, M.C., Otago Infantry Battalion.
Lieut. G. R. Blackett, Canterbury Mounted Rifles.
Captain D. B. Blair, M.C., Canterbury Mounted Rifles (N.Z. Staff Corps).
8/1370 Sergt.-Major P. C. Boate, D.C.M., Otago Infantry Battalion.
7/311 Trooper J. M. Boocock, Canterbury Mounted Rifles.
†Lieut.-Colonel W. G. Braithwaite, C.M.G., D.S.O. (Royal Welsh Fusiliers).
Major (temp. Lieut.-Colonel) C. H. J. Brown, D.S.O., Canterbury Infantry Battalion (N.Z. Staff Corps).
2nd Lieutenant R. T. R. P. Butler, M.C., N.Z. Engineers (Royal Engineers).
9/129 Sergeant J. Campbell, D.C.M., Otago Mounted Rifles.
10/706 Private A. V. Carbines, Wellington Infantry Battalion.
8/911 Sapper S. Carlyon, N.Z. Engineers.
13/535 Trooper N. D. Champney, Auckland Mounted Rifles.
Major F. Chapman, Auckland Mounted Rifles.
Lieut.-Colonel A. B. Charters, C.M.G., Wellington Infantry Battalion.
Colonel E. W. C. Chaytor, C.B., N.Z. Staff Corps.
2/83 Fitter N. Clark, D.C.M., N.Z. Field Artillery.
3/158 Private J. Comrie, D.C.M., N.Z. Field Ambulance.
Lieutenant A. E. Conway, Canterbury Infantry Battalion.
Captain C. F. D. Cook, Wellington Infantry Battalion.
11/520 Corporal F. R. Corrie, Wellington Mounted Rifles.
Lieutenant J. G. Cowan, Otago Infantry Battalion.
Major E. P. Cox, Wellington Infantry Battalion.
13/606 Private L. Crawford-Watson, D.C.M., N.Z. Field Ambulance.
Captain A. C. B. Critchley-Salmonson, D.S.O., Canterbury Infantry Battalion (Royal Munster Fusiliers).
10/729 Private C. Crone, Wellington Infantry Battalion.
Major W. H. Cunningham, Wellington Infantry Battalion.
Captain G. E. Daniell, M.C., N.Z. Field Artillery (Royal N.Z. Artillery).
12/1185 Private D. Davidson, Auckland Infantry Battalion.
*Major T. H. Dawson, Auckland Infantry Battalion.
4/506 Sapper B. L. Dignan, D.C.M., N.Z. Engineers.
Rev. P. Dore, M.C., Chaplain, 4th Class, N.Z. Chaplains' Department.
10/966 Corporal A. G. Duncan, Wellington Infantry Battalion.
3/144 Private A. F. D. East, N.Z. Medical Corps.

New Zealanders Mentioned in Despatches.

Captain T. R. Eastwood, M.C., Headquarters Staff, N.Z. Expeditionary Force (Rifle Brigade, Prince Consort's Own).
Captain H. M. Edwards, N.Z. Engineers (Royal Engineers).
7/800 Trooper J. Edwards, Canterbury Mounted Rifles.
Major J. McG. Elmslie, Wellington Mounted Rifles.
Major (temp. Lieut.-Colonel) J. J. Esson, C.M.G.
Major N. S. Falla, D.S.O., N.Z. Field Artillery.
Captain T. Farr, M.C., N.Z. Field Artillery.
Major F. A. Ferguson, N.Z. Engineers (Royal Engineers).
*6/227 Private A. J. Findlay, D.C.M., Canterbury Infantry Battalion.
Lieut.-Colonel J. Findlay, C.B., Canterbury Mounted Rifles.
Captain B. S. Finn, D.S.O., N.Z. Medical Corps.
Lieut.-Colonel N. Fitzherbert, Wellington Infantry Battalion.
7/441 Sergeant R. A. Fleming, Canterbury Mounted Rifles.
2nd Lieutenant E. N. Gabites, Otago Infantry Battalion.
Lieutenant L. J. Gibbs, Canterbury Infantry Battalion.
6/234 Sergeant D. D. Gill, Canterbury Infantry Battalion.
*Major-General (temp. Lieut.-General) Sir A. J. Godley, K.C.B., K.C.M.G., General Officer Commanding N.Z. Expeditionary Force.
2nd Lieutenant T. M. P. Grace, Wellington Infantry Battalion.
9/465 Sergeant-Major L. S. L. L. Graham, D.C.M., Otago Mounted Rifles.
Major S. A. Grant, Auckland Infantry Battalion (N.Z. Staff Corps).
Rev. W. Grant, Chaplain, 3rd Class, N.Z. Chaplains' Department.
A. Greene, Chaplain, 4th Class (Salvation Army), M.C., N.Z. Chaplains' Department.
7/340 Sergeant A. R. Greenwood, Canterbury Mounted Rifles.
3/251 Private J. Greenwood, N.Z. Medical Corps.
Major R. R. Grigor, D.S.O., Otago Mounted Rifles.
Captain R. N. Guthrie, M.C., N.Z. Medical Corps.
Lieutenant W. Haeata, Auckland Mounted Rifles.
2nd Lieutenant C. St. C. Hamilton, Otago Infantry Battalion.
*Lieut.-Colonel N. C. Hamilton, D.S.O., N.Z. Army Service Corps (Army Service Corps).
7/516 Corporal G. G. Harper, D.C.M., Canterbury Mounted Rifles.
7/517 Sergeant R. P. Harper, D.C.M., Canterbury Mounted Rifles.
Captain E. S. Harston, Wellington Infantry Battalion.
Major H. Hart, D.S.O., Wellington Infantry Battalion.
Major N. F. Hastings, D.S.O., Wellington Mounted Rifles.
Major W. H. Hastings, Headquarters Staff, N.Z. Expeditionary Force (92nd Punjabis, Indian Army).
Captain B. S. Hay, Otago Mounted Rifles.
10/723 Private H. E. Hayden, Wellington Infantry Battalion.
Lieutenant C. Hayter, Canterbury Mounted Rifles.
3/170 Private W. Heaver, N.Z. Field Artillery.
Captain P. B. Henderson, M.C., Headquarters N.Z. Mounted Rifles Brigade (N.Z. Staff Corps).
8/1504 Private W. J. Henry, D.C.M., N.Z. Field Ambulance.
2/147 Sergeant J. Hill, D.C.M., N.Z. Field Artillery.
4537a Sergeant P. Hill, N.Z. Maori Contingent.
Captain F. L. Hindley, Canterbury Mounted Rifles.
Major (temp. Lieut.-Colonel) J. G. Hughes, C.M.G., D.S.O., Canterbury Infantry Battalion (N..Z. Staff Corps).
Major E J. Hulbert, N.Z. Engineers.
Major H. C. Hurst, D.S.O., Canterbury Mounted Rifles Regiment.
Major G. F. Hutton, Canterbury Mounted Rifles (Royal Welsh Fusiliers).
2/115 Bombardier D. Inglis, D.C.M., N.Z. Field Artillery.
Captain W. Janson, Wellington Mounted Rifles.

7/128 Trooper D. Jenkins, Canterbury Mounted Rifles.
10/824 Company Sergt.-Major A. Johnson, Wellington Infantry Battalion.
*Major (temp. Brigadier-General) G. N. Johnston, N.Z. Field Artillery (Royal Artillery).
10/392 Private S. Johnston, Wellington Infantry Battalion.
3/180 Private H. W. Keesing, N.Z. Medical Corps.
Captain V. A. Kelsall, Wellington Mounted Rifles.
Captain G. A. King, D.S.O., Headquarters N.Z. Mounted Rifles Brigade (N.Z. Staff Corps).
2nd Lieut. J. B. Le Mottée, Canterbury Infantry Battalion.
Captain R. Logan, Wellington Mounted Rifles.
Rev. J. A. Luxford, Chaplain, 3rd Class, C.M.G., N.Z. Chaplains' Department.
10/2228 Private F. Mahoney, D.C.M., Wellington Infantry Battalion.
*Lieut.-Colonel W. G. Malone, Wellington Infantry Battalion.
Colonel N. Manders, N.Z. Medical Corps (Royal Army Medical Corps).
12/1710 Private C. J. Maroni, Auckland Infantry Battalion.
9/445 Sergeant-Major V. Marshall, Otago Mounted Rifles.
13/272 Trooper A. Mason, Auckland Mounted Rifles.
Lieutenant-Colonel W. Meldrum, C.M.G., Wellington Mounted Rifles.
8/33 Sergeant F. Mitchell, D.C.M., Otago Infantry Battalion.
3/269 Warrant-Officer F. W. Moor, D.C.M., N.Z. Medical Corps.
Lieutenant-Colonel A. Moore, D.S.O., Otago Infantry Battalion (Royal Dublin Fusiliers).
Captain K. McCormick, N.Z. Medical Corps.
Reverend A. Macdonald, Chaplain, 4th Class, N.Z. Chaplains Department.
Major C. McGilp, N.Z. Field Artillery.
2nd Lieutenant E. J. McGregor, Auckland Mounted Rifles.
Temp. 2nd Lieutenant R. McPherson, M.C., N.Z. Field Artillery.
10/1109 Private J. Neale, Wellington Infantry Battalion.
Major C. R. Neale, N.Z. Veterinary Corps.
4/655 Sergeant S. Neels, N.Z. Engineers.
Lieutenant M. G. R. Newbold, N.Z. Engineers.
Major C. N. Newman, N.Z. Field Artillery.
4/115 Sergeant H. W. Newman, N.Z. Engineers.
Lieutenant T. H. Nisbet, Otago Infantry Battalion.
12/606 Private E. L Noakes, Auckland Infantry Battalion.
Lieutenant A. N. Oakey, M.C., N.Z. Engineers.
*Major E. J. O'Neill, D.S.O., M.B., N.Z. Medical Corps.
Major P. J. Overton, Canterbury Mounted Rifles.
2nd Lieutenant W. T. Palmer, Auckland Mounted Rifles.
16/407 Corporal Tau Paranihi, D.C.M., N.Z. Maori Contingent.
Lieutenant-Colonel W. R. Pearless, N.Z. Medical Corps.
4/827 Sergeant A. G. Picken, N.Z. Engineers.
Major W. R. Pinwill, Headquarters Staff, N.Z. Expeditionary Force (Liverpool Regiment).
*Lieutenant-Colonel A. Plugge, C.M.G., Auckland Infantry Battalion.
8/1048 Sergeant-Major A. W. Porteous, M.C., Otago Infantry Battalion.
Captain C. Guy Powles, D.S.O., Headquarters, N.Z.M.R. Brigade (N.Z. Staff Corps).
Lieutenant A. H. Preston, Wellington Infantry Battalion.
Lieutenant-Colonel G. R. Pridham, N.Z. Engineers (Royal Engineers).
7/108 Sergeant F. L. Rees, Canterbury Mounted Rifles.
Major H. G. Reid, N.Z. Army Service Corps (Army Service Corps).
10/778 Private J. R. Reid, Wellington Infantry Battalion.
Lieutenant A. T. G. Rhodes, Headquarters Staff, N.Z. Expeditionary Force (Grenadier Guards).

New Zealanders Mentioned in Despatches. 315

Major (temp. Lieutenant-Colonel) G. S. Richardson, C.M.G., Headquarters Staff, N.Z. Expeditionary Force (N.Z. Staff Corps), attached Royal Naval Division (Staff).
Captain J. M. Richmond, M.C., N.Z. Field Artillery (N.Z. Staff Corps).
11/442 Sergeant W. Ricketts, D.C.M., Wellington Mounted Rifles
13/438 Trooper R. R. E. Rollett, Auckland Mounted Rifles.
11/736 Sergeant B. Ronaldson, Wellington Mounted Rifles.
Captain J. M. Rose, M.C., Wellington Infantry Battalion (N.Z. Staff Corps).
*Colonel (temp. Brigadier-General) Sir A. H. Russell, K.C.M.G.
4/208a Corporal C. W. Salmon, D.C.M., N.Z. Engineers.
4/60a Corporal C. W. Saunders, D.C.M., N.Z. Engineers.
6/1399a Sapper E. G. Scrimshaw, D.C.M., N.Z. Engineers.
Captain L. M. Shera, M.C. N.Z. Engineers.
Captain A. V. Short, N. Z. Medical Corps.
9/343 Corporal A. Simon, Otago Mounted Rifles.
3/95 Lance-Corporal W. Singleton, D.C.M., N.Z. Field Ambulance.
8/1837 Lance-Corporal H. D. Skinner, D.C.M., Otago Infantry Battalion.
Major G. S. Smith, D.S.O., Otago Infantry Battalion.
Captain R. B. Smythe, Headquarters N.Z. and A. Division (N.Z. Staff Corps).
12/1799 Sergeant H. Spencer, D.C.M., Auckland Infantry Battalion.
Major I. T. Standish, D.S.O., N.Z. Field Artillery (Royal N.Z. Artillery).
Lieutenant W. H. Stainton, M.C., N.Z. Maori Contingent.
Major F. H. Statham, Otago Infantry Battalion.
3/447 Lance-Corporal G. Steedman, D.C.M., N.Z. Medical Corps.
13/237 Trooper K. M. Stevens, Auckland Mounted Rifles.
Captain H. Stewart, M.C., Canterbury Infantry Battalion.
Lieutenant-Colonel D. McB. Stewart, Canterbury Infantry Battalion.
6/1156 Private T. Stockdill, D.C.M., Canterbury Infantry Battalion.
Lieutenant J. K. D. Strang, Otago Mounted Rifles.
6/770 Lance-Corporal W. H. Studley, Canterbury Infantry Battalion.
10/1674 Corporal J. W. Swan, D.C.M., Wellington Infantry Battalion.
Major (temp. Lieutenant-Colonel) F. B. Sykes, D.S.O., N.Z. Field Artillery (Royal Artillery).
Lieutenant-Colonel F. Symon, C.M.G., N.Z. Field Artillery (Royal N.Z. Artillery).
6/157 Lance-Corporal B. N. Tavender, D.C.M., Canterbury Infantry Battalion.
Lieutenant G. N. Taylor, Canterbury Mounted Rifles.
23/1213 Private G. A. Tempany, D.C.M., Auckland Infantry Battalion.
Major A. C. Temperley, Headquarters Staff, N.Z. Expeditionary Force (Norfolk Regiment).
Captain N. W. B. B. Thoms, M.C., Headquarters Staff, N.Z. Expeditionary Force (N.Z. Staff Corps).
6/1131 Private A. Thomson, Canterbury Infantry Battalion.
2/146 Bombardier J. P. Thomson, D.C.M., N.Z. Field Artillery.
8/494 Corporal T. A. Timpany, Otago Infantry Battalion.
9/91 Trooper A. K. Topi, Otago Mounted Rifles.
12/267 Bugler D. B. Treacher, Auckland Infantry Battalion.
Lieutenant F. K. Turnbull, M.C., Wellington Infantry Battalion.
Major W. McG. Turnbull, D.S.O., Otago Infantry Battalion (N.Z. Staff Corps).
Lieutenant F. M. Twistleton, M.C., Otago Mounted Rifles.
16/161 Company Sergeant-Major H. R. Vercoe, N.Z. Maori Contingent.
*Major F. Waite, D.S.O., N.Z. Engineers.
Lieutenant W. H. Walker, N.Z. Maori Contingent.

4/72a Sergeant A. Wallace, N.Z. Engineers.
Captain J. A. Wallingford, Auckland Infantry Battalion (N.Z. Staff Corps).
12/1020 Corporal F. W. Watson, D.C.M., Auckland Infantry Battalion.
*Major J. H. Whyte, D.C.M., Wellington Mounted Rifles (N.Z. Staff Corps).
11/654 Sergeant J. W. Wilder, Wellington Mounted Rifles.
Lieutenant G. L. Wilson, Otago Infantry Battalion.
Captain E. R. Wilson, Wellington Infantry Battalion.
14/76 Lance-Corporal J. Wimms, D.C.M., N.Z. Divisional Train.
11/941 Trooper J. H. Winter, D.C.M., Wellington Mounted Rifles.
Captain F. A. Wood, M.C., Auckland Mounted Rifles (N.Z. Staff Corps).
*Lieutenant-Colonel R. Young, C.M.G., D.S.O., Wellington Infantry Battalion.

The Place-Names of Anzac.

Some unfortunate tracts of country are destined from their situations to be the battlegrounds of the world. Old world names, before this war but the memory of former campaigns, have once again become household words. So Mons and St. Quentin, Kantara and Damascus, have become familiar to the boys of the present generation, for have not their elder brothers been on police picket in the back streets of every one of them?

But war sometimes chances to descend on poor, unsettled and otherwise unimportant territory. Such a place was Anzac—rough and hungry clay hillsides, no habitations in its area except the lonely Fishermen's Hut near the mouth of the Sazli Beit Dere, and a poor shepherd's hut at the foot of Monash Gully. Into this desolate country, with only a few ridges and watercourses important enough to be marked on the map, came legions of foreign soldiers who peopled every scrubby ridge and winding gully.

The necessity for place-names became very pressing. Retaining such of the native ones as were shown on the maps, a multitude of Australian and New Zealand names appeared spontaneously at Anzac, just as the English and French names appeared at Helles.

Difficulties often arose. An Australian unit holding a part of the line had local names for every place within the sector, whereas a New Zealand unit taking over manufactured or evolved names quite different. The preparation of a trench map or operation orders written by the Staff fixed the name for all time. Place-names like "The Sphinx" are evidence of this.

Ismail Oglu Tepe with its wavy crestline, naturally became the "W" Hills of Anzac. From Walker's Ridge the description point—"W" Hills—never failed to be recognized.

Most places in Anzac are named after men or units. This is natural. But sometimes accidents crept in here, too. For instance, an attack of measles made what might have been "Johnston's Ridge," into "Walker's Ridge."

The word "Anzac" arrived in quite a different way. "Anzac" obviously suggested itself. But numerous stories are current as to its origin, and doubtless many of the stories are correct. Statements on this subject have been made by the two most important Generals connected with the campaign, and their claims may easily be reconciled.

1. In the "Anzac Book" General Birdwood stated that when he took over the command of the Australian and New Zealand Army Corps in Egypt, he was asked to select a telegraphic code address for his Army Corps, and adopted the word "Anzac." Later on, after the landing, he was asked by General Headquarters to suggest a name for the beach, and in reply he christened it "Anzac Cove."
2. General Ian Hamilton wrote in his preface to "Crusading at Anzac, A.D. 1915," by Signaller Ellis Silas: "As the man who first, seeking to save himself trouble, omitted the five full stops and brazenly coined the word "Anzac," I am glad to write a line or two in preface to sketches which may help to give currency to that token throughout the realms of glory."

In compiling this list of place-names and their origins, the aim has been to set down only those names that were generally accepted and used at Anzac. Official trench maps, operation orders, books, pamphlets, and captured Turkish maps have been searched and verified. I am greatly indebted to the work of my friend Sapper Moore-Jones in his unrivalled "Sketches Made at Anzac." Besides being works of art, these sketches are particularly valuable as showing in faithful detail the land features of the Anzac area, with many of the place-names in use during the operations.

It is not necessary to burden this volume with a complete Turkish dictionary, but the following words, with their equivalents in English, may be found of value:—

Bair	-	-	Spur	Kuchuk	-	-	Small
Biyuk	-	-	Large	Kuyu	-	-	Well
Burnu	-	-	Cape	Ova	-	-	Plain
Chair	-	-	Meadow	Sirt	-	-	A Summit
Dagh	-	-	Mountain	Tepe	-	-	Hill
Dere	-	-	Valley with stream	Tekke	-	-	Shrine
Kale	-	-	Fort				

Abdel Rahman Bair.—The great northern spur of the Sari Bair range.

Anafarta.—(1) The Turkish name for the Suvla front.
    (2) There are two villages inland from Suvla Bay called Biyuk Anafarta and Kuchuk Anafarta.
    (3) A long-range gun firing from the hills was called "Anafarta Annie."

Anzac.—Formed from the initial letters of Australian and New Zealand Army Corps. First used (written A. and N.Z.A.C.) in Egypt, when the Army Corps was formed. It soon became A.N.Z.A.C., and the new word was so obvious that the full stops were omitted.

Anzac Cove.—The little bay where the principal landing was made on April 25, 1915.

The Apex.—High up on Rhododendron Spur, and the furthest point inland retained by the Anzac forces after the attack on Chunuk Bair. An earlier name, little used, was "The Mustard Plaster."

Ari Burnu.—The northern horn of Anzac Cove. The Turk called the Anzac area the Ari Burnu front.

Asma Dere.—One of the upper reaches of the Azmak Dere, starting in the foothills of the Abdel Rahman Bair.

Azmak Dere.—A watercourse leading from Biyuk Anafarta, running to the south of Ismail Oglu Tepe and debouching on to the Suvla flats. There is another Azmak flowing into the north of the Salt Lake at Suvla.

Australian Valley.—One of the northern branches of the Aghyl Dere, named after the 4th Australian Infantry Brigade.

Baby 700.—A Turkish position between The Nek and Battleship Hill.

Battleship Hill.—High ground within the Turkish lines between Baby 700 and Chunuk Bair. Turkish reserves sheltered behind it, and were frequently shelled by the warships.

Bauchop's Hill.—A hill between the Aghyl Dere and the Chailak Dere. Named after the gallant colonel of the Otago Mounted Rifles, who was mortally wounded here on August 8.

Beach Road, The.—The road running along the sea beach from Ari Burnu toward No. 2 Post.

Bedford Ridge.—A ridge opposite Cheshire Ridge on which were situated our three isolated posts: Newbury's Post, the southern one; Franklin Post, the central one; Warwick Castle, the northern one.

Blamey's Meadow.—Overlooked by Tasmania Post. Named after Major Blamey, an Intelligence Officer who carried out extensive reconnaissances in Turkish territory towards Maidos.

Blockhouse, The.—A Turkish position opposite the Apex. This blockhouse was built after the Turks swept us off Chunuk Bair in August.

Bloody Angle.—The gully between Dead Man's Ridge and Quinn's Post. The 4th Australian Brigade and the battalions of the Royal Naval Division suffered heavy losses here on the night of May 2/3.

The Place-Names of Anzac.

Bolton's Hill.—Named after Colonel Bolton, 8th A.I. Battalion. On the extreme right flank; part of the front line of the Australian position.

Biyuk Anafarta.—See Anafarta.

Braund's Hill.—A hill behind the centre of the Australian line on the right, and overlooking Shrapnel Valley. Named after Colonel Braund, of the 2nd Australian Infantry Battalion. Colonel Braund was a member for Armidale in the New South Wales Paliament, and was killed soon after the landing.

Broadway.—The wide sunken road leading from the top of Walker's Ridge round the back of the firing line on Russell's Top.

Bridges' Road.—A road leading to the right from Shrapnel Valley towards Wire Gully. Named in memory of General Bridges, the Australian Divisional Commander, who was mortally wounded in Shrapnel Valley.

Brighton Beach.—The long stretch of beach running southwards from Hell Spit towards Gaba Tepe. Brighton is the well-known watering place near Melbourne, named after the English seaside resort.

Brown's Dip.—A depression just behind the Australian trenches opposite Lone Pine, where the Turkish and Australian dead were buried after the struggle for Lone Pine. The lower part of Brown's Dip was known as Victoria Gully.

Bully Beef Gully.—A gully running up from the centre of Anzac Cove past Army Corps Headquarters. As stores on the beach would be threatened by rough weather, beef and biscuits were stacked in this valley.

Bully Beef Track.—A communication trench running from the right of Russell's Top to the head of Monash Gully.

Bully Cut.—A deep communication trench cut to enable troops to avoid a much-sniped section of the Aghyl Dere.

Camel's Hump.—A Turkish position just below Snipers' Nest.

Canterbury Gully.—A small gully between Plugge's Plateau and Shrapnel Valley, where the Canterbury Infantry Battalion rested when in reserve from Quinn's Post. Often shown on the map as Rest Gully.

Canterbury Slope.—On the slopes of Rhododendron Spur.

Canterbury Knob.—A famous machine gun position on the right flank of the Apex position and overlooking the head waters of the Sazli Beit Dere. Known to machine gunners as Preston's Top after the gallant Lieut. Preston (killed in France) who first placed machine guns there on August 7.

Canterbury Ridge.—A name given to Rhododendron Spur during the early days of August. The Canterbury Infantry occupied this ground on the morning of August 7.

Chailak Dere.—A narrow valley falling down from Chunuk Bair, past the north side of Table Top and between Bauchop's Hill and "Old No. 3 Post."

Chatham's Post.—The southern limit of the Anzac line. Named after Lieut. Chatham, of the 5th Australian Light Horse.

Chessboard, The.—A criss-cross network of Turkish trenches opposite Pope's Hill and Russell's Top.

Cheshire Ridge.—A ridge between the upper reaches of the Chailak Dere and the southern fork of the Aghyl Dere. Named after the 8th Cheshires who were in the 40th Brigade of the 13th Division. Its respective parts were known as Upper and Lower Cheshire. Durrant's Post was in the centre.

Chocolate Hills.—A range of hills inland from Suvla Bay, south of the Salt Lake. These hills were brownish red, and later swept with fire. One part was covered with scrub and, not being burnt, was known as Green Hill.

Chunuk Bair.—A ridge about 860 feet high on the Sari Bair, below Hill Q, and above Rhododendron Spur.

Clarke Valley.—Between Victoria Gully and Shell Green. Colonel Clarke had the 12th Australian Infantry Battalion.

Cornfield, The.—A small patch of cultivated ground on the right flank just above Shell Green.

Courtney's Post.—One of the three famous posts at head of Monash Gully. Lieut.-Colonel R. E. Courtney, of the 14th Australian Infantry Battalion, was in command here in May. He died at Melbourne on October 22, 1919.

Daisy Patch, The.—A piece of old meadow at Cape Helles.

Damakjelik Bair.—On the left of the Anzac line; the objective of the Left Covering Force on August 6.

Dawkins' Point.—On Brighton Beach, about 600 yards south of Hell Spit. Named after an officer of the Australian Engineers.

Dead Man's Ridge.—A much-contested Turkish salient running in between Pope's Hill and Quinn's Post. So called because of the bodies of New Zealanders, Australians, and men of the Royal Naval Division which lay there from May 2/3 until the Armistice.

Destroyer Hill.— A small hill overlooking the Sazli Beit Dere and midway between Rhododendron Spur and No. 1 Post. Often heavily shelled by the torpedo destroyers.

Durrant's Post.—A post on Cheshire Ridge. Major Durrant was an officer in the 4th Australian Infantry Brigade.

Farm, The.—A hotly contested corner of the Chunuk Bair battlefields. Just underneath the ridge of Chunuk Bair. It eventually remained in the hands of the Turk.

Fishermen's Hut.—A rude hut or huts near the coast, at the foot of the Sazli Beit Dere.

Gaba Tepe.—A headland about a mile and a quarter south of the Anzac right flank. The Anzac landing was originally known as the Gaba Tepe landing. Most of the earlier gazetted decorations were prefaced "in the neighbourhood of Gaba Tepe," which really means Anzac.

Gillespie Hill.—A part of Hill 60. On the left of the Anzac theatre. Named after Lieut.-Colonel Gillespie, of the South Wales Borderers.

Hampshire Lane.—A communication trench leading from the Aghyl Dere towards Sandbag Ridge.

Happy Valley.—The valley just north of Walker's Ridge, and immediately below Turk's Point. In the spring the lower reaches were a mass of flowering shrubs, beautiful grasses, and fragrant wild thyme.

Hay Valley.—A southern arm of the Aghyl Dere; branching to the left it was known as Stafford Gully, and to the right, Hotchkiss Gully. Captain Bruce Hay, N.Z.S.C., was killed while leading a squadron of the Otago Mounted Rifles in the attack on Bauchop's Hill.

Hell Spit.—The southern horn of Anzac Cove. Jutting out into the sea, it was a convenient mark for the Turkish gunner of the Olive Groves and Gaba Tepe.

Hill Q.—Sometimes known as Nameless Peak. Midway between the heights of Hill 971 and Chunuk Bair. About 280 feet.

Hill 60.—The height in metres of the hill known as Kaiajik Aghala, near which was the important well Kabak Kuyu.

Hill 100.—High ground between the Asma Dere and the head of the Kaiajak Dere; held by the Otago Mounted Rifles at the evacuation.

Hill 112.—Ismail Oglu Tepe, which see.

Hill 971.—The most important tactical feature on Gallipoli Peninsula. The highest Peak of the Sari Bair range, 971 feet high. Known to the Turk as Koja Chemen Tepe, and shown on the later maps as Hill 305, from its height in metres.

THE PLACE-NAMES OF ANZAC. 321

Hotchkiss Gully.—See Hay Valley.
Howitzer Gully.—The northernmost gully running up towards Plugge's Plateau from Anzac Cove. Here the 4.5 Howitzer Battery, under Major Falla, made its welcome appearance the morning after the Anzac landing.
Hughes Gully.—Part of the Sazli Beit Dere running to the north opposite Destroyer Hill, towards the front of Table Top. Lt.-Col. J. G. Hughes, C.M.G., D.S.O., was in command of the Canterbury Battalion during the August offensive.
Ismail Oglu Tepe.—See "W" Hills.
Johnston's Jolly.—A Turkish position between Lone Pine and German officers' trench. Named after Colonel G. J. Johnston, Brigadier of the 2nd Australian Artillery Brigade.
Koja Chemen Tepe.—See Hill 971.
Koja Dere.—A Turkish village two miles due east of Lone Pine. Here were concentrated a large proportion of the enemy's reserves. Koja Dere (sometimes spelt Kurija Dere) was the site of the Turkish Army Headquarters in the southern sector of the Ari Burnu front.
Kaiajik Aghala.—See Hill 60.
Kuchuk Anafarta.—See Anafarta.
Kabak Kuyu.—A valuable well in the neighbourhood of Hill 60.
Kur Dere.—A valley between Chunuk Bair Hill Q, on the enemy's side of the watershed. Mentioned as one of the objectives in the operation order for August 6.
Lala Baba.—The highest ground between Nibrunesi Point and the Salt Lake. This observation post was raided several times by New Zealanders before the Suvla landing. On it a German flag was flown after the evacuation.
Leane's Trench.—A set of Turkish trenches near Tasmania Post, taken on July 31 by Western Australian troops under Major Leane, who was killed during the operations.
Little Table Top.—A small, flat-topped hill north of the original "Table Top," which was sometimes called "Big Table Top."
Long Sap, The.—A communication trench running from Anzac Cove, near Ari Burnu, along the foothills out to No. 2 Post.
Lone Pine.—A set of Turkish trenches south of Johnston's Jolly, taken and held by the Australians during the August fighting. Seven Victoria Crosses were won here by Australians.
Malone's Gully.—A dry watercourse between Happy Valley and No. 1 Post, leading up towards Baby 700. Named after the gallant Colonel of the Wellington Infantry Battalion.
Mal Tepe.—A small hill inland from Gaba Tepe, on which the Turks had guns. One of the objectives mentioned in the operation order for the Anzac landing.
Monash Gully.—See Shrapnel Valley. Brigadier-General Monash commanded the 4th Australian Infantry Brigade, which first held the head of Monash Gully.
Mortar Ridge.—A ridge behind German Officers' Trench. Under the reverse slope of Mortar Ridge were innumerable dugouts protecting the Turkish reserves.
Mule Gully.—A ravine running up behind Walker's Ridge. Under the shelter of the high banks the mules of the Indian Supply and Transport Corps were protected from fire.
Mustard Plaster, The.—See the Apex.
Maclagan's Ridge.—The ridge running from Plugge's Plateau down to Hell Spit. Named after the landing in honour of Colonel Sinclair Maclagan, D.S.O.

Maclaurin's Hill.—Just south of Steel's Post. Colonel Maclaurin, the Brigadier of the 1st Australian Infantry Brigade, was killed in Monash Gully two days after the landing.

McCay's Hill.—On the right flank, north of White Valley. Named after the Brigadier of the 2nd Australian Infantry Brigade.

No. 1 Post.—On the left flank of Anzac. Sometimes known as Maori Post, from it being garrisoned by the Maori contingent.

No. 2 Post.—Called Nelson Hill in the earlier days because held by the 10th (Nelson) Mounted Rifles; then taken over by the Otago Mounted Rifles; eventually became Divisional Headquarters for the August operations.

No. 3 Post.—Established just north of No. 2 Outpost, when Old No. 3 was abandoned.

Nameless Peak.—See Hill Q.

Nek, The.—A narrow tongue of No Man's Land, running from Russell's Top towards the Turkish trenches.

Nelson Hill.—See No. 2 Post.

Nibrunesi Point.—The southern horn of Suvla Bay, shown on some Turkish maps as Kuchuk Kemekli.

North Beach.—See Ocean Beach.

Ocean Beach.—The stretch of sea shore between Ari Burnu and No. 2 Post. Sometimes known as North Beach.

Old No. 3 Post.—High ground above Fishermen's Hut. Captured and held for two days by the N.Z.M.R. in May, but eventually abandoned to the Turks; retaken during the August advance.

Olive Groves.—Clumps of trees inland from Gaba Tepe. "Beachy Bill" and other obnoxious Turkish guns were "dug in" in the vicinity.

Otago Gully.—Near No. 3 Post. The Otago Mounted Rifles had their headquarters hereabouts during June and July.

Overton Gully.—A gully named to commemorate Major Overton, Canterbury Mounted Rifles, a keen officer who directed the scouting and reconnoitering on the left flank. He was killed on August 7 while leading Cox's Indian Brigade up the Aghyl Dere.

Owen's Gully.—A gully in Turkish territory between Johnston's Jolly and Lone Pine; named after Brigadier-General Cunliffe Owen, the artillery commander of the A.N.Z.A.C.

Phillip's Top.—Near the bottom and on the southern side of Shrapnel Valley there was a low ridge called "The Razor Back," which, running up towards the firing line, became known as Phillip's Top, after Major Phillips, of the Australian Field Artillery.

Pimple, The.—A salient in the Australian line just opposite the Turkish Lone Pine trenches; this Pimple became the Lone Pine Salient.

Pine Ridge.—A Turkish position opposite the extreme right flank of Anzac.

Plugge's Plateau.—The high ground immediately inland from Anzac Cove, the southern spur running down to Hell Spit being named Maclagan's Ridge. Plugge's Plateau is called after the O.C. Auckland Infantry Battalion.

Point Rosenthal.—On the ridge below Bolton's Hill. Colonel Rosenthal commanded the 1st Australian Artillery Brigade.

Pope's Hill.—An isolated post at the head of Monash Gully; on its right was Dead Man's Ridge; on its left a deep canyon separating Pope's from Russell's Top. Colonel Pope was the gallant white-haired commander of the famous 16th Australian Infantry Battalion.

Poppy Valley.—There were many "Poppy" Valleys and "Poppy" Fields in the Anzac area, but the only one to get on the map was in the Turkish territory between Harris' Ridge and Pine Ridge, on the extreme southern flank of Anzac.

Queensland Point.—That lower part of Maclagan's Ridge which resolves itself into Hell Spit. The Queensland Infantry landed here early on April 25.

Quinn's Post.—At the head of Monash Gully; the most famous post in Anzac, the salient of the Anzac line. Named after Major Quinn, of the 15th Australian Infantry Battalion, who was killed defending the post. For the first few days this ground was held by Major Rankine ("Bobby") of the 14th Battalion A.I.F. He then handed over to Major Quinn.

Reserve Gully.—A "rest" gully in the low ground between Plugge's Plateau and the Sphinx. It eventually became unsafe, being periodically searched by the guns from the "W" Hills.

Rest Gully.—See Canterbury Gully.

Rhododendron Spur.—A prominent spur running westward from Chunuk Bair, and between the Chailak Dere and the Sazli Beit Dere, the point nearest Chunuk Bair being called the Apex. It was first called Rhododendron Spur by Major Overton, who saw in the scrubby arbutus some resemblance to a rhododendron.

Rose Hill.—A northern underfeature of Bauchop Hill, below Little Table Top and above Hotchkiss Gully. Guns placed here defended the ground between The Blockhouse and our position on the Apex. Major Rose was a New Zealand machine gunner in charge of the 4th Australian Infantry Brigade machine guns.

Russell's Top.—The highest point of Walker's Ridge, where Brigadier-General Russell, commanding the New Zealand Mounted Rifles, had his headquarters during May, June, and July.

Ryrie's Post.—On the right of the Australian line; named after Brigadier-General Ryrie, 2nd Light Horse Brigade.

Sandbag Ridge.—A salient in the new Anzac line near Hill 100.

Sari-Bair.—The tangled mass of hills and watercourses inland from Anzac and Suvla, culminating in Hill 971.

Sazli Beit Dere.—A watercourse, dry in summer, originating in the slopes of Chunuk Bair, and entering the sea near Fishermen's Hut.

Scimitar Hill.—A round hill north of the "W" Hills, on which was a curved strip of yellow earth resembling a Turkish sword; shown on some maps as Hill 70, from its height in metres.

Scrubby Knoll.—A Turkish position about 1500 yards due east of Courtney's Post.

Shell Green.—A small area of cleared cultivable ground on the extreme right of Anzac, between Clarke Valley and Ryrie's Post.

Shrapnel Valley.—The road to the centre of the Anzac position; heavily shelled by the Turkish artillery from the first day. Known to the Turks as Kamu Kapu Dere. The upper portion of the valley was known as Monash Gully.

Snipers' Nest.—A scrubby hill about 1000 yards from the sea, from which Turkish snipers made the beach north of Ari Burnu unsafe for bathing or traffic.

Smyth's Post.—A post in the Australian sector, named after an Australian officer.

Sphinx, The.—A peculiar knife-edge spur jutting out seawards from Walker's Ridge. During the early days it was known by many names such as the Sphinx, the Knife Edge, the Cathedral, the Snipers' Crevice, &c., until it was entered on the map as the Sphinx. A legend that from a crevice a sniper picked off men for the first few days, until shot by Captain Wallinford, the well-known machine gunner, has no foundation in fact, except that some wild pigeons which had their home there were thought to be carriers.

Stafford Gully.—See Hay Valley.

Steel's Post.—The post south of Courtney's, named after Major Steel, of the 14th Australian Battalion. For the first week, Courtney's and Steel's were included in Steel's Post; but Lt.-Col. Courtney took over the left section which was renamed Courtney's.

Susuk Kuyu.—A well just north of Hill 60, where the Anzac forces got in touch with the Suvla forces after the Suvla landing.

Table Top.—A flat-topped hill, 1400 yards inland from the sea, just south of Chailak Dere and at the foot of Rhododendron Spur; captured by the Wellington Mounted Rifles on the night of August 6/7.

Tasmanian Post.—A post held by the Tasmanians on the right of the Anzac front line, just north of Ryrie's Post.

Taylor's Hollow.—A depression just below Bauchop's Hill; named after Lieut. Taylor, of the 10th (Nelson) Mounted Rifles, who made numerous reconnaisances in the vicinity.

Turks' Hump.—A Turkish position on the lower slopes of Gunners' Hill, opposite Canterbury Knob.

Turk's Point.—Part of the left of the original Anzac line, overlooking the head of Malone's Gully.

Valley of Despair, The.—A valley in Turkish hands opposite our extreme right flank, running from near Lone Pine down towards the sea.

Victoria Gully.—See Brown's Dip.

Walden's Point.—North of Taylor's Hollow. Waldren, whose name was always mis-spelt "Walden," was a very daring sniper who did much reconnoitering on the Suvla Flats as a machine gun officer of the Maoris. He was killed on the Apex.

Walker's Ridge.—The left flank of the original Anzac line. Brigadier-General Walker was attached to Army Headquarters, but as Colonel Johnston was down with measles on the morning of the Anzac landing, General Walker took command of the Brigade.

Walker's Pier.—A wharf erected north of Ari Burnu, between Mule Gully and Reserve Gully.

Wanliss Gully.—A gully breaking the Anzac line just opposite German Officers' Trench. This section was at one time under the command of Colonel Wanliss, 5th Australian Infantry Battalion.

Warley Gap.—The gap in the line at Sandbag Ridge.

Waterfall Gully.—A small sheltered gully in Bauchop's Hill, where newcomers bivouacked. The Headquarters of a Turkish unit was captured here on August 6/7.

Watson's Pier.—The first wharf built at Anzac Cove by the New Zealand Engineers. Captain Watson was an officer of the Australian Signal Service, who overlooked the work when N.Z.E. officers could not be spared.

Wellington Terrace.—The cliff side under the shadow of the Sphinx, studded with dugouts; originally a rest camp for the Wellington Regiment, who saw some resemblance to their native hillsides.

White's Valley.—A valley turning to the right off Shrapnel Valley, north of McCay's Hill; named after Lieut-Colonel White, of the 8th Australian Light Horse.

Wine Glass Ridge.—A Turkish position opposite the Anzac right flank.

Williams Pier.—A pier on North Beach.

"W" Hills.—A low ridge 112 metres high, about a mile due north of Hill 60; shown on Turkish maps as Ismail Oglu Tepe, but better known to the Anzac troops as the "W" Hills. When looking north from Russell's Top, the spurs of this feature formed the line W, while the re-entrants formed the shadows.

A Gallipoli Diary.

War has many phases. Within the compass of a volume such as this, it is not possible to describe in detail all those events bearing on the subject of the Gallipoli campaign. Neither is it possible—though the temptation is great—to deal with the glorious achievements of our silent Allied Navies, and the accomplishments of our heroic French, British, Indian and Australian comrades.

The following diary has been compiled so that the bearing of all the multifarious happenings:—naval, military, and political—may be seen in their proper setting in regard to the campaign.

1914.

June 28. Assassination of Archduke Ferdinand at Serajevo.
July 28. Austria declared war on Serbia.
  30. Preliminary arrangements made in New Zealand for a volunteer Expeditionary Force.
Aug. 2. Germany declared war on Russia. Germans entered France. Russians entered Germany.
  3. Germany declared war on France.
  4. Britain declared war on Germany.
  5. "Goeben" and "Breslau" at Messina, Italy.
  7. The New Zealand Government cabled to the Imperial Government offering the services of an Expeditionary Force.
  8. British Expeditionary Force landed in France.
  10. "Goeben" and "Breslau" reported at Constantinople.
  12. Services of N.Z.E.F. accepted by Imperial Authorities.
  15. Samoan Force of 1350 New Zealanders and four guns sailed.
  28. German Samoa surrendered.
Sept. 24. Main Body embarked on transports.
  25. Force ordered to await a more powerful escort.
Oct. 14. "Minotaur" and "Ibuki" arrived in Wellington Harbour.
  15. Main Body again embarked on transports.
  16. Convoy sailed from Wellington.
  21. Arrived at Hobart.
  22. Left Hobart for Albany.
  28. Arrived at Albany.
Nov. 1. Australian and New Zealand convoy left Albany. British Naval defeat at Coronel.
  2. Martial law proclaimed in Egypt. First shelling of the Dardanelles Forts by French and British Squadrons.
  5. Britain and France officially declared war on Turkey.
  9. H.M.A.S. "Sydney" destroyed the "Emden" at the Cocos Islands.
  13. Convoy crossed the Equator; the "Hampshire" joined the convoy.
  15. Arrived at Colombo.
  17. New Zealand transports left Colombo for Aden.
  25. New Zealand transports arrived at Aden.
  26. Combined Australian and New Zealand convoy left Aden for Suez.
  28. Received wireless to prepare for disembarkation in Egypt.
  30. Arrived at Suez.

Dec.	1.	New Zealand ships passed through the Suez Canal.
	3.	Commenced disembarkation at Alexandria.
	4.	First troop train arrived at Helmieh station for Zeitoun Camp.
	8.	German Naval defeat at the Falkland Islands.
		Australian Light Horse Brigade and Ceylon Planters Rifle Corps attached to N.Z.E.F.
	12.	British Section trained on Salisbury Plain left Southampton for Egypt.
	13.	Lieut. Holbrook in BII. torpedoed the "Messoudieh" in the Dardanelles.
	14.	Second Reinforcements left New Zealand.
	18.	18. Proclamation of a British Protectorate in Egypt; the Khedive Abbas deposed.
	19.	High Highness Prince Hussein proclaimed Sultan of Egypt.
	23.	March of N.Z. Troops through the streets of Cairo.
	24.	British Section arrived at Zeitoun Camp.
	25.	Christmas Day spent on the Desert.

1915.

Jan.	18.	Division now styled the "New Zealand and Australian Division."
	25.	N.Z. Infantry Brigade ordered to Suez Canal.
	26.	Infantry Brigade left Zeitoun for Ismailia and Kubri.
Feb.	1.	Advance parties 4th Aust. Inf. Bde. arrived at Zeitoun.
	3.	Turks attacked Suez Canal. New Zealanders engaged; one man died of wounds and one wounded.
	14.	Third Reinforcements left New Zealand.
	19.	Naval attack on the forts at the entrance of the Dardanelles.
	26.	N.Z. Infantry Brigade returned from Suez Canal to Zeitoun.
March	18.	End of Dardanelles Naval attack. "Queen," "Irresistible" and "Bouvet" sunk.
	26.	Third Reinforcements, consisting of 63 officers and 2417 other ranks arrived at Zeitoun.
	29.	Inspection of Division by Sir Ian Hamilton.
April	9.	N.Z. & A. Division, less mounted units, entrained for Alexandria.
	10.	First transports left for Mudros.
	15.	Transport "Lutzow" with Divisional Headquarters on board arrived in Mudros Harbour.
	17.	Fourth Reinforcements left New Zealand.
	24.	French, British, Australian and New Zealand transports left Mudros Harbous.
	25.	French landed at Kum Kale.
		British landed at Cape Helles.
		A. & N.Z. Army Corps landed at Anzac Cove; 3rd Australian Infantry Brigade forced a landing at dawn.
		N.Z. Divisional Headquarters and details ashore at 10 a.m.; Auckland Battalion all ashore by 12 noon; No. 1 Field Company N.Z. Engineers and Canterbury and Otago Infantry came ashore during the afternoon.
		Wellington Infantry landed during the night.
	26.	6 a.m. two guns of N.Z. Howitzer Battery landed and came into action.
		Turkish counter attacks beaten off at Anzac.
	27.	2nd Battery N.Z.F.A. landed at 3 a.m.
		Heavy attack against centre and Walker's Ridge beaten off 9.30 a.m.
	28.	Portsmouth and Chatham Battalions (Royal Marine Brigade) arrived 6 p.m.
		No. 2 Company Divisional Train arrived at night.

A Gallipoli Diary.

April 29. Heavy Turkish attacks all along the Anzac Line.
A Naval Brigade (Nelson and Deal Battalion) arrived at night.

May 2. Turkish observation post destroyed at Lala Baba by New Zealanders.
2/3. Our attack at head of Monash Gully failed.
3. Turk warship in straits fired on transports; "Annaberg" hit.
4. Australian attack on Gaba Tepe beaten off.
5/6. N.Z. Infantry Brigade and 2nd Australian Brigade left for Cape Helles.
6. 3rd Reinforcements arrived Anzac—sent down to Helles.
Combined French, British and Colonial Forces commenced attack on Krithia.
7. New Zealanders in support of 29th Division.
Sinking of "Lusitania" in the Atlantic.
8. Great attack on Krithia not successful.
10. Australians at head of Monash Gully attacked Turks, but withdrew.
12. N.Z. Mounted Rifles (1500 men) arrived at Anzac to fight as Infantry.
Gen. Chauvel with 1400 men of the Australian Light Horse arrived.
14. H.M.S. "Goliath" sunk at mouth of straits.
Queenslanders made a sortie from Quinn's Post.
15. General Birdwood slightly wounded in the head at Quinn's Post.
General Bridges mortally wounded.
16. 6-inch Howitzer with R.M.L.I. crew arrived in support of the Division.
Machine Gun detachment Otago Mounted Rifles arrived.
17. 2nd Australian Infantry Brigade returned. 3 guns of 2nd Battery N.Z.F.A., man-handled up to Plugge's Plateau.
18. Heavy Turkish attacks.
German Taube flew over Anzac.
19. Turks fail to drive A.N.Z. Corps into the sea.
N.Z. Infantry Brigade returned from Helles.
20. Otago Mounted Rifles (dismounted) arrived.
Turks first ask for an armistice.
24. Armistice Day to bury dead.
25. H.M.S. "Triumph" torpedoed off Gaba Tepe.
27. H.M.S. "Majestic" torpedoed off Cape Helles.
28. Late at night Turks fire mine in front of Quinn's Post.
Canterbury Mounted Rifles take "Old No. 3 Post."
29. Attack on Quinn's Post—Major Quinn killed.
Major Bruce, 26th Indian Mountain Battery killed.
31. Turk blockhouse blown up in front of Quinn's by two sappers.

June 3. 2nd Field Company, N.Z.E., arrived.
4. Slight advance made at Cape Helles.
Canterbury Infantry raided from Quinn's Post late at night.
5. Another sortie against German Officers' Trench opposite Courtney's post.
7. Fourth Reinforcements arrived Anzac Cove.
Sortie from Quinn's Post night of 7/8th.
8. First Monitor appeared off Anzac.
10. Scouting parties of N.Z.M.R. driven back to No. 2 Post.
12. 4.5 Howitzer taken from Howitzer Gully up to Plugge's Plateau.
21. French captured the Haricot Redoubt at Cape Helles.

June	28.	A marked advance made in the Helles sector.
	29/30.	Turks again unsuccessfully endeavoured to drive the infidels into the sea. The last Turkish attack on Anzac.
July	2.	Determined Turkish attack at Helles unsuccessful.
	4/5.	Another heavy attack beaten off the British at Cape Helles.
	10.	Turks at Cape Helles asked for Armistice to bury their dead. Armistice refused.
	11.	N.Z. Hospital ship "Maheno" left Wellington.
	12.	General Masnou, commanding the 1st French Division at Helles, mortally wounded.
	31.	200 men of the 11th West Australian Battalion took Turkish trenches opposite Tasmania Post.
Aug.	3.	13th (New Army) commenced landing at Anzac.
	5.	Fall of Warsaw.
	6/7.	British delivered holding attack at Cape Helles. Australians made heroic attack at Lone Pine, Quinn's Post and Russell's Top. Old No. 3 Post retaken and Table Top and Beauchop's Hill taken by N.Z.M.R. Damakjelik Bair captured by Left Covering Force.
	7.	New landing at Suvla Bay before dawn. Rhododendron Spur in the hands of New Zealanders.
	8.	New Zealanders storm Chunuk Bair. New Army remains inactive at Suvla. Fifth Reinforcements reach Anzac and go into the firing line.
	9.	Ghurkas reach the Saddle between Hill Q and Chunuk Bair. New Zealanders cling to the shoulder of Chunuk Bair; relieved at night by New Army Troops.
	10.	New Army Troops driven from Chunuk Bair by Turkish counter attack.
	11.	Advance from Suvla definitely held up.
	14.	Sixth Reinforcements left New Zealand.
	21.	First attack on Hill 60. Italy declared war on Turkey.
	26.	"Maheno" arrived off Anzac.
	27.	Battle renewed for the possession of Hill 60.
	28.	New Zealanders held on to and consolidate their position on Hill 60.
Sept.		Troops go to rest camp at Sarpi.
	19.	Von Mackensen renewed attack on Serbia.
	20.	Bulgaria Treaty with Turkey announced, thus opening the Balkan corridor.
	29.	British and Indian troops enter Kut-el-Amara.
	30.	10th (Irish) Division left Suvla for Salonika.
Oct.	3.	2nd French Division left Helles for Salonika.
	7.	Britain offered Cyprus to Greece.
	9.	Belgrade captured by Austro-Germans.
	11.	Lord Kitchener asked Sir Ian Hamilton the estimated cost of evacuation.
	12.	Sir Ian Hamilton replied that evacuation was unthinkable.
	14.	In the House of Lords, Lord Milner and Lord Ribblesdale urged the evacuation of Gallipoli.
	15.	Britain declared war on Bulgaria.
	16.	Lord Kitchener telegraphed recalling Sir Ian Hamilton.
	17.	Sir Ian Hamilton issued his farewell order.
	20.	General Munro, in London, received instructions to proceed to the near east and take over command of the M.E.F.
	30.	General Sir Charles Munro first visits the Peninsula.
	23.	Wreck of Marquette—10 nurses drowned.

Nov.	2.	4th Australian Infantry Brigade arrived from Sarpi Rest Camp.
	6.	Nish captured by the Austro-Germans.
	10.	N.Z. Mounted Rifles arrived from Mudros Rest Camp.
	13.	Lord Kitchener visited Anzac.
	13.	Mr. Winston Churchill resigned from the British Cabinet.
	17.	Lt.-Col. Braithwaite, D.S.O., assumed command of N.Z. Infantry Brigade.
	22.	Batle of Ctesiphen.
	24.	Period of silence ordered: lasted 72 hours. Major General Russell took over N.Z. and A. Division.
	26.	Major General Godley assumed command of Army Corps.
	27/28.	Commencement of the **Great Blizzard**.
Dec.	3.	General Townshend besieged at Kut-el-Amara.
	8.	General Munro ordered General Birdwood to proceed with the evacuation of Anzac and Suvla.
	10/11.	All sick, wounded, surplus troops, vehicles and valuable stores removed.
	12.	Announced at Anzac that a winter rest camp would be formed at Imbros. Surplus guns removed.
	15.	Detailed orders issued for the evacuation.
	16.	All ranks were warned of the impending operations.
	19.	The last night of the evacuation of Anzac and Suvla.
	20.	Evacuation of Anzac and Suvla completed by daylight. Troops disembarked at Lemos.
	21.	Brig.-Gen. F. E. Johnston returned to Mudros and took over N.Z. Infantry Brigade; Lt.-Col. W. G. Braithwaite proceeded to Egypt to take over N.Z. Rifle Brigade. Col. E. W. C. Chaytor took over N.Z. Mounted Rifle Brigade.
	25.	Christmas Day mostly spent at sea on transports returning to Egypt. Troops transferred to Egypt between December 21 and 31.

1916.

Jan.	9.	Evacuation from Cape Helles completed.

1918.

Sept.	29.	Surrender of Bulgaria.
Oct.	31.	Surrender of Turkey.

A Note by the Author.

Thanks are due, and are here tendered, to Generals Sir Ian Hamilton and Sir William Birdwood for their most interesting forewords. They with their authority and special knowledge, have said what might have been difficult for a New Zealand officer.

I might also be permitted to say that from Sir James Allen I have received most sympathetic encouragement. Any criticisms that I have made appear without alteration, as the opinion of myself speaking for the soldiers. My only aim has been to put the case before the people of New Zealand as it occurred to the soldiers serving overseas.

The writing of this volume has not been easy. The records of the New Zealanders at Gallipoli are far from complete, as Embarkation Rolls, War Diaries and Returns of Casualties were kept by soldiers who frequently became casualties; often the stress was so great that the continuity of these records was broken. As the Company or Regimental records box was sometimes lost altogether, it is difficult to reconstruct the story. But by the aid of diaries, soldiers' letters, personal experience and the willing assistance of old comrades, this story of the New Zealanders at Gallipoli has been written. It would be easier to write a history of the Crimean war, for the soldiers who fought at Inkerman are nearly all dead, but many of the veterans of Gallipoli happily survive and are keen critics. I can only throw myself on their charity.

For considerable help, particularly in the later chapters, I am indebted to Major Wallingford, M.C., Lt.-Colonel Powles, C.M.G., D.S.O., Lt.-Colonel Grigor, D.S.O., Major Lampen, D.S.O., Major Blair, D.S.O., M.C., and Colonel Findlay, C.B.; to my thousand and one other helpers—distinguished generals, unknown soldiers, and harassed typists—I can only say "Thank you!" They will understand that a record of their names would be almost a nominal roll of the Main Body and the Staff of Base Records.

The photographs are unique in that they were all taken by soldiers serving in the line. Working on my own collection as a basis I was fortunate enough to secure those of Captain Boxer, N.Z.M.C., and Sergeant Tite, N.Z.E., whose beautiful photographs will be found duly acknowledged. Just before going to Press I received a number of photographs taken by members of the Canterbury Mounted Rifles, in December 1918, and to Colonel Findlay and Captain Douglas Deans special thanks are due. Wherever possible photographs have been acknowledged, but some of which I cannot trace the owners are included. From these I shall be glad to hear, so that acknowledgment may be made in future editions. It is only right to say that whenever I have asked a soldier or a sailor for permission to use photographs, that permission has been freely given. In not one case has there been a refusal—for that is the way of the men of Anzac.

My rough maps and sketches have been transformed into works of art by A. E. West, Esq., and W. Bedkober, Esq. Through an error on my part the scale on the map of Anzac, page 111 is wrong. All distances in the Anzac area should be measured on the large folded map at the end of the volume.

I cannot say how indebted I am to J. Jeffery, Esq., of Anderson's Bay, Dunedin, for valuable suggestions, and to W. Slater, Esq., who has helped me with the proofs.

In a work of this kind—a pioneer effort—there must necessarily be slight inaccuracies. I shall be glad to hear from any reader who detects such.

Fred Waite

November, 1919.

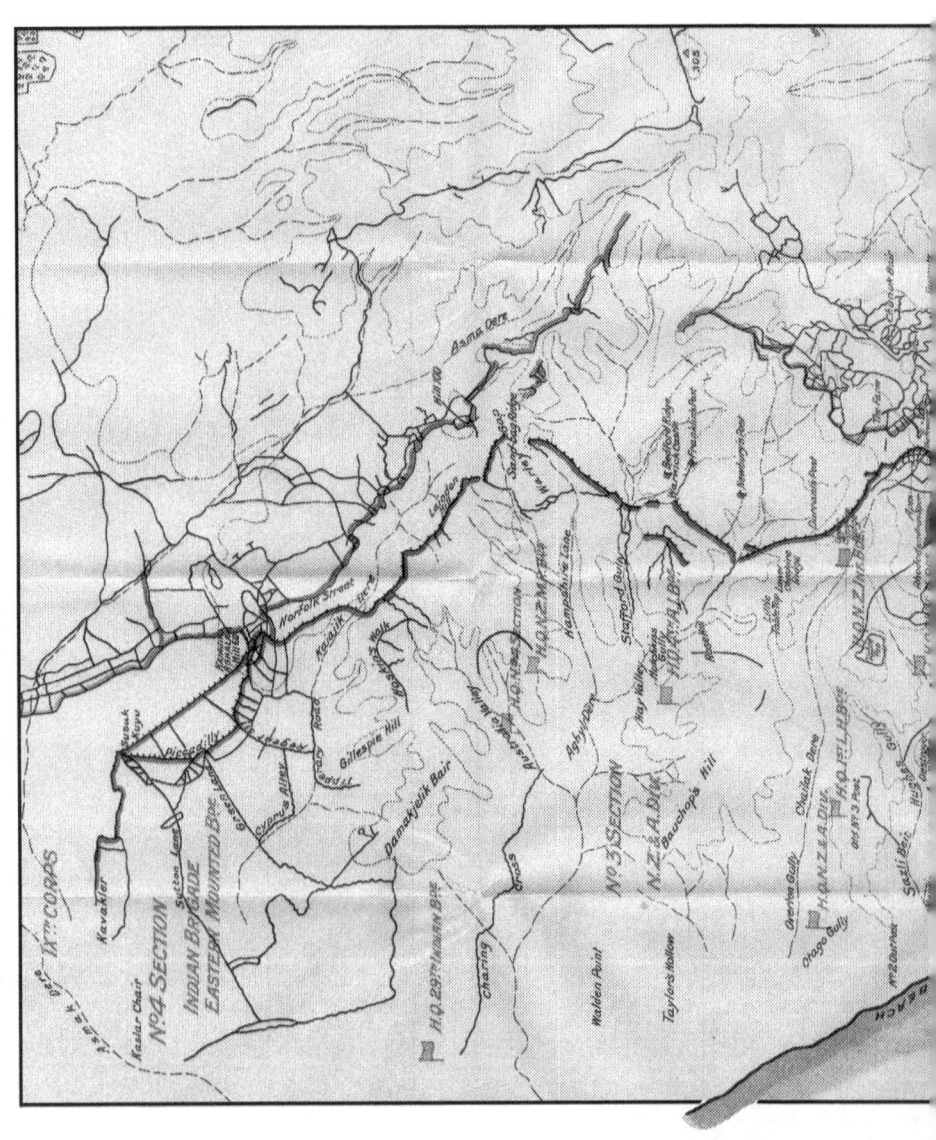

www.ingramcontent.com/pod-product-compliance
Lightning Source LLC
Chambersburg PA
CBHW021830220426
43663CB00005B/196